Kubrick

MICHEL CIMENT

Translated from the French
by Gilbert Adair

Holt, Rinehart and Winston
New York

In memory of my father

Library of Congress Cataloging in Publication Data
Ciment, Michel, 1938–
Kubrick.
Filmography: p.
Bibliography: p.
1. Kubrick, Stanley.   I. Title.
PN1998.A3K736513   791.43 ' 0233 ' 0924   82-6224
ISBN: 0-03-061687-5   AACR2

First American Edition

Designed by Bernard Père
for Chantal Noetzel-Aubry

Photoset in Rockwell Light by
MS Filmsetting Limited, Frome, Somerset, England

Printed in the United States of America
10 9 8 7 6 5 4 3 2 1

Grateful acknowledgment is made to Hawk Films, Hawk/Peregrine
Productions, Metro-Goldwyn-Mayer Film Co., United Artists Corporation, Universal Pictures and Warner Bros. Inc. for permission to use
the photos and motion picture stills in this book.

The following photos are from the MGM release *Lolita* © 1961 A.A.
Productions Ltd. Copyright assigned 1962 to Metro-Goldwyn-Mayer Inc.:
Pages 18–19; page 41 (taken during filming of the picture); page 58;
page 71, photo 3; page 78, photo 1; page 83, photo 2; page 88, photo 1;
page 92, photos 1 and 2; page 102, photo 3; page 118, photo 1; page 202,
photo 2; page 203.

The following photos are from the MGM release *2001: A Space Odyssey*
© 1968 Metro-Goldwyn-Mayer Inc.: Pages 22–23; page 52, photos 1 and 2
(taken during filming of the picture); page 60, photo 1; page 64, photo 2;
page 66, photo 2; page 72, photos 1 and 2; pages 76–77; page 86, photo 1;
pages 86–87, photo 3; page 98, photos 1 and 2; page 113, photo 2; page
114, photo 1; page 118, photo 2; page 123; pages 126–134; pages 138–139;
page 142, photo 2; page 144.

ISBN 0-03-061687-5

Contents

Foreword

Every critic, I feel sure, who has attempted to come to terms with Stanley Kubrick's work has been made painfully aware of the limits of his own discourse. To describe film in words – which is to say, to present to the reader in conceptual terms a series of associations of animated images – is in itself a challenge. With films which their maker has always described as 'a non-verbal experience' the task is rendered even more difficult. And the refusal often shown by Kubrick to comment on his art comes from his desire to conserve a margin of mystery and uncertainty. His is an oeuvre that both demands and defies analysis.

As long as I can remember, by recalling my own encounters with his films – in particular, the night I wandered through the streets of London after my first viewing of *2001: A Space Odyssey*, trying to collect my thoughts after an experience unique in my years of film-going – I have dreamt of a book about Kubrick in which images would play an essential role.

Such is the spirit in which this album has been conceived. The illustrations (often frame enlargements rather than a set photographer's stills, as was Kubrick's request for his later work) will not only conjure up a shot or lighting effect, a composition or gesture, but provide a critical commentary through unexpected analogies or internal rhymes. And the text itself both influenced and was influenced by the choice of photographs. The book does not claim to be exhaustive, but proposes a series of converging approaches with the aim of reaching the central, unchanging core of Kubrick's art. Apart from a detailed bibliography and filmography, it consists of seven sections. In five of these (Kubrick's odyssey; Reflections on an oeuvre in evolution; Kubrick and the fantastic; Interviews with Stanley Kubrick; Interviews with colleagues), both words and pictures are used. In the other two (Eleven films; Directing), only pictures.

Afterwards, it will be up to the reader–viewer to pursue his own personal thoughts and impressions of one of the most demanding, most original and most visionary film-makers of our time.

Stanley Kubrick (filming A Clockwork Orange*)*

1953

1. Paul Mazursky
2. Frank Silvera, Steve Coit, Kenneth Harp
3. Steve Coit, Kenneth Harp

Fear and Desire

1. Irene Kane
2. Irene Kane, Jamie Smith
3. Jamie Smith
4. Frank Silvera, Jamie Smith
5. Frank Silvera

Killer's Kiss

1956

1. Marie Windsor
2. Ted de Corsia, Joe Sawyer,
Elisha Cook, Sterling Hayden,
Jay C. Flippen
3. Elisha Cook

The Killing

1958

1. George Macready, Kirk Douglas
2. George Macready, Adolphe Menjou, Richard Anderson
3. Timothy Carey, Ralph Meeker, Joseph Turkel, Richard Anderson (from behind)
4. Ralph Meeker
5. Kirk Douglas

Paths of Glory

1960

1. The slaves escape
2. Kirk Douglas, Woody Strode
3. Kirk Douglas
4. Laurence Olivier, Jean Simmons
5. Charles Laughton, Peter Ustinov,
Jean Simmons

Spartacus

3

4

5

1962

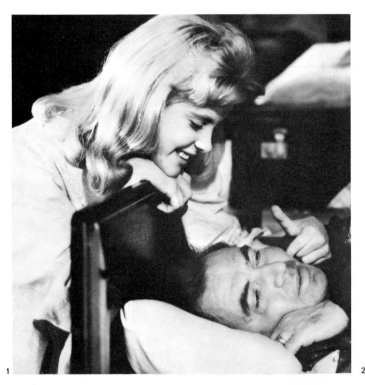

1. Sue Lyon, James Mason
2. James Mason, Shelley Winters
3. James Mason, Sue Lyon
4. James B. Harris, Marianne Stone,
Peter Sellers, Sue Lyon

Lolita

1. Sterling Hayden
2. George C. Scott
3. Peter Sellers
4. The War Room

Dr Strangelove

4

1968

1. *The Dawn of Man*
2. Orion, *Space Station 5 and the earth's surface*
3. *Gary Lockwood*

2001 : A Space Odyssey

3

1971

1. and 2. Malcolm McDowell
3. Miriam Karlin
4. Warren Clarke

A Clockwork Orange

3

4

1975

1. Ryan O'Neal, David Morley
2. Marisa Berenson
3. Dunleary camp
4. Hardy Krüger

Barry Lyndon

1980

1. Shelley Duvall,
Danny Lloyd,
Jack Nicholson
2. Shelley Duvall,
Danny Lloyd
3. The Overlook
Hotel
4. Jack Nicholson

4

Stanley Kubrick
1. *Filming* Dr Strangelove
2. *Filming* Barry Lyndon

There's a man lives in London town,
Makes movies, he's world renowned,
Yes, he's really got the fame,
Stanley Kubrick is his name.
He does it all, he does it all,
Stanley does it all . . .
He's a man who looks ahead
To make you think he raised the dead
And he cuts all his flicks.
He's a genius with his tricks.
He does it all, he does it all.
I'm telling y'all, Stanley does it all.

(Song written during the making of *The Shining*
by Scatman Crothers, who played the role of Hallorann.)[193]

SLOK 455F-27A

[1] the numbers refer to the bibliography at the end of the book

Kubrick's odyssey

Milestones

Stanley Kubrick was born on 26 July 1928 in the Bronx, New York. His parents were American Jews of Central European origin. He has one sister, Barbara, six years his junior. His father, a well-known doctor, introduced him to chess at the age of twelve and to photography the following year when he gave him his first camera – a Graflex – for his birthday. The gift took Kubrick's mind off another of his youthful enthusiasms, jazz, and his dream of becoming a professional drummer. At school – William Howard Taft High School in the Bronx – the only good grades he received were in physics (science was his favourite subject) and he left at seventeen with a poorish average of sixty-seven. He was therefore refused entry to college, especially as in 1945 the return of thousands of young GIs from the war made standards of enrolment in higher education even more strict.

While still at high school, Kubrick had taken numerous photographs – he was actually made the official school photographer – and a few of these were exhibited. One morning in April 1945, on his way to school, he chanced to snap the haggard features of a newspaper vendor beside headlines announcing the death of Franklin D. Roosevelt; he then sold the photograph for twenty-five dollars to *Look* magazine, which offered him ten more than the *New York Daily News*. Shortly after, he proposed two other features to *Look* and both were accepted. One of these involved his English teacher, Aaron Traister, who had aroused his interest by playing all the roles in *Hamlet* and other Shakespeare plays himself (a fascination with multiple-role-playing which will later be found in his films).

Though he enrolled in evening classes at New York's City College in the hope of eventually being eligible for university, his involvement in photography was given a boost when Helen O'Brian, the head of *Look*'s photographic department, found him a place on the magazine's team. He worked there for four years, travelling all over the country and even to Portugal, his camera concealed inside a shopping bag so that he would not be taken for a tourist or a journalist.

During these years of apprenticeship – when his independence, his stamina and his bright ideas were already such that he came to be regarded as one of the magazine's best photographers – Kubrick applied himself to the avid study of a wide range of books that would contribute to his intellectual development in every possible field of knowledge. Because of this thirst for facts and ideas, he enrolled as a non-matriculating student at New York's Columbia University, where he sat in on classes given by Lionel Trilling and Mark Van Doren.

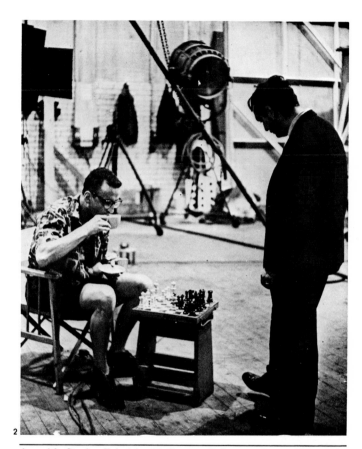

1. and 2. Stanley Kubrick with George C. Scott on the set of Dr Strangelove

Though they were destined to give way to the cinema, the young Kubrick's three favourite activities (two of which, chess and photography, are often viewed as frivolous pastimes) left a lasting mark on him. From chess, which he would continue to practise between takes (with George C. Scott, for example, during the filming of *Dr Strangelove*), came the mathematical precision of his plots, his enthusiasm for abstract speculation, and his view of life as a game in which one wrong move could be fatal. Photography, of course, gave him a feel for composition and an interest in visual effects, qualities evident in all of his films: he controls their photographic textures by working in close collaboration with his lighting cameramen, and occasionally shoots certain hand-held camera sequences himself. Jazz, finally, gave him a grounding in rhythm, in editing and in the art of selecting the right musical accompaniment for a scene, a talent which will have struck everyone who has seen his films.

In 1949, Kubrick and his first wife, Toba Metz (whom he had known at Taft High School and married at the age of eighteen), moved to Greenwich Village. He furthered his newly acquired ambition of becoming a film-maker by assiduously attending screenings at the Museum of Modern Art. His tastes were – and have remained – eclectic, his curiosity ever alert and his interest in formal problems constant. He admits that at that period Eisenstein's books had not impressed him, and adds: 'Eisenstein's greatest achievement is the beautiful visual composition of his shots and his editing. But as far as content is concerned his films are silly, his actors are wooden and operatic. I sometimes suspect that Eisenstein's acting style derives from his desire to keep the actors framed within his composition for as long as possible; they move very slowly, as if under water ... Actually anyone seriously interested in comparative film techniques should study the difference in approach of two directors, Eisenstein and Chaplin. Eisenstein is all form and no content, whereas Chaplin is content and no form[14].'

When the American magazine *Cinema* asked him in 1963 to name his favourite films, Kubrick listed the following titles: 1. *I Vitelloni* (Federico Fellini, 1953), 2. *Wild Strawberries* (Ingmar Bergman, 1958), 3. *Citizen Kane* (Orson Welles, 1941), 4. *The Treasure of the Sierra Madre* (John Huston, 1948), 5. *City Lights* (Charles Chaplin, 1931), 6. *Henry V* (Laurence Olivier, 1945), 7. *La Notte* (Michelangelo Antonioni, 1961), 8. *The Bank Dick* (W. C. Fields, 1940), 9. *Roxie Hart* (William Wellman, 1942), 10. *Hell's Angels* (Howard Hughes, 1930). In this choice one can detect a broadminded attitude towards very dissimilar aesthetic experiences, with a preference nevertheless for European art films strongly coloured by a pessimistic view of life (Fellini, Antonioni, Bergman); and a predilection for American directors known for their larger-than-life personalities, as also for their marginal position with regard to the system (Welles, Huston, Chaplin, W. C. Fields, Howard Hughes, Wellman). Which should not surprise us from the future director of *Dr Strangelove*.

The absence of one name, however, is striking: that of Max Ophüls, for whom Kubrick has always had the greatest esteem and about whom he said some years earlier: 'Highest of all I would rate Max Ophüls, who for me possessed every possible quality. He has an exceptional flair for sniffing out good subjects, and he got the most out of them. He was also a marvellous director of actors.' All of these qualities are to be found in Kubrick's work, along with the elaborate camera movements characteristic of the director of *Le Plaisir*. Finally, one might mention his admiration for Elia Kazan, whom he considered in 1957 'without question the best director we have in America. And he's capable of performing miracles with the actors he uses.' By his bold choice of themes (adapted from Tennessee Williams, as with *A Streetcar Named Desire*, or straight from the headlines, as with *On the Waterfront*), by his introduction of a new approach to acting (via the Actors Studio), and by his desire to keep his distance from Hollywood (filming *Waterfront* with the independent producer Sam Spiegel in New York's dockland), Kazan in the early fifties could hardly fail to attract the attention of a young director with aspirations to independence and originality.

For Kubrick in 1950 was determined to take the plunge and become a film-maker. He spent his leisure hours (and augmented his modest income) playing chess at the Marshall and Manhattan Clubs and in Washington Square, proving to be one of the finest experts there. He would put his strategic gifts to the test by changing boards at nightfall: 'If you made the switch the right way you could get a table in the shade during the day and one nearer the fountain under the lights, at night.' This he confided to a physicist, Jeremy Bernstein, who

visited him on the set of *2001*: a chess enthusiast himself, the scientist claimed that he always won every fifth game. Intrigued, Kubrick challenged him. They played twenty-five games together, Bernstein gathering valuable information for an article by drawing Kubrick out during the breaks.

It was through meeting a former school friend, Alexander Singer (a future director himself), that he was given his first chance to direct a film. Singer worked as office boy at *March of Time* (a famous newsreel company) and had discovered that his employers would spend 40,000 dollars on films lasting only eight or nine minutes. Kubrick and he decided to make the same kind of film for a tenth of the cost. The subject of their first documentary was the middleweight boxer Walter Cartier, on whom Kubrick had already done a photo-feature for *Look* entitled *Prizefighter*. The result was a 35mm film, *Day of the Fight*, whose musical score was written by another friend, Gerald Fried (subsequently a collaborator on Kubrick's early features, then a notable Hollywood composer). Kubrick endeavoured to sell the film, but was offered less than its cost price of 3900 dollars. When *March of Time* went into liquidation, RKO bought the documentary for a

Filming Fear and Desire

On the set of Dr Strangelove

Refused by all the major studios, it was finally distributed by Joseph Burstyn, who screened it at one of his cinemas, the Guild Theater in New York. *Fear and Desire* garnered critical attention, which encouraged Kubrick to direct a second film – adopting the same means of financing, with 40,000 dollars put up mostly by Morris Bousel, a Bronx chemist to whom he was related. *Killer's Kiss* was shot in 1954 in the streets of New York, edited and mixed over a period of ten months and featured his second wife, Ruth Sobotka, who played the role of a dancer in one brief sequence. Though for the critics it confirmed the young director's importance, it too failed to recover its costs.

A meeting with James B. Harris gave new impetus to Kubrick's career. Alexander Singer had known Harris in the Signal Corps where he was making training films for the Korean War. The son of the owner of Flamingo Films, a cinema and television distribution company, he had hopes of becoming a producer and was on the lookout for a talented director. He made contact with Kubrick through their mutual friend Singer; and, after seeing *Killer's Kiss*, decided to give him his chance. They were both twenty-six when they co-founded Harris–Kubrick Pictures. Together they produced *The Killing* in 1956. Though appreciative of Kubrick's abilities, the distribution company, United Artists, agreed to take over most of the budget (its investment amounted to 200,000 dollars) only after receiving a completed screenplay and the assurance that some well-known actor would be cast – in the event Sterling Hayden, who had confidence in the young film-maker.

The Killing attracted the attention of Dore Schary, head of production at MGM, who invited Harris and Kubrick to select a subject from one of the novels in which the studio owned the rights. Kubrick and Calder Willingham wrote a screenplay based on Stefan Zweig's *The Burning Secret*, but the project aborted when Schary was dismissed. After *Paths of Glory* (1957), also produced by Harris and filmed in Munich, they

Filming The Shining

Filming The Shining

derisory sum (one hundred dollars more than its production cost), but offered an advance of 1500 dollars on a second documentary, *Flying Padre*. After the violence of sport, this gave Kubrick a chance to deal with another of his favourite subjects, aviation: the film centred on a priest in New Mexico who used to fly from one Indian parish to another in a Piper Cub. Having recovered his costs, Kubrick decided in 1953 to direct his first feature and resigned from *Look*. He was encouraged by Joseph Burstyn, a New York distributor and exhibitor who was one of the first to introduce the idea of 'art-house cinemas' in the United States at a period when European and independent films were impossible to see there. Kubrick scraped together 9000 dollars, borrowing from family and friends, in particular from his father and his uncle, Martin Perveler. He commissioned a screenplay from one of his poet friends in Greenwich Village, Howard Sackler (later to be the author of *The Great White Hope*), and set off to film *Fear and Desire* in the San Gabriel Mountains near Los Angeles, as the severe New York winter precluded any exterior shooting on the East Coast. The crew consisted of three Mexican workers to transport the equipment, a few friends and his wife Toba. Kubrick was director, lighting cameraman and editor. For twenty-five dollars a day he rented a Mitchell camera, whose owner taught him how to use it. But post-synchronization expenses amounted to three times the shooting costs and the film failed to make its money back.

announced several projects for which scripts were written but never filmed: *The German Lieutenant*, a World War II story by Richard Adam; *I Stole 16,000,000 Dollars*, the autobiography of a former safecracker, Herbert Emerson Wilson; *The 7th Virginia Cavalry Raider*, which recounted the adventures of a Union Cavalry officer, John Singleton Mosby, during the Civil War, with Gregory Peck slated for the leading role. During this same period, Kubrick spent six months preparing *One Eyed Jacks*, for and with Marlon Brando, but the actor finally decided to direct it himself.

In 1960 the producer of *Spartacus*, Kirk Douglas (also the star of *Paths of Glory*), asked Kubrick after one week's shooting to replace Anthony Mann, with whom he had had serious disagreements (Mann had directed the opening sequence and prepared the gladiatorial bouts). However remarkable his achievement, *Spartacus* is an exception in Kubrick's oeuvre: he did not contribute to the screenplay (as he invariably does), had no control over casting, and so simply had to accommodate himself to a project which he had not initiated.

He once more collaborated with James B. Harris on *Lolita*. Because of the exertion of pressure by various leagues of decency and the possibility of easier financing, Kubrick shot the film in Britain, then settled there for good. The interest aroused by an adaptation of Nabokov's novel placed him in a strong bargaining position, and he signed an agreement with MGM which would henceforth guarantee him real financial independence. After *Lolita* he and Harris separated, the latter branching out as a director (*The Bedford Incident*). Thanks to the commercial success of *Lolita*, it was Kubrick himself who produced his subsequent films, *Dr Strangelove* (1964), *2001: A Space Odyssey* (1968), *A Clockwork Orange* (1972), *Barry Lyndon* (1975) and *The Shining* (1980), five unique works, all of them bearing the stamp of a single man who had mapped out a private, artificial space for himself in which to pursue his preoccupations. In the sixties and seventies, Kubrick enjoyed absolute security, the product of a hard-won independence.

Free to choose his projects, supervising each stage of their creation, he is able to make whatever films he pleases. He has often been compared to Orson Welles, and indeed there are parallels in their independence of character, moral preoccupations, extraordinary visual invention and showmanship. As their careers developed, however, they could scarcely be more different. Both of these young prodigies turned to film direction at the age of twenty-five. But Welles began at the very top of the pyramid – Hollywood and its huge technical crews – and was offered *carte blanche* on his first film, *Citizen Kane*, without the least interference from the studio; whereas Kubrick directed his first film on a tiny budget. Yet, never having had *economic* control of his films, Welles has always been at the mercy of his producers. Kubrick's strength derives from his realisation that if the film-maker is not in charge of every element of his product – from the original rights via the screenplay down to the advertising campaign that will launch his film and the very cinemas in which it will be screened – three or four years' work may go for nothing.

But Kubrick appeared on the film scene ten years after Welles, and in the decade beginning in 1950 significant changes took place which he, unlike his brilliant precursor, was able to turn to his advantage. The fifties marked the decline of the hierarchical, all-powerful major studios, outside of which nothing could be achieved in Hollywood. The growing popularity of television, coupled with the movement of urban populations away from the inner cities, would deprive the cinema of its regular audience. In order to regain it, the studios sought out younger talents bursting with new ideas (the generation which started in television: Frankenheimer, Lumet, Ritt, Mulligan, Penn), while according a greater degree of independence to its most prestigious directors who now became their own producers (Hitchcock, Wilder, Kazan, Preminger, Mankiewicz, etc.). Making *The Killing*, which would be distributed by United Artists, allowed Kubrick to step into this breach. His case is both unique and exemplary, however, and may be compared rather to the future French New Wave (*Killer's Kiss*, shot in 1954 in the New York streets, predated *A Bout de souffle* by six years). Unlike his confrères, Kubrick was not the product of TV, the theatre or film school; nor had he ever been an assistant director, producer or actor. He was an independent who learned everything on the spot, starting out with whatever means were available and ending up with absolute control over highly sophisticated technical equipment.

He has never really been absorbed into a system on which he is nevertheless financially dependent; jealous of his autonomy, juggling with millions of dollars, he probably enjoys greater freedom now than in the straitened circumstances in which he started his career. And today all his efforts are channelled into preserving the same autonomy which he had in his first films so that, instead of becoming the victim of the means at his disposal, he can on the contrary make them serve his own purpose, one which has never changed: self-expression. This is how he summed up his personal experience: 'The best education in film is to make one. I would advise any neophyte director to try to make a film by himself. A three-minute short will teach him a lot. I know that all the things I did at the beginning were, in microcosm, the things I'm doing now as a director and producer. There are a lot of non-creative aspects to film-making which have to be overcome and you will experience them all when you make even the simplest film: business, organization, taxes etc . . . It is rare to be able to have an uncluttered artistic environment when you make a film and being able to accept this is essential.

'The point to stress is that anyone seriously interested in making a film should find as much money as he can as quickly as he can and go out and do it.'

There is no doubt that Kubrick's ideas were confirmed by his period in Hollywood. The years spent there waiting for the go-ahead from MGM on *The Burning Secret*, as well as on his other projects, made him suspicious of production companies which kept directors in a permanent state of inactivity. Similarly, the filming of *Spartacus* – on which, as he himself phrased it, he was just a 'hired hand' – could only make him more determined that it should never happen again. In fact, it was after *Spartacus* – whose commercial success, the first for him of such a magnitude, helped him to gain his independence – that he opted definitively to work in London. It is as if his geographical separation from the United States might henceforth be a metaphor for the distance which he was determined to keep between himself and the Mecca of cinema.

With Kirk Douglas (filming Spartacus*)*

Standards

Everyone knows how exacting Kubrick can be, how he insists on being in sole command of a film from its preparation and shooting to the editing process. 'Stanley is an extremely difficult and talented person. We developed an extremely close relationship and as a result I had to live almost completely on tranquillizers[216],' remarked one of his set designers, Ken Adam. And Arthur C. Clarke, the scenarist of *2001*, added, 'Every time I get through a session with Stanley, I have to go lie down[103].' In effect, Kubrick submits his scenarists (Jim Thompson, Calder Willingham, Vladimir Nabokov, Terry Southern and Arthur C. Clarke) to a gruelling work schedule in which he himself actively participates (he wrote *A Clockwork Orange* and *Barry Lyndon* on his own), devoting between six months and a year to the preparation of the script. But his view of screenplays remains pragmatic: 'Thinking of the visual conception of a scene at script stage can be a trap that straitjackets the scene. I find it more profitable to just try to get the most interesting and truthful business going to support the scene and then see if there's a way to make it interesting photographically. There's nothing worse than arbitrarily setting up some sort of visual thing that really doesn't belong as part of the scene[10].'

Kubrick has no interest in theories and, like all American directors, gives prominence to his actors. Shooting a film is the natural extension of writing it and actors are the essential means by which a director can give flesh to his vision. 'Writers tend to approach the creation of drama too much in terms of words, failing to realize that the greatest force they have is the mood and feeling they can produce in the audience through the actor. They tend to see the actor grudgingly as someone likely to ruin what they have written rather than seeing that the actor is in every sense their medium[19].' James Mason, Sterling Hayden, Marie Windsor and Kirk Douglas have all recognized Kubrick as a great director of actors, who is willing to spend his 'breaks' in lengthy discussions with them. Much has been written about the number of takes which he requires for each shot in his search for perfection; but none of his actors has ever questioned the merits of this method, however much he might have suffered from it. As Lady Lyndon's spiritual adviser, Murray Melvin recalls having played one scene fifty times. 'I knew he had seen something I had done. But because he was a good director he wouldn't tell me what it was. Because if someone tells you you've done a good bit, then you know it and put it in parentheses and kill it[177].' Jack Nicholson adds, 'Stanley's demanding. He'll do a scene fifty times and you have to be good to do that. There are many ways to walk into a room, order breakfast or be frightened to death in a closet. Stanley's approach is: how can we do it better than it's ever been done before? It's a big challenge. A lot of actors give him what he wants. If you don't he'll beat it out of you – with a velvet glove, of course[193].' Malcolm McDowell has spoken of the long discussions he had with Kubrick about his character, emphasizing the degree to which the director, far from browbeating the actor, leaves him free to invent gestures and suggest variations: Kubrick even borrowed from him the notion of using 'Singin' in the Rain' to accompany one of *A Clockwork Orange*'s most violent sequences. 'This is why Stanley is such a great director. He can create an atmosphere where you're not inhibited in the least. You'll do anything. Try it out. Experiment. Stanley gives you freedom and he is the most marvellous audience. I used to see him behind the camera with the handkerchief stuffed in his mouth because he was laughing so much. It gave me enormous confidence[213].'

1. With Tony Curtis and Laurence Olivier (filming Spartacus)
2. With Kirk Douglas (filming Paths of Glory)
3. With Peter Sellers (filming Dr Strangelove)

Anthony Harvey, who edited *Lolita* and *Dr Strangelove*, has noted how Kubrick would adjust the editing to the performances: 'If an actor gives something terribly exciting in terms of performance, I think it is important to stay on his face, even though the conventional thing is to cut every so often to the person he is talking to. I think the audience can imagine the other character's reactions for themselves. There was a scene in *Lolita* where Sue Lyon is talking to James Mason and they are alone in the room: she was so extraordinary that we remained on her for the entire scene without cutting to him at all[217].' The shooting script of *Dr Strangelove*, though regarded by Harvey as the most brilliant and most perfectly constructed he had ever read, was also modified at the editing stage. Once the film had been shot, they realised that the rhythm was not sufficiently varied and the tension did not develop properly. They therefore decided to delay each change of scene in order to gain clarity and sustain interest.

For Kubrick to maintain such autocratic control over the work in hand, he needs total isolation. Pursuing his Pascalian reflections on the infinity of space during *2001*, he cloistered himself in a private, protected estate far removed from any distractions. He lives in a country house about twenty miles

1. *With Malcolm McDowell, from behind (filming* A Clockwork Orange*)*
2. *With Sue Lyon watched by James Mason, left in profile (filming* Lolita*)*

from London with his third wife, the former German actress Susanne Christian (who played the café singer in *Paths of Glory* and is now a well-known painter), his three daughters and lots of cats and dogs. There he leads a real family existence, with everyone interested in what everyone else is doing – and he only very occasionally goes up to town. He travels as rarely as possible, forbids his chauffeur to drive faster than 40 miles an hour, and while filming *2001* wore his safety helmet rather more often than was necessary. His clothes are famous for their simplicity (baggy trousers, open-necked shirt and anorak – 'a balloon vendor' his wife says), and his working-day meals for their frugality: he has no time to waste.

For his whole life seems to be a race against the clock, a battle against the relentless passage of time. He has, for example, turned part of his garage into an editing room so that he can continue working at home; he has had a 35mm projection room installed in which, with voracious curiosity, he has the latest films screened for him; and he communicates essentially by telephone, telex, video, tapes and brief memos. He employs an entourage of technicians, secretaries and assistants to form an empire within the vaster empire of the company which distributes his work, but from which this parallel power allows him to retain his independence. There is no affectation in such an attitude (social standing means nothing to him and he has no interest in acquiring it; money serves exclusively to guarantee him independence): wholly absorbed in his work, he is not the kind of person to make capital out of his inaccessibility. When, on the release of a film, he agrees to be interviewed by a few critics, he does so with good grace and modesty. I observed, on the occasions we met, how measured and methodical were his replies to my questions, his obvious concern being to get down to essentials without either showing off or spouting paradoxes. His features are alert and extraordinarily intense, their authority accentuated by his beard and dark, lined eyes. He is soft-spoken, with a crisp, surprisingly youthful voice, alternately serious and humorous in tone. Later, he will insist on checking each sentence entrusted to the tape-recorder. What could be more natural, given that so many remarks are distorted then quoted again and discussed without the speaker having any further say in the matter? His sole contact with the press, then, takes place every four or five years. A chauffeur drives the chosen few (Kubrick would be happy to arrange more of these meetings, but his other activities make it impossible . . .) to a roadside pub near the director's home, or to his office, or even to the editing-room – piled high with cans of film, newspapers, files and card-indexes, like some enormous artist's loft in Montparnasse or Greenwich Village – where this 'eternal student' can work away in privacy.

Since Kubrick sees only those who may, in one way or another, be of assistance to the career of his films – his principal concern – he has been spared the increasingly frequent globe-trotting to which his less fortunate colleagues have to resign themselves in order to launch their films, repeating the same remarks over and over again (how they must envy him!). He prefers to prepare a project, collect material for it over a period of months, even years, pore over books and magazines with the systematic curiosity of an autodidact, monitor the seating capacity and average takings of cinemas in each foreign capital or the design and deployment of posters or even the distance between seats and screen at press shows, not to mention the size of newspaper ads and the rates of currency exchange. He also has the subtitles of every foreign version of his films completely re-translated into English to make certain that nothing crucial has been omitted, supervises all dubbed versions, and checked out the quality of the seven hundred prints of *The Shining* which were released the same day in the United States.

He may interrupt the interview to ask you about some technical detail or plot point of a film which he has never seen. Alexander Walker, the critic who has written about him best, described how on a single evening in Kubrick's company the conversation ranged over an incredible variety of subjects, all of which required his close attention. 'An evening's conversation with him has covered such areas as optical perception in relation to man's survival; the phenomenon of phosphene; German coastal gun emplacements in Normandy; compromised safety margins in commercial flying; Dr Goebbels' role as a pioneer film publicist; the Right's inability to produce dialecticians to match the Left's; the Legion of Decency's pressures during the making of *Lolita*; S.A.M.-3 missiles in the Arab–Israeli conflict; Irish politics and the possibility of similarities in the voice prints of demagogues; and, of course, chess[6].'

We have become too accustomed to the romantic image of the artist as someone creating in an ivory tower not to entertain doubts about such indefatigable attention to economic, technical or administrative questions. But in Kubrick's case one can draw no strict line between his work and this kind of super-technician's existence. Some film-makers find their inspiration in the contemplation of nature, others from the study of news items, still others in constant contact with the world at large. Kubrick's films reflect his perfectionism, his inordinate taste for technology, his fascination with diagrams and statistics, but also his fear of any flaw in a totally programmed system, of an excessive dependence on machines. It should be understood that the power which Stanley Kubrick has acquired within the film industry (he not only has the right to the final cut – that goes without saying; but he also, in the case of *Barry Lyndon* and *The Shining*, received millions of dollars from Warners, the distributors, without being obliged to screen either film to the studio heads more than ten days in advance of their release date) he means to exploit solely in furtherance of his work. Unlike Coppola, who has extended his empire to include real estate, newspapers and distribution, Kubrick's only concern is an artistic one. At the centre of the extraordinary organization which he has created, he remains as much a craftsman writing, photographing, directing and editing his films as the young amateur who started out in the streets of New York – if now with infinitely greater means at his disposal. And the painstaking care he brings to the release of his films simply reflects his concern to see them presented in the best possible conditions without their being compromised by a bad print, faulty projection or flat dubbing. Kubrick, who in his youth sensed the arrival of TV as a dangerous competitor, has undoubtedly understood that, if the cinema is to compete with the small screen, it must make each film an 'event' displayed to advantage in technically perfect conditions.

Thus his career has been guided by logic and lucidity, since they alone can guarantee his freedom vis-à-vis a system which he has succeeded in beating at its own game.

For if the major studios – MGM and Warners – have for twenty years given him *carte blanche* on his most unconventional projects and most extravagant budgets, it is because he has enjoyed an unbroken string of commercial successes, with the exception perhaps of *Barry Lyndon* (even though that too, in the long term, should prove profitable). Of course, *Dr Strangelove*'s takings (5 million dollars to the United States distributor), *Barry Lyndon*'s 10 million, *A Clockwork Orange*'s 15 million and *2001*'s 25 million cannot compare, even if one takes inflation into account, with *Star Wars*' 175 million, *Jaws*' 135 million and the 85 million each of *The Exorcist* and *The Godfather*. But they represent an undeniable and enduring financial success for what are exceptionally personal works, blockbuster 'auteur films', projects so much riskier and more original than those of Hollywood's Movie Brats (who venerate Kubrick no less for his independence than for the films themselves).

The director of *2001* appears to have mastered the subtle game of art and finance that was the downfall of his celebrated predecessors. I refer to those powerful and ambitious artists who seem to surface every ten years in Hollywood to shake it up, rebel against its conventions and revitalise its genres. Griffith at the beginning of the century, Stroheim in the twenties, Sternberg in the thirties, Welles in the forties, Kazan in the fifties, Kubrick in the sixties and Altman in the seventies. In the past, each of them found himself virtually forced into retirement or exile. Orson Welles (a man not given to fulsome praise) recognized this lineage when he remarked in 1965: 'Among the younger generation Kubrick strikes me as a giant.' With Griffith Kubrick shares a penchant for super-

productions (*2001* is his *Intolerance*, *Barry Lyndon* his *Birth of a Nation*) and for the primacy of the image; with Stroheim the relentless search for the telling detail and a taste for novelistic length (his dream of a film lasting twenty hours and the '*Greed* in high society' aspect of *Barry Lyndon*); with Sternberg the fusion of visual invention with detached irony; with Welles the influence of expressionism, the sense of deep focus and mobile camerawork; and with Kazan the pleasure of letting the actor contribute by drawing out what is most deeply rooted in him.

If the general public has had no difficulty appreciating such a rebel and individualist, his relations with the critics have always been ambiguous – at least since *Lolita*, which is to say for the last twenty years – after they had been virtually unanimous in their praise of his first features, *The Killing* and *Paths of Glory*. With hindsight, the vast majority of critics have acknowledged his importance. When in 1978 the Cinémathèque royale in Belgium polled 200 international specialists (film-makers, critics, historians, etc.) on the most important films in the history of the American cinema, Kubrick's name was cited 138 times, preceding that of every other post-war director and figuring in sixteenth place. In the same year, 300 readers of the French magazine *L'Avant-scène du cinéma* established their ideal film Pantheon and placed *2001* at the top of their list ahead of *Citizen Kane*, *Les Enfants du Paradis*, *Modern Times* and *Battleship Potemkin*. Finally, at the end of the seventies, the Parisian weekly *Les Nouvelles littéraires* questioned about forty well-known personalities on what they considered the outstanding films of the preceding decade: both *A Clockwork Orange* and *Barry Lyndon* were listed, with Kubrick and Fellini coming out on top.

Stanley Kubrick
1. Filming Barry Lyndon
2. Portrait by his wife Christine at the period of Barry Lyndon

But such a consensus is deceptive, as the admiration which it appears to reflect is scarcely borne out by the reception accorded his films on their initial release, a reception which their subsequent prestige has consigned to oblivion. Who now remembers the firing-squad directed at *2001: A Space Odyssey* by New York's 'establishment': 'It's a monumentally unimaginative movie' (Pauline Kael, *Harper's* magazine); 'A major disappointment' (Stanley Kaufman, *The New Republic*); 'Incredibly boring' (Renata Adler, *The New York Times*); 'A disaster' (Andrew Sarris, *The Village Voice*)? *Variety*, the American show-business Bible, is the most reliable barometer of the profession's suspicion of any unique, unconventional artist. It could hardly have foreseen *2001*'s enormous success when it wrote prior to its release: '*2001* is not a cinematic landmark. It compares with, but does not best, previous efforts at film science-fiction; lacking the humanity of *Forbidden Planet*, the imagination of *Things to Come* and the simplicity of *Of Stars and Men*. It actually belongs to the technically slick group previously dominated by George Pal and the Japanese'; and, as the ultimate criticism, 'Film costs too much for so personal a film.' Seven years later, writing of *Barry Lyndon*, it noted: 'The point which seems to be made is that some people are hustlers, a few succeed, life goes on, the sun still comes up in the East. Well, we knew all that walking in' (17 December 1975). As for *The Shining*, it was demolished in almost parodic fashion, with *Variety* complaining above all that Warners 'not having learned its lesson with *Barry Lyndon* was silly enough to let him do it' (28 May 1980).

The reaction of the Hollywood community at Oscar time perfectly illustrates the ambivalence of Kubrick's status. Because of his ambition and commercial success they are obliged to recognize him, but his refusal to become one of the 'family' and the distance which he maintains from Hollywood have wrecked his chances of ever being honoured. Nominated Best Director for four films in succession (*Dr Strangelove*, *2001*, *A Clockwork Orange* and *Barry Lyndon*), he shares with Charlie Chaplin, Josef von Sternberg, Orson Welles and Robert Altman (rebels, all of them!), but also with Fritz Lang, Alfred Hitchcock, Howard Hawks and Ernst Lubitsch, the unique distinction of never once having received an Academy Award for Best Direction.

The explanation for his equivocal position vis-à-vis critics and film people lies in the very nature and personality of his art. Disturbing both stylistically and thematically, refusing ever to do what is expected of him though sometimes infiltrating traditional cinematic genres (the war movie, science-fiction, horror), ceaselessly experimenting yet prepared to play the commercial game, preferring spectacle and fantasy to moral complacency and philosophical certitudes, Stanley Kubrick, as an intellectual and an artist, has contrived to win over the public without sacrificing any of his ambitions. Which is surely because, as a visionary film-maker bringing his most personal obsessions to life on the screen of his fantasy, he has been able to apprehend the underlying tensions of his period and tap its collective unconscious.

2

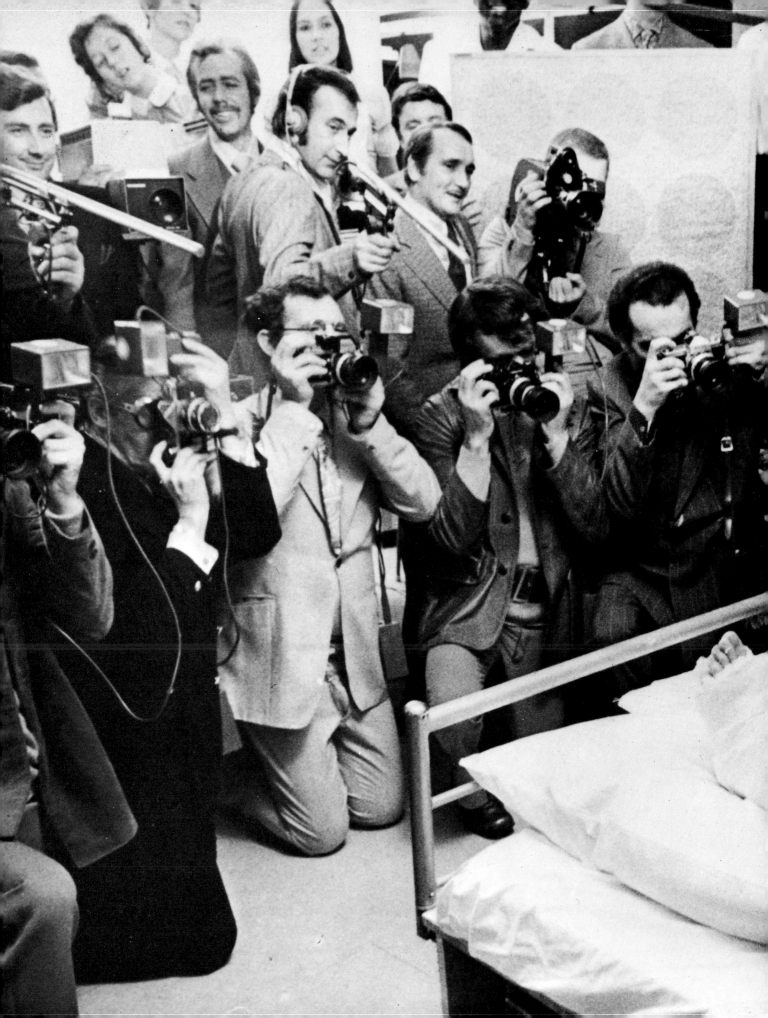

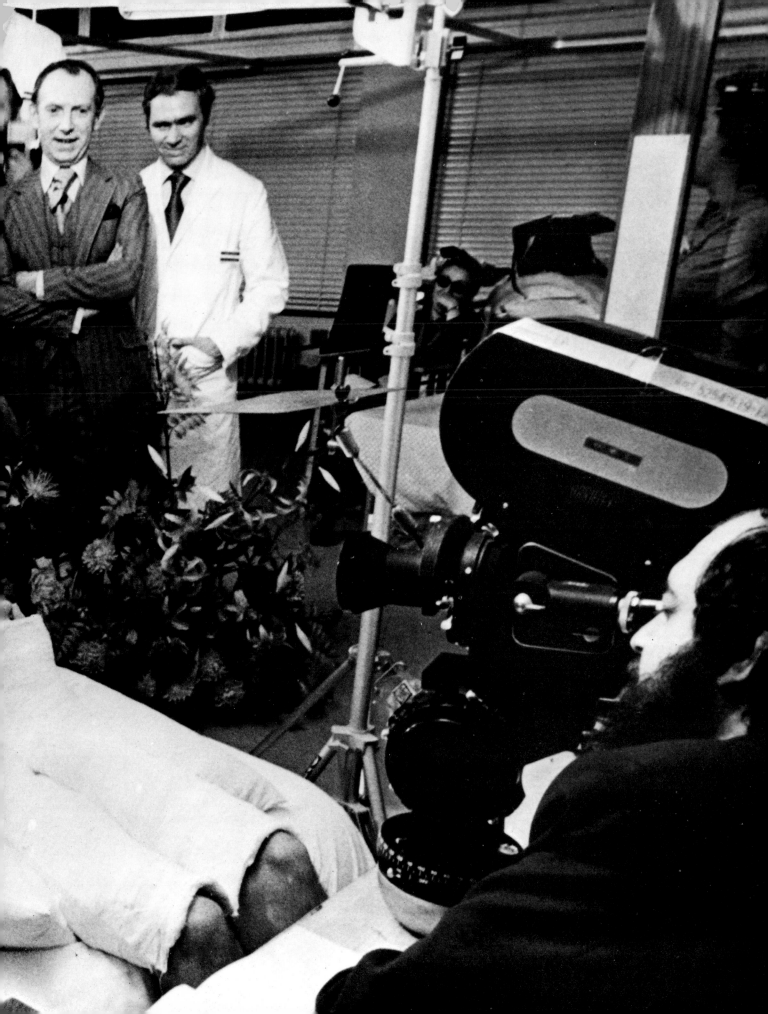

Preceding page: Stanley Kubrick (right) filming A Clockwork Orange
Stanley Kubrick
1. *Filming* Dr Strangelove
2. *Filming* A Clockwork Orange
3. *Filming* The Shining
4. *Filming* A Clockwork Orange

Directing

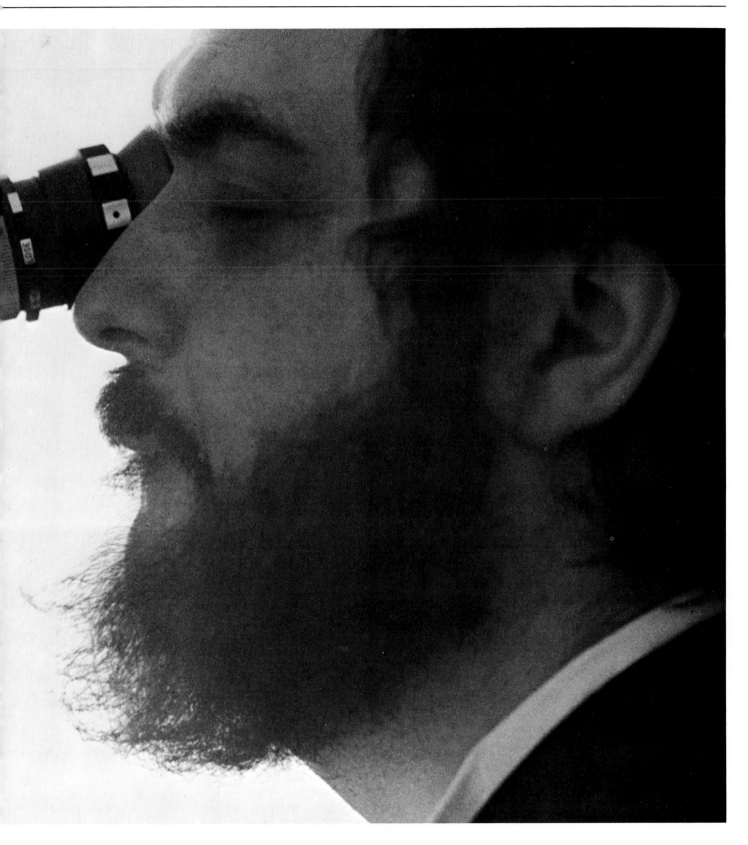

The crew of Fear and Desire. *First and only photograph of Kubrick with all his collaborators (13 – a lucky number). In the foreground: the actors Kenneth Harp, Steve Coit, Paul Mazursky, Frank Silvera*
Second row: workers
Back row: to the left of the camera Steven Hahn, assistant director, to the right Stanley Kubrick and his first wife, Toba Metz
2. With Peter Sellers (filming Dr Strangelove)

*1. 2. and 3. Stanley
Kubrick (filming
Dr Strangelove)*

2

1. and 2. Filming 2001: A
Space Odyssey
Filming A Clockwork
Orange:
3. With Adrienne Corri
and Malcolm McDowell
4. With Patrick Magee

3 4

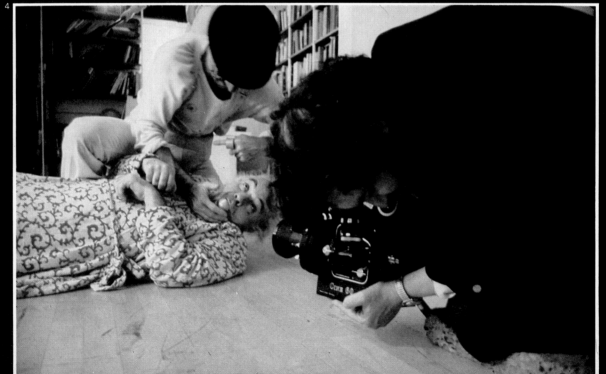

1

2

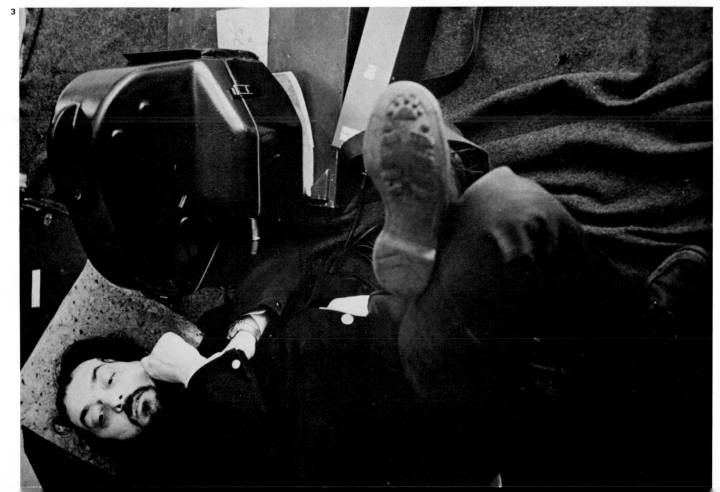

3

1, 2 and 3. Filming A Clockwork Orange
Filming Barry Lyndon
4. With Ryan O'Neal (right)
5. and 6. With Pat Roach and Ryan O'Neil

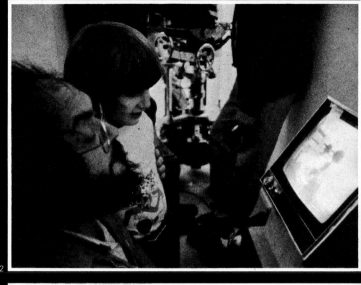

Stanley Kubrick
1. Filming Barry Lyndon
2, 3, and 4. At work on The Shining
Following page: Sue Lyon and James Mason (Lolita)

Between reason and passion

Reflections on an oeuvre in evolution

'The despair of his imagination exceeded the negativity of his period.'

(Adorno on Alban Berg)

1

One indication of Kubrick's modernity is his taste for surprise and diversity; even more than certain obvious themes of his futurist trilogy (the nuclear threat, the conquest of space, the problem of violence), this is what betokens his originality. He seems activated by a desire to astonish himself as much as to astonish other people. Since *Lolita*, his work has constantly aimed at confounding our expectations. What could be further from *Dr Strangelove* – with its gratingly farcical tone, the scope given its cast to invent incisive caricatures and the uncompromising linearity of its screenplay – than the poetic reverie of an experience as non-verbal as *2001: A Space Odyssey*? *A Clockwork Orange* in its turn proved to be the antithesis of *2001*, as if by some dialectical progression whose every stage contradicts the one preceding it. And the failure of Anglo-Saxon critics to appreciate *Barry Lyndon* can partly be explained by their perplexed reaction to a story of love and war as bereft of sex and ultra-violence as *A Clockwork Orange* was saturated with them. It is as if Kubrick were obsessed with contradicting himself, with making each work a critique of the previous one.

2

Modern art has, of course, accustomed us to innovation (which is too often what it can be reduced to), but only on condition that, once the artist has found his style, he will stick to it, affording his admirers the regular gratification of being able to 'recognize' his signature. Hence the striking contrast between the idiosyncratic experiments and mania for perpetual change of the avant-garde and the single-mindedness of a number of individual oeuvres. Kubrick has no desire to be a Bresson or a Janscó. The changes he proposes are bound up in his own evolution and so deprive experts of the satisfaction of instant identification. Perhaps this explains why some critics have denied him any personality at all, regarding him solely as a brilliant and versatile 'inventor'.

I believe, on the contrary, that in Kubrick's work can be found a very real individuality, an internal coherence which is difficult to elucidate because of the abundance and diversity of his formal experiments and his tendency to adapt works of literature.

These two characteristics would seem to provide Kubrick with the possibility of putting on a mask, of shielding himself behind artistic constraints or faithfulness to some literary model. His distaste for interviews is well-known; and on the rare occasions when he does agree to answer questions, one is conscious of how wary he is of opening up. As a Bronx Jew with a Central European background, he shares with his co-religionists – the Viennese émigré film-makers Wilder, Lang, Sternberg and Preminger – a reluctance ever to explain his intentions. In this they differ from Catholic or Mediterranean artists, who are always ready to make confession, or from Protestants given to self-analysis, as if haunted by the recollection of a little bearded man who, precisely in Vienna at the turn of the century, managed to detect in an innocent painting by Leonardo da Vinci a vulture that brought a childhood memory to light. By shedding such a light on the shadow zones of the personality, psychoanalysis is capable of blocking the creative process and paralysing artists with the fear of revealing too much of themselves. The figure of the psychiatrist appears only twice in Kubrick's work – as either sinister or grotesque. In *Lolita*, when Quilty (Peter Sellers) disguises himself as Professor Zempf in order to fool Humbert; in *A Clockwork Orange* where, under orders from the authorities, a doctor carries out tests to check whether Alex has really come to his senses.

3

I have spoken of Kubrick's concern to be original. But the etymology of this term, which means 'independent' or 'unique', paradoxically refers to a totally opposed concept, that of origin and therefore of tradition. The paradox, however, is only a superficial one. To affirm one's difference it is important to preserve a historical conscience, a sense of being linked with the past. Other artists – painters, writers, composers – discovered this a long time ago. Like those civilizations which know that they are mortal, as Valéry said, they see themselves as links in the chain of time. And this recognition of time and the evolution of forms is undoubtedly one of the characteristics of modern art. Film-makers took a long time to reach such a stage of awareness. When they finally realized that the cinema had a history, they lost their innocence. Godard was perhaps the most remarkable example of this transformation, but the American cinema in its turn has begun to interrogate its past. As with American literature, Hollywood has been aesthetically dependent on

1 This text was written before the release of *The Shining*. Rather than subject it to a hasty revision, I have preferred to reserve my comments on Kubrick's latest film for a special chapter (p. 135) where I shall attempt to demonstrate its place in the continuity of his work and how it confirms the general tendencies discussed above.

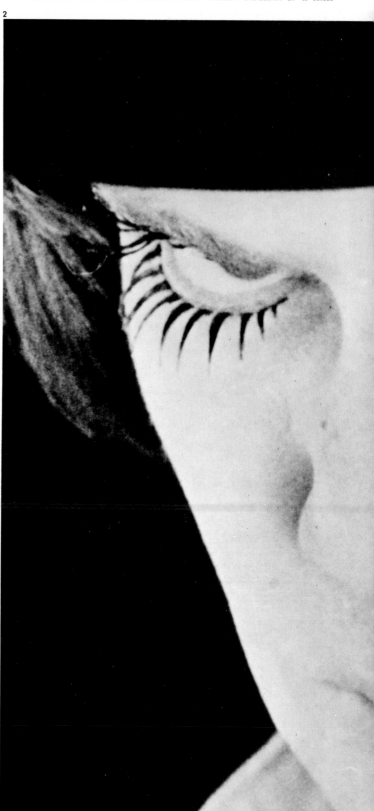

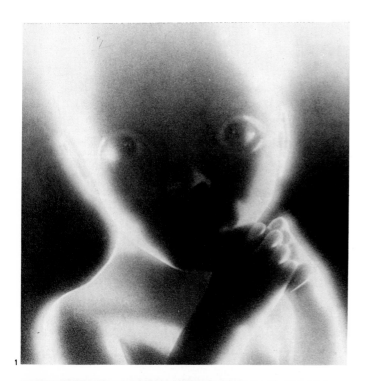

genres, accepted models whose (fairly) strict codes bear witness to a tradition of classicism. One means of distancing oneself from this tradition is to call its genres into question. This is the approach of another great creator, Robert Altman – a centrifugal approach by which the strongholds of cinema are invaded and undermined from within. Altman is a film-

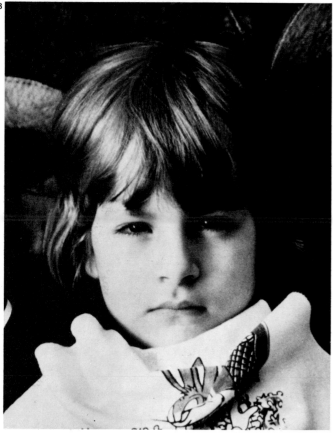

The eye of the foetus at the end of 2001: A Space Odyssey *(1) prefigures the close-up in* A Clockwork Orange *(2) of the eye of the mutant Alex (Malcolm McDowell) before the appearance of the child of light (Danny Lloyd) in* The Shining *(3)*

maker of dispersion, of organized confusion. Kubrick's approach on the contrary is centripetal. Based on concentration, its aim is to create an autarchic system. Note how each work refers back to its predecessor. Quilty drapes himself in a toga at the beginning of *Lolita* and declares, 'I am Spartacus'. The cosmic explosion at the end of *Dr Strangelove* is a prelude to *2001*. The foetus's eye at the end of that film prefigures *A Clockwork Orange*'s close-up on the eye of the mutant Alex. The tramp's song at the beginning of the latter film – 'Men on the moon and spinning around the earth . . . and there's not no attention paid to earthly law and order no more' – alludes explicitly to *2001*, as does the record sleeve in the

drugstore visited by Alex. Barry Lyndon buys a painting by an artist called Ludovico, which is the name of the treatment inflicted on Alex in prison. Alex sees himself in an old movie seducing his wife's servants, just as Barry deceives his own wife with whores. As for the gentry dressed in Victorian clothes who applaud Alex's sexual exploits in the last shot of *A Clockwork Orange*, mightn't they be the future readers of Thackeray revelling in Barry's rakish escapades?

But this self-preoccupation can also be taken as summing-up, as an end to art (in Hegel's sense when he spoke of an end to history). Kubrick's perfectionism, the passion with which this insatiable *cinéphile* undertakes each of his projects, may be said to derive from a dissatisfaction with what was limited or left unfinished in previous films. Hence his iconoclasm retains close links with cultural traditions. Though, possessing neither forerunners nor successors, *Dr Strangelove* and *A Clockwork Orange* are *sui generis*, *2001: A Space Odyssey* might well be the film which Méliès dreamt of while making *Voyage dans la lune* (*A Trip to the Moon*), and *Barry Lyndon* the culmination of Griffith's work on the historical film in *America.*

His love of innovation is therefore accompanied by a refusal (one founded on reason?) to see innovation imposed *at any cost.* Insubordination and revolt have become the snares of modernity. Those who believed it possible to identify Kubrick with *A Clockwork Orange* will have to think again. Its jaundiced negativity could not become stereotyped as what it expressed was a fundamental pessimism, a nostalgia rooted in a meditation on history.

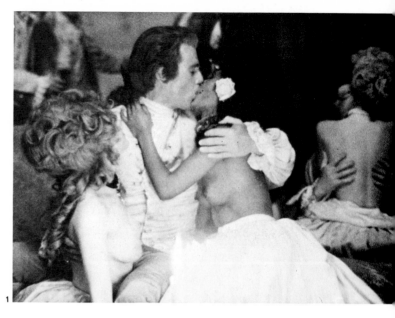

1. *Barry Lyndon* (Ryan O'Neal) *deceives his wife with whores just as* Alex (Malcolm McDowell) *dreamt of seducing his wife's servant girls in a historical movie* (A Clockwork Orange) *(2)*

3. *The festivities of* Barry Lyndon *(Ryan O'Neal, centre, Philip Stone, right) a costume film anticipated by the last shot of* A Clockwork Orange *(4)*

The first reviewers of *Barry Lyndon* were no less baffled by Kubrick's choice of Thackeray's novel than they had been by the Louis XVI décor in the final section of *2001: A Space Odyssey*. In fact, novel and décor share the same historical context: the eighteenth century. Arthur C. Clarke, the scenarist of *2001*, once conjectured that the astronaut Dave Bowman might have been placed under observation by extraterrestrial beings who, to put him at ease, furnished the room out of his own memory. *Barry Lyndon* offers an explanation as to why his memory should have focused on the eighteenth century, but one cannot help remarking how often, on those rare occasions when the past has been present in Kubrick's work (with the exception of *Spartacus*, a project not originated by him), it is this period that has engaged his interest. There was the Gainsborough-like portrait behind which Quilty died, riddled with bullets, in *Lolita*; the château in *Paths of Glory* whose civilized opulence made a startling contrast with the butchery of trench warfare; and the abandoned casino and pastoral fresco which framed the violent brawl between Alex's gang and Billyboy's in *A Clockwork Orange*. The latter film makes explicit reference in its overall structure to the Voltairean philosophic tale (*Candide*); and to Swift with 'nadsat', the language of the 'droogs', in which the word for 'head' is 'gulliver'. In these scenes, violence and death are invariably juxtaposed with the art or architecture of the eighteenth century, as was the old man's death agony in *2001* before his resurrection as an astral foetus.

It was not to be expected, then, that Kubrick's view of the eighteenth century would be the conventional one, mythical and make-believe, made up of lightness and lechery, frivolity and soft-focus contentment. *Barry Lyndon* restores sobriety and historical weight to the period: in many respects, the modern world is directly descended from the century of enlightenment and Kubrick, after concerning himself with the future for ten years, was patently going to be drawn back to

1

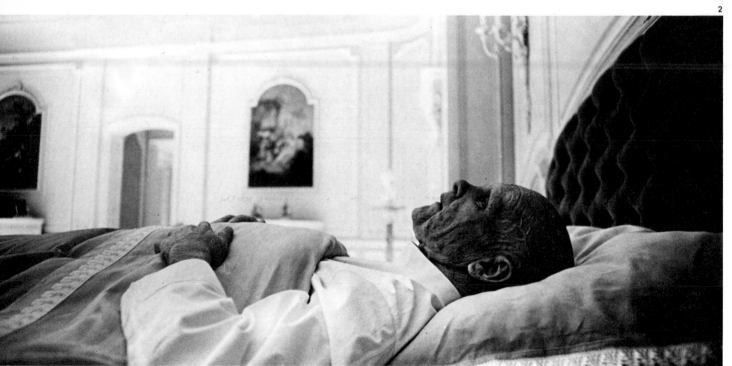

2

3

4

In Kubrick's work, death and violence are linked to the eighteenth century:
1. Timothy Carey, Ralph Meeker, Joseph Turkel and the hall of the château in Paths of Glory
2. Keir Dullea in the room of 2001: A Space Odyssey
3. The Seven Years War (Godfrey Quigley in the foreground, Ryan O'Neal in Barry Lyndon)
4. The Seven Years War (Barry Lyndon)

its origins. For him, a work of art is a dialogue between past and future from which the present – which is to say, life – has been excluded. The principle of creation is death, and all art is informed with a destructive and disturbing quality. As Vienna was for Sternberg, Stroheim and numerous artists of the Hapsburg period, for Kubrick the eighteenth century is rotten to the core, an age awaiting its impending destruction; behind the façade of gaiety, luxury and pleasure, death and disintegration are already lurking.

Kubrick planned to adapt two 'Viennese' novels, Stefan Zweig's *The Burning Secret* and Arthur Schnitzler's *Rhapsody: A Dream Novel*. He employed the waltz for both the ball sequence in *Paths of Glory* and the spacecraft in *2001*, and he has obvious affinities with the whole Viennese spirit. Note, for example, the resemblances between *Barry Lyndon* and another historical film, Sternberg's *The Scarlet Empress*, in their use of music and commentary, in their direction of actors and their irony.

Barry Lyndon's life, as it grows darker and darker in the film's second half, therefore becomes the metonym of the century, tracing a parabola which leads to nothingness.

5

The eighteenth century also saw the conjunction of reason and passion. As will be shown, these are the two poles of Kubrick's universe. Reason can be found in the philosophy of enlightenment, in architecture, in the birth of science and technology (before conquering space, man learns to fly), in a taste for automata (Vaucanson's duck, Kempelen's chess-player) – that encounter between the living and the mechanical whose most advanced form in the cinema is HAL 9000, the computer in *2001* – in the ceaseless thirsting after knowledge of the encyclopaedists, with whom an autodidact like Kubrick can be compared in the way he methodically and systematically explores the various disciplines covered by his films. Man's power is dependent on his knowledge, and the domination of the world (or the cinema) knows no bounds. But this taste for logic and symmetry is accompanied by the glorifying of the emotions, just as Palladian architecture might be surrounded by an English garden. Laclos, a ballistics

The Viennese waltz
1. George Macready (Paths of Glory)
2. Aboard Aries (2001 : A Space Odyssey)

expert and inventor of the shell, and Beaumarchais, a clockmaker and inventor of the lever watch, were no less skilled in the depiction of feelings. As Jean Starobinski noted: 'From the beginning of that "rationalistic" century, the theorists of reason willingly recognized the absolute domination of passion in the field of poetry and the fine arts.' And further: 'The rule always invoked by the period was that of the pleasure of the soul: the pleasure of the overview in symmetry, the pleasure of perpetual renewal in variety and contrast[241].' Kubrick's tireless activity, the way he will pursue every project to its ultimate limit, his rational yet fanatical exploration of knowledge, are nurtured by an enthusiasm that can never be satisfied. The perfection principle laid down by the theorists of progress anticipates the notion of the mind's evolution to which nineteenth-century philosophers were so attached: two ideas that are closely linked in *2001*.

But, as *2001* and *Dr Strangelove* demonstrate, pure rationality may end up as totally irrational. Both the German scientist and the computer HAL 9000 decline into madness and delirium. There, too, reason and passion are locked in ruthless combat, a fruitful one for the artist if we are to believe Freud, for whom 'there is in madness not only method but a fragment of historical truth'.

6

The rigidly logical construction of Kubrick's works is the sign of a deep-seated anxiety against which it represents perhaps the final refuge. The very titles of *Fear and Desire*, *Killer's Kiss*, *The Killing* and *Dr Strangelove* embody the link between love and death which is the essence of his films. In *Killer's Kiss* the night-club proprietor ardently kisses a young woman while revelling in the massacre of the hero by his opponent in a televised boxing match; in *The Killing* the impotent gangster fires his revolver at the woman who deceived him; in *Lolita* Humbert's passion is one long act of self-destruction ending in Quilty's murder; in *Dr Strangelove* General Jack D. Ripper decides to annihilate the enemy which, he claims, is polluting the earth's water, and prefers to abstain from sexual relations; in *A Clockwork Orange* Alex's erotic ballets with Mrs Alexander and the Cat Lady are also dances of death; and in *Spartacus* Crassus desires Varinia, a woman loved by the man who haunts him and whose image pursues him.

In a different sense, though still linked to the same obsession, one remembers the scene in *Spartacus* where the leader of the freed slaves and his friend Antoninus are condemned to fight each other to the death, the victor then having to die by crucifixion. To spare the young man from even more suffering, Spartacus kills him, embracing him with the words 'I love you'. And Varinia's last words to the crucified Spartacus are 'Oh, my love – my life. Please die.' The omnipresent violence (fields strewn with corpses in *Spartacus* and *Barry Lyndon*, the final butchery of *The Killing*, the attack by night in *Paths of Glory*, the gang-fights, rapes and muggings in *A Clockwork Orange*, the duels in *Barry Lyndon*, the slowly executed murder in *Lolita*, Bowman's struggle with HAL 9000 which mirrors the battle of the apes for possession of the waterhole in *2001*, the nuclear explosion in *Dr Strangelove*) is linked to a sexual malaise, to a 'strange love' whose only possible outcome is a no less strange form of death. Kubrick's vision of history is a nightmare, illustrated by ordinary, everyday terror, executions '*pour encourager les autres*', the atomic holocaust, the savagery of the Roman legions, and the corruption and brutality of American society. Like Turgidson or Ripper, Dr Strangelove is *literally* in love with death. Eroticism is displaced from woman to death; and if in American society death tends to be treated as a taboo, the

Hand-to-hand combat:
1. Jamie Smith, right (Killer's Kiss)
2. Sterling Hayden, right (The Killing)
3. Ryan O'Neal (from behind), Norman Mitchell, Pat Roach (Barry Lyndon)

Duels:
1. Malcolm McDowell, right (A Clockwork Orange)
2. Steven Berkoff (from behind), Ryan O'Neal (Barry Lyndon)
3. The first duel in Barry Lyndon, the death of the father

power élite nevertheless operates through institutionalized violence. In his masterly essay, *Life Against Death*, Norman O. Brown examines the relation between the life (and love) instinct and the death instinct, demonstrating that the history of mankind is that of a neurosis linked to man's sense of guilt. But, now that the annihilation of mankind has become possible, the struggle between Eros and Thanatos may well end with the victory of death. Given his preoccupations, it was logical that Kubrick would eventually film the nuclear conflict of *Dr Strangelove*; as Freud wrote in *Civilization and Its Discontents*: 'Men today have advanced so far in their mastery of the forces of nature that, with their help, mutual extermination down to the very last human being has been made easy. Their awareness of this fact explains much of their present agitation, their unhappiness and anxiety'. Speaking of Swift, Norman Brown noted that what was more important than interpreting his works as the symptoms of his own individual neurosis was to observe the insight which he brought to the universal neurosis of mankind, and one can see Kubrick as a similar exponent of his period. Certainly, Swift's excremental vision is close to that of Kubrick's. Along with the biting irony which reduces men to the level of grotesque puppets, the use of names in *Dr Strangelove* recalls that of *Gulliver's Travels*: the Laputa base, the Russian minister Kissov, Ambassador de Sadesky, General Turgidson, Colonel Bat Guano, President Murkin Muffley and the bomber 'Leper Colony.' The satiric force of Kubrick's imagery is equivalent to those verbal witticisms whose relation to the subconscious has been defined by Freud, with his belief that humour was also a means of exploring the universal neurosis. The humour of *Dr Strangelove* culminates in its final shot in which a nostalgic ballad of the forties 'We'll meet again, don't know where, don't know when . . .' is warbled over imagery of radio-active clouds and death. This further association of love and death mirrors the film's opening shots in which bombers 'copulate' in the sky, and a later image of Major Kong astride a phallic hydrogen bomb.

The satire is no less biting in *A Clockwork Orange*, where Alex inflicts tortures on his victims to the strains of 'Singin' in the Rain'. And to interpret the climax of *Paths of Glory* along humanistic lines – in the spirit of, say, Renoir's *La Grande Illusion* – is to misunderstand Kubrick's intentions. After the execution of their three innocent comrades, the other soldiers move off rather passively to listen to a café-singer who manages to bring tears to their eyes with a complacently sentimental song. It's an ironic coda to a film in which burlesque is a crucial element, sometimes implicitly, sometimes overtly as in the scenes involving the High Command. The 'grotesque' Kubrick cannot be separated from the 'serious' Kubrick, which is how he tended to be viewed prior to *Dr Strangelove*. One has only to remember the mask attached to Johnny Clay's face during the heist in *The Killing*; the French general ordering his own troops to be fired upon and the inspection of the trenches by beribboned old fogeys in *Paths of Glory*; Peter Ustinov as the gladiators' master, the central figure of a corrupt world, in *Spartacus*; the outrageous caricatures in *Dr Strangelove*; and the folding bed, the character of Charlotte and the condolences offered Humbert in his bath in *Lolita*.

3

4

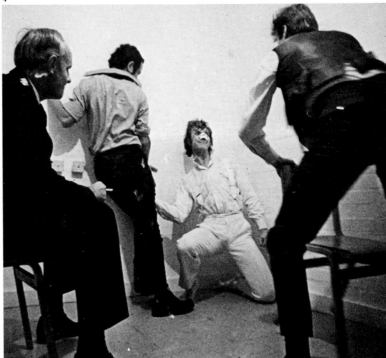

Violence:
1. *Kirk Douglas* (Paths of Glory)
2. *Kirk Douglas* (Spartacus)
3. *James Mason* (Lolita)
4. *Malcolm McDowell* (A Clockwork Orange)

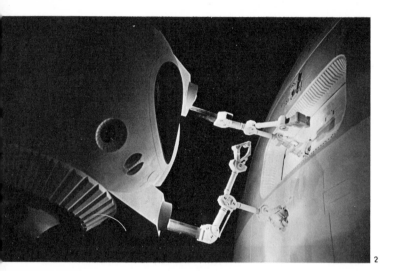

The death instinct
1. *The Dawn of Man* (2001: A Space Odyssey)
2. *The sphere and the spacecraft* Discovery (2001: A Space Odyssey)
3. *Billyboy's gang* (A Clockwork Orange)
4. *Slim Pickens* (Dr Strangelove)

SL 9198

7

Kubrick's world is forever on the brink of collapse, whether it be that of an individual or a society. In this respect, it is worth noting that he has disowned the happy ending of *Killer's Kiss*, a film whose tone throughout is that of a waking nightmare. The atmosphere of *The Killing* is Hustonian, but the bitterness of defeat is not even redeemed by the glory of having at least fought: what prevails is a sense of waste and destruction. In as early a film as *Fear and Desire*, four soldiers engaged in a symbolic war infiltrate behind enemy lines, clear a path through the forest, massacre a detachment and attack an enemy post, only to discover that their exploit has been meaningless and that they are in precisely the same situation as when they started out. Kubrick's is a universe that alternates between pursuit and stagnation, as expressed in the bric-à-brac and weird décors of his films; lamps, blinds and eerie shadows in *The Killing*; a basement crammed with mannequins in *Killer's Kiss*; the jumble of suitcases, statues, glasses, bottles and paintings in the Ali Baba's den which serves as Quilty's abode in *Lolita*; the fallen trees, the landscape strewn with detritus in *Paths of Glory*.

It is all stiflingly claustrophobic; and though, on Kubrick's part, one senses a desire to open up his sets as far as possible (as with the immense War Room in *Dr Strangelove*), they nevertheless remain prisons. Which is why he has had such frequent recourse to a kind of movement that may be termed baroque in the way it dynamically articulates the filmic space (in his early work by a somewhat systematic use of lateral tracking shots, and much more radically since *2001* when his primary concern has been for an ever greater distillation and purity of style). The confined space which Kubrick's camera movements endeavour to pulverize has its correlative in the sweat and painful breathlessness of his characters. One has only to think of the respiratory difficulties suffered by the boxer in *Killer's Kiss*, or the poison gas victims in *Paths of Glory*, or Humbert who died, after all, of a heart attack; one thinks, too, of the *angina pectoris* whose anxiety symptoms plague the astronauts in *2001*, and the patients who, when subjected to Dr Brodsky's treatment in *A Clockwork Orange*, experience a feeling of suffocation close to death. If Spartacus (a hero imposed on Kubrick) alone manages to rise above this despair, it is because he dreams of changing the world and attains both love and liberty by sundering his chains (except that asphyxiation is also what one dies of on the cross and it was at the director's own suggestion that the final crucifixion was added to Dalton Trumbo's original script).

8

Kubrick's fascination with machinery can be traced to the same dream as that of the makers of automata, analysed by Starobinski: the creation of a machine which would accomplish almost everything of which nature is capable. 'Might not the processes of reason inspire inanimate matter with the breath of life?' Thus the demiurgic temptation to which Faust succumbed and which would give rise to the myth of the Golem originated with the development of the sciences. And the cinema itself might be seen as another expression of the desire to dominate and reproduce. Chinese shadows and optical toys were an eighteenth-century craze. They were at the source of that preoccupation with illusionism which was to culminate in the cinema, with *Morel's Invention*, as imagined by the Argentinian novelist Bioy Casares, remaining the inaccessible goal. The cinema, and prior to it the realistic novel of the eighteenth century (of which Thackeray's *Barry Lyndon*, written a century later, is clearly a pastiche), pose more acutely than ever the epistemological problem of the correspondence between a work of art and the reality it imitates. A problem raised by Alex during the Ludovico treatment in *A Clockwork Orange* when he exclaims: 'It's funny how the colours of the real world only appear really real when you viddy them on the screen?'

Kubrick, more than any other contemporary film-maker, has immersed himself in the problems of art and technology. Like the medium's pioneers (Griffith, Murnau), and with a zeal comparable to theirs, he recognized that the intensification of realism on the screen was dependent on the development of technological artifice. His experiments with transparencies, models and other special effects for *2001*, with direct sound recording on lightweight microphones for *A Clockwork Orange* and with lighting for *Barry Lyndon* have all engendered technological improvements and accentuated the impression of reality. They can be compared with Griffith exhorting his cameraman Billy Bitzer to improve the lighting of his films or Murnau forcing Karl Freund to invent a more mobile camera. And the painstaking attention – worthy of that other 'primitive', Stroheim – which he brings to set and costume design (constructing an exact replica of a B-52 interior for *Dr Strangelove* at a cost of 100,000 dollars; studying the history of eighteenth-century art for *Barry Lyndon*) is part of the same obsession with authenticity. But it would be a mistake to suppose that Kubrick was aiming for some kind of superficial naturalism. Like Hegel in this respect, yet again, he reverts to the real as a means of avoiding the arbitrary and the conventional. This is how one should read his desire to know and reproduce the forms and figures of reality in their most infinitesimal nuances. But the imitation of nature must not lead to *trompe-l'oeil*. It remains inseparable from the significant expression of an idea. 'It is the expression of spirituality that must prevail. That is what naturalism is incapable of achieving and therein lies its impotence. Nature and reality are wells from which art must draw its inspiration. The ideal, too. For the ideal is not something nebulous, general or abstract. ... Art occupies the middle ground between pure sensibility and pure thought.' (Hegel's *Aesthetics*) Kubrick's art is both conceptual and concrete. He begins with a concept and exploits the finite and particular only as a means of returning to the universal and abstract. Thus the impact of his films derives from the way their powerful physical presence and materiality is underpinned by an almost mathematical logic.

The power possessed by images is evoked by Kubrick in the Ludovico treatment. It is with images that Alex is conditioned, his brain washed. Every artist is in his fashion an illusionist. In *Barry Lyndon* the conjuror convinces little Bryan that he is his own master when, in fact, like every spectator, the child is being manipulated. He predicts the future, appears to be laying his *cards on the table* (and his forecast overlaps the film's own commentary, informing the spectator of Bullingdon's feelings towards his stepfather), but the real action is taking place elsewhere. The film-maker is also a magician – he plays with retinal persistence, making us believe we are perceiving movement when we are not – and his illusions recall those of the conjuror's sleight-of-hand. This image of the prompter and the 'theatre of society' is introduced in the film's first section when, at Dunleary Camp, Thomas 'prompts' Barry on how best to annoy Toole, who has insulted him.

A world on the brink of collapse (Paths of Glory)

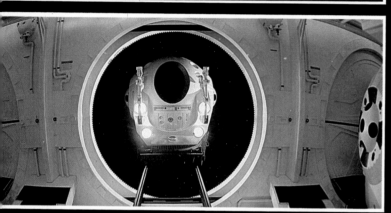

Kubrick's fascination with machines (2001 : A Space Odyssey)

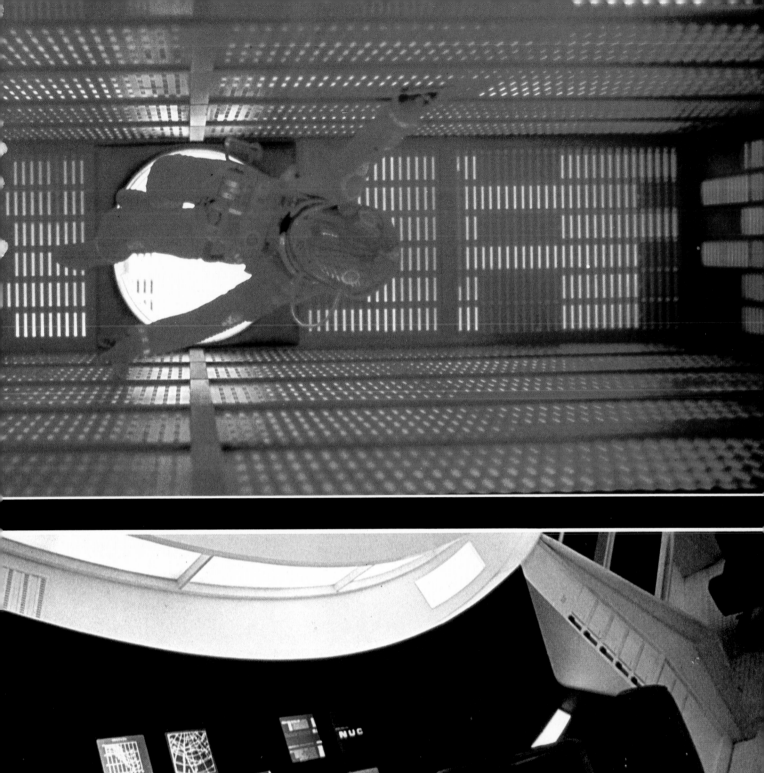

9

Theatre – indeed, theatricality in every form – has always been one of the principal references in Kubrick's work: the café-singer entertaining the troops in *Paths of Glory*, the high-school play in *Lolita*, the concert and conjuring tricks in *Barry Lyndon*, the dolls, puppets and mannequins in *Killer's Kiss* and *A Clockwork Orange*. *Barry Lyndon* in its entirety may be seen as the portrait of a play-acting society: festivities and banquets, ceremonies and mere encounters all seem to obey strictly formalized rules and rituals. War itself becomes the expression of choreographed violence: the troops advance and retreat like so many automata in accordance with a strategy whose meaning now escapes us. But it is above all in *A Clockwork Orange* that Kubrick subjects the very function of theatricality to critical scrutiny. Not only does Alex directly address the public – taking it to one side, as it were – but he becomes an actor himself; his brawl with Billyboy's gang is as choreographed as a ballet and takes place on the stage of an abandoned casino. Later, to demonstrate the effects of the Ludovico treatment, the Minister presents the guinea-pig Alex to a crowd of spectators; and on a platform the young hooligan, now cured, licks his aggressor's shoe and resists

Theatre:
1. *Sue Lyon, centre (Lolita)*
2. *Malcolm McDowell (A Clockwork Orange)*
3. *Marisa Berenson (Barry Lyndon)*
4. *Suzanne Christian, today Stanley Kubrick's wife (Paths of Glory)*
5. *Woody Strode (from behind) and Kirk Douglas (Spartacus)*
6. *Virginia Weatherell, Malcolm McDowell (A Clockwork Orange)*

the advances of a half-naked blonde, thereby proving that he has sworn off sex and violence. Alex's visions while listening to the Ninth Symphony in his bedroom or reading in prison are influenced by Hollywood: he imagines himself as Dracula, a centurion scourging Christ, an oriental prince savouring the delights of the flesh as in the 'historical' films of Cecil B. De Mille (or Kubrick's *Spartacus*?). And, as part of his cure, Dr Brodsky forces him to watch American action movies and Nazi newsreel footage.

At first glance, Kubrick would appear to be criticizing facile, irresponsible entertainments. But isn't he himself titillating the spectator with what he is supposed to be attacking? In fact, the visual style of *A Clockwork Orange* was clearly adopted to frustrate any such possibility of identification. Instead of aiming for narrative fluidity, Kubrick uses various devices to fragment the image: speeded-up motion for the orgy with the two girls, slow-motion when Alex reasserts his authority over his droogs, a series of brief shots during the off-screen murder of the Cat Lady, and a rapid, almost mechanical montage of statues of Christ in Alex's bedroom. Alex himself is little more than a cartoon character, almost a shadow or silhouette, as in the tunnel where he assaults a tramp or on the prison stage.

Like all of Kubrick's work, *A Clockwork Orange* feeds on the same popular culture of which it offers a critique. Already in *The Killing* he cast each of the actors for his mythic aura, his roots in the *film noir* tradition: Sterling Hayden (from *The Asphalt Jungle*), Ted de Corsia and Colleen Gray (from *Kiss of Death*), Elisha Cook Jr. (from *The Maltese Falcon*) and, of course, Marie Windsor. In *Spartacus* he took full advantage of the ironic, if not entirely unjustified, casting of American actors (Kirk Douglas, Tony Curtis, Woody Strode) as the slaves opposite British actors (Laurence Olivier, Charles Laughton, Peter Ustinov) as the patrician class. In *Dr Strangelove* Slim Pickens, who straddles the bomb (named 'Lolita' in Peter George's original novel!) with a stetson on his head, was well-known for his appearances in Westerns; and Keenan Wynn, Colonel 'Bat' Guano, comically at odds with a Coca-Cola bottle, used to play Red Skelton's sidekick on television. The popular songs used in *Dr Strangelove* – 'Try a Little Tenderness' over credit-title imagery of bombers in flight; 'When Johnny Comes Marching Home' for the pilots

Alex's dreams, influenced by Hollywood movies à la DeMille, or possibly by Spartacus?
1. *Malcolm McDowell, extreme right* (A Clockwork Orange)
2. *The revolt of the slaves* (Spartacus)
3. *Malcolm McDowell* (A Clockwork Orange)

Role-playing: Kirk Douglas (Spartacus)

going to their death and who precisely will not come marching home; 'We'll Meet Again' as accompaniment to the final holocaust – operate as a sardonic counterpoint drawn from the stockpile of 'golden oldies'. In this resides the ambiguity of Kubrick's position vis-à-vis popular culture: on the one hand, as we have seen[32], he recognises its vital importance (even when the example is as provocative as the pornography of *A Clockwork Orange*); on the other, he questions its values by demonstrating just how easily it can cause the spectator to lose touch with reality.

10

'Play-acting' is also present in Kubrick's work in the form of disguise. Masks, as Georges Buraud has noted, infuse new energy into us. 'The wearing of a mask galvanizes us into taking action, exerting ourselves, surpassing ourselves[221].' The grotesque disguises sported by Alex and his droogs correspond to carnival masks; they represent a rejection of civilization and reversion to animal pleasures, a kind of mental panic which in this case turns to destructive rage. Western society has increasingly tried to repress the libido; and in the eighteenth century the last vestiges of the mask were prettified into the rouge and powder which give the characters of *Barry Lyndon* the appearance of livid ghosts in a kingdom of shadows. Such make-up reappears in the 'public lives' of Alex and Lolita.

More significantly, Kubrick knows how to expose the inner mask of an individual, a mask which ends by rising to the surface, organizing the features of the face into a unique expression. The uneasiness caused by his generals, preachers, politicians and careerists derives either from the

Masks:
1. James Marcus, Adrienne Corri (A Clockwork Orange)
2. Sterling Hayden (The Killing)

Make-up:
1. Malcolm McDowell (A
Clockwork Orange)
2. James Mason, Sue Lyon (Lolita)

intensity of their features or from their caricatural mobility. According to Buraud's analysis, to experience ambition or love, to dominate another creature or assure one's future through selfish calculations, means withdrawing into the illusory present, repressing the depths of one's being so that only a shallow façade will be visible on the surface.

11

In more general terms, the mask, the theatre and theatricality are all forms of game-playing. Competitive games (including sport) constitute an autonomous world on the fringe of reality but also reflecting it, whose strict codes and precise, universally respected rules offer a startling contrast to the anarchy and confusion of the world. In a sense, games represent the ideal of every society, the fulfillment of a civilisation, towards which man has always tended. As closed, disciplined systems,

The face as mask:
1. *Patrick Magee* (A Clockwork Orange)
2. *George C. Scott* (Dr Strangelove)
3. *Peter Bull* (Dr Strangelove)
4. *Leonard Rossiter* (Barry Lyndon)
5. *Jack Nicholson* (The Shining)

eliminating chance from life, they are the embodiment of the eighteenth century – even if, as *Barry Lyndon* shows, that period never quite succeeded in concealing the submerged violence which it claimed to have suppressed. Games are also, according to Roger Caillois, 'doomed to create nothing and produce nothing, their essence being precisely to negate results whereas work and science capitalise on theirs and, if possible, transform the world[223].' Game-playing and play-acting on one side, work and science on the other, pleasurable activity and material productivity, all of Kubrick's films reflect these antitheses. They are punctuated by boxing

matches (*Killer's Kiss*, *Barry Lyndon*, Poole's shadow-boxing and even the judo on television in *2001*), duels (*Killer's Kiss*, *Spartacus*, *Barry Lyndon*), card games (*The Killing*, *Barry Lyndon*), billiards (*A Clockwork Orange*), Ping-Pong (*Lolita*) and horse-racing (*The Killing*).

And inevitably, chess, the director's favourite pastime, in which, as he has said (see the interview on *The Shining*), intuition and calculation are equally combined. Chess reveals the duality proper to every game: the evaluation of available resources and the calculation of probable consequences, the accepted risk and the anticipated result. There are actual games of chess played in *The Killing* (at Maurice's club), *Lolita* (between Humbert and Charlotte) and *2001* (between Bowman and HAL 9000); but, more important, the majority of Kubrick's films are based on power struggles, calculations of probability calling for both caution and daring. The hold-up of *The Killing*, the military strategy of *Paths of Glory*, *Spartacus* and *Dr Strangelove*, the political manoeuvring of *A Clockwork Orange* and the personal manoeuvring of *Lolita* and *Barry Lyndon*, all follow the same pattern: a regular advance, interspersed with shows of strength, also becomes a battle against time and, therefore, against death. In *Paths of Glory*, General Mireau measures the percentage of human loss against the ground gained in yards as a means of calculating his own chances of promotion. *The Killing* is structured as a series of flashbacks which recount the same day from the vantage points of various characters, allowing us each time to retrace the steps of the gangster obsessed with

2

1

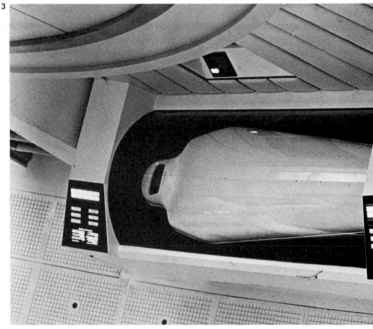

3

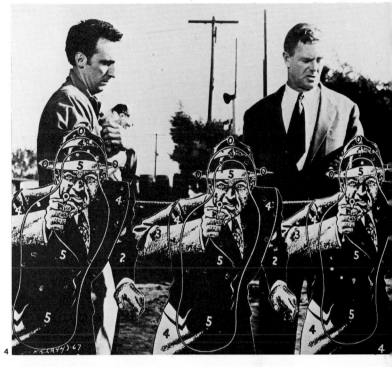

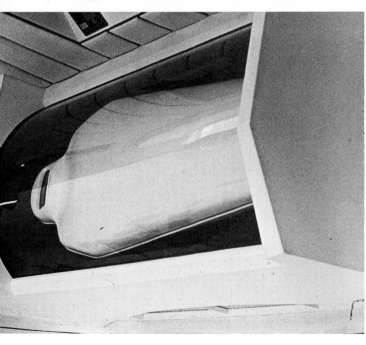

Man and his facsimiles: diving-suits, mannequins, mummies, human targets, sculptures:
1. The astronauts on the moon in 2001: A Space Odyssey
2. Frank Silvera (from behind), Jamie Smith (Killer's Kiss)
3. The astronauts in hibernation aboard the Discovery (2001: A Space Odyssey)
4. Timothy Carey, Sterling Hayden (The Killing)
5. Michael Tarn, Warren Clarke, Malcolm McDowell, James Marcus (A Clockwork Orange)

his hold-up and view the event from different angles. In his own fashion, Humbert fights against time to seduce a Lolita who is becoming (too rapidly for his liking) an adult.

Dr Strangelove is an exemplary illustration of this perfect logic, too perfect in fact not to be thrown out of kilter by some unforeseen error. The gambler in Kubrick was fascinated by the possibilities of an accidental nuclear war, by the situation of the world's two superpowers; and, to demonstrate the kind of problem he was portraying, he used the analogy of a game: 'Two men get on a train in different cars – they know the rules but they can't communicate. And the game is this: that if they both get off at the first station, man A gets ten dollars and man B gets three dollars. If they both get off at the second station, man B gets ten dollars and man A gets three dollars. But if they don't get off at the same station, in other words if they get off differently, neither one of them gets anything. So here you have a situation where you have mutual conflict and mutual interest and great chances for misunderstanding, even under the circumstances where one side was willing to give a little more than the other, or than he was willing to take[10].'

The symbolism of chess, a game that originated in India, bears a resemblance to that of military strategy. It represents a conflict between black and white pieces, between shadow and light, between the Titans and the Gods ... What is at stake in the conflict is the supremacy of the world. A normal chessboard has sixty-four squares (sixty-four being the number of the fulfillment of cosmic unity) and is the symbol of existence. The conflict can be transposed onto the existential plane where the player's skill coincides with universal intelligence[234]. There was nothing fortuitous about Kubrick's collaboration with another great lover of chess, Nabokov (whose *Laughter in the Dark* he also considered adapting), and Edmond Bernhard has analysed the themes of the novel *Lolita* in terms of the game.

Games:
1. James Mason, Sue Lyon, Shelley Winters (Lolita)
2. Ryan O'Neal (from behind), Gay Hamilton
Following pages:
Ryan O'Neal (from behind), Murray Melvin, Marisa Berenson (Barry Lyndon)

12

Lolita (1962) is a great but greatly misunderstood film. Few critics defended it on its release and yet every viewing confirms its status as not only a decisive turning-point for Kubrick but as one of the keys to his inner universe. Sue Lyon, it was objected, was physically too mature for the role. To be sure, it would have been difficult for Kubrick to show in the cinema, at the period when the film was made, what in literature is after all transformed by the abstraction of Nabokov's language and his allusive, elliptical style. But it should also be remembered that little girls in America dress and make themselves up like women and that the age difference would therefore be less distracting than one might think. It is when Humbert at last rediscovers his Dolly married and pregnant that Sue Lyon appears too young for the role of wife and mother. But if Kubrick certainly could not hope to rival Nabokov in terms of eroticism, the film is imbued with an undeniable malaise. The spectator feels a certain uneasiness which he cannot pin down if he has not read the book. Lolita is no longer a nymphet, but the book's equivocal atmosphere continues to linger, creating an impression all the stranger for being apparently without reason. Similarly, in *L'Education sentimentale* the description of the Arnoux couple tends to unsettle the reader for a reason he cannot understand because it is never revealed (and it would have been impossible for Flaubert to do so, given that he himself did not know that the couple on whom he based his characters were not married, even if he could sense the peculiar nature of their relationship).

That Sue Lyon is no nymphet also makes Humbert's despair more complex since it is no longer exclusively based on a social taboo. The malaise in *Lolita* is already perceptible in the character of Humbert as written by Nabokov, but Kubrick has invested it with an unbearable current of anxiety and morbidity. The director intentionally imprisoned his film in a flashback inspired by the novel's concluding chapter, as the shooting of Quilty through the portrait of a hauntingly beautiful woman would set the requisite tone of black humour. Death is also present in the person of the deceased husband making himself felt between Mrs Haze and Humbert, then in the body of Mrs Haze herself coming between Humbert and Lolita.

In a way, Quilty becomes the central character of *Lolita*. Because of Peter Sellers' overpowering performance, his presence was widely regarded as a superfluity, but he represents one of Kubrick's most deeply rooted obsessions: the double. Quilty is Humbert's double, just as Humbert Humbert is a double name. Already in Kubrick's first short, *Day of the Fight*, the boxer had a twin brother. In *Fear and Desire*, Kubrick emphasized – none too subtly – the bizarre and ambiguous presence of another self or its own negation: two soldiers killed an enemy general and his aide-de-camp and each of the victims was played by the same actor who played his killer. In *Spartacus* the idea of a hundred slaves answering with one voice to the hero's name must have appealed to the director. In *2001* Bowman literally sees himself at various stages of the ageing process. In *A Clockwork Orange* Mr Alexander is a reflection of Alex (as suggested by his very name, his facial resemblance to Beethoven, his doorbell which chimes the opening notes of the Fifth Symphony). In *Barry Lyndon* Barry's name phonetically echoes that of Bullingdon, his stepson, and Balibari, his protector.

In *Lolita*'s satirical travelogue of America, Quilty is a lurking threat, a pursuing shadow, the spy of a society that hunts witches but whose own corruption surpasses that of its victims. Incarnating three faces of the same character, Peter Sellers prefigured his creation of Dr Strangelove, particularly in the role of Dr Zempf, the school psychologist whose thick German accent recalls that of the mad professor (note Kubrick's ambiguous feelings towards Germany: his admiration for its culture, its music above all, from Beethoven to Richard Strauss; and his fear of its demonstrations of power: Zempf in *Lolita*, Strangelove, the Nazi newsreel footage in *A Clockwork Orange*). It was by inventing a police convention in *Lolita* that Kubrick was able yet again to assail the representatives of authority. Authority is also the superego which prevents his characters (notably Humbert) from living freely and obeying their personal instincts. The state of despair induced by their obsessive fear of having infringed the taboos of their society culminates in madness (Humbert struggling in the hospital corridor, the pleasure he takes in murdering Quilty), just as Quilty's dialogue on normality borders on delirium. Like General Broulard in *Paths of Glory*, Crassus in *Spartacus*, Dr Strangelove, the Minister and Dr Brodsky in *A Clockwork Orange*, Quilty is a super-technician, a manipulator, the incarnation of power.

Peter Sellers' disguises in Lolita *foreshadow his roles in* Dr Strangelove
1. Peter Sellers, James Mason (Lolita)
2. Marianne Stone, Peter Sellers, Shelley Winters (Lolita)
3. Preparatory photographs for Dr Strangelove. Clockwise: the President of the United States, Dr Strangelove, Group-Captain Mandrake, Major T. J. 'King' Kong (a role eventually played by Slim Pickens following an accident to Peter Sellers)

3

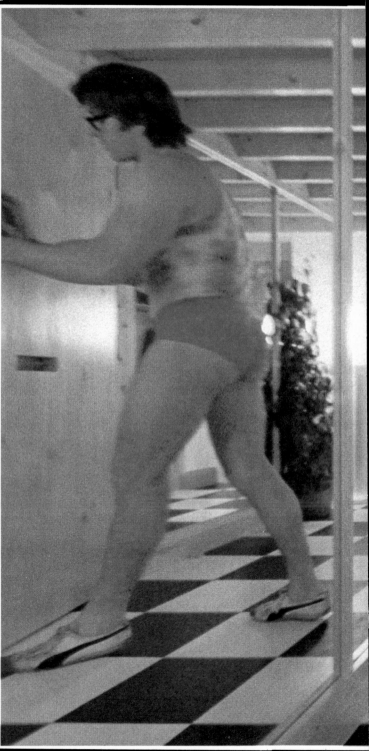

Symmetry:
1. *Margaret Tyzack, Patrick Magee, David Prowse, John Savident*
(A Clockwork Orange)
2. *David Prowse, Malcolm McDowell* (A Clockwork Orange)

13

In a brilliant essay[141], Robert Benayoun has demonstrated how close the libertarian position taken by Stanley Kubrick in *A Clockwork Orange* is to that of Stirner who, in *The Ego and His Own,* posed the crucial question raised by the film: 'How can one liberate man without, at the same time, setting free the non-man?' By refusing to gloss over the horror of Alex's behaviour, Kubrick actually heightens his condemnation of a government whose methods of conditioning horrify us *even* when applied to such a character. In this he is only being consistent, for such criticism of the State is to be found in all his films, from the position of Colonel Dax in *Paths of Glory* who quotes Dr Johnson's celebrated phrase 'Patriotism is the last resort of the scoundrel' to the denunciation of the high military command in *Dr Strangelove*, without forgetting Spartacus's revolt in a film that Kubrick has disowned because it was not he who initiated the project, but whose themes coincided with his own.

Power struggles are symbolized in visual terms by the setting of the action: the contrast between the château of the generals and the trenches of the infantrymen in *Paths of Glory*, the patrician abodes and the slave camp in *Spartacus*, Quilty's luxurious mansion and Charlotte Haze's lower-middle-class apartment in *Lolita*, the War Room and Burpelson Base in *Dr Strangelove*, Mr Alexander's trendy residence and Alex's council flat in *A Clockwork Orange*. The

In Kubrick's work, however, revolt ends in failure. Each of his films tells a story of fragmentation and disintegration. Often a group is gradually dispersed, with the loss of every one of its members (*Fear and Desire*, *The Killing*, *Paths of Glory*, *2001*, *A Clockwork Orange*); or else the family unit, sometimes the couple, breaks up (*Lolita*, *Barry Lyndon*, *The Shining*); and even the characters' bodies may be injured, mutilated or disabled.

2

1

3

urge to subvert this arrangement is accompanied by a no less great fear of chaos, as if Kubrick wished to preserve a spirit of revolt while remaining sceptical about the possibilities of more radical change. *2001*, though, proceeds by a series of disruptions, symbolized by the way the monolith (a rectangular form) is set in opposition to curved forms or circles, which, as we know, represent eternity (cf. the theological definition of God: 'A sphere whose centre is everywhere and whose circumference is nowhere'). From the pit inside which the apes huddle in the prologue to the astral foetus revolving around the earth, from craters to planets, from spacecraft to celestial wheels, Kubrick sets the figures of order in motion. And Jean-Loup Bourget has noted in a remarkable analysis how *A Clockwork Orange* (to begin with its title) rings every possible change on the circle: a bowler hat adorning a round head, mothballs and billiard balls, convicts exercising in the prison yard, and women's breasts, notably Mrs Alexander's, which are peeled like oranges[142].

To the theme of the circle may be added Kubrick's fascination with symmetry. The screenplay of *A Clockwork Orange* is a model of balance – three sections lasting forty-five minutes each, with the central panel of the triptych (the prison and the cure) separating two trajectories each of whose elements is matched in the other if in a different order (the encounter with the tramp, the visit to Mr Alexander, the fight with the droogs, the scene 'at home'). In the same way, *Barry Lyndon* is constructed on a rising and falling pattern, with antitheses both within each of the sections (two 'positive' captains, two 'negative' captains) and between them (four matching duels). More oppressively, the same kind of symmetry (one thinks again of a chessboard) can be found in the chequered floor of the court-martial hall in *Paths of Glory* and the circular table in *Dr Strangelove*. According to Caillois, it is present at 'every level of the world, in the most infinitesimal atomic particles as at the human stratum with right and left and their continuance in the subconscious and so on up to the vast configuration of nebulae and galaxies[222].' The aim of Kubrick's recourse to temporary if violent dissymmetry is to force the lock by which symmetry closes itself off from evolution. As an artist, Kubrick himself proceeds no differently, attempting to subvert the established order and inner equilibrium of styles and genres; and if he stops short of total dissolution, it is because he knows only too well how quickly the status quo would re-establish itself.

Circular forms:
1. *Keir Dullea aboard* Discovery *(2001: A Space Odyssey)*
2. *The vessel* Aries *(2001: A Space Odyssey)*
3. *The War Room* (Dr Strangelove)

The film noir *influence*:
1. *Wayne Morris, Ken Dibbs, Ralph Meeker* (Paths of Glory)
2. *Sterling Hayden, Peter Sellers* (Dr Strangelove)
3. *Paul Farrell (on the ground), Warren Clarke, Malcolm McDowell,
James Marcus, Michael Tarn* (A Clockwork Orange)

14

In the photography of Kubrick's films we can see the same kind of contrast. It oscillates between meticulous realism and wilfully flamboyant expressionism. Both Kubrick's early work as a photographer and his essays in the crime movie genre clearly contributed to the evolution of a visual style for his subsequent work. Absorbed (no less today) by problems of optics and lighting, he managed in *Killer's Kiss* and *The Killing* – even in *Fear and Desire* and *Paths of Glory*, war movies influenced by the aesthetics of the *film noir* – to evolve a style that could encompass both fidelity and distortion. *Film noir* photography reduces indirect lighting, thereby creating strong contrasts and shadows; it hardens the features and facilitates unusual camera angles. But it also rejects the day-for-night technique in favour of a more authentic kind of darkness and employs depth of focus to situate a character within the frame. As a result, it is forced to use narrow lenses, since any increase in the source of light would fail to achieve a realistic nocturnal atmosphere.

These characteristics are to be found in Kubrick's first films, but also in *Lolita* and even *Dr Strangelove* and *A Clockwork Orange*. However, just as he will use décor to play on the contrast between humdrum banality and decorative excess (*Dr Strangelove*, *A Clockwork Orange*), so Kubrick is careful always to vary the symbolism of his lighting to prevent it from congealing into the cliché of evil obscurity versus positive clarity. In *Paths of Glory*, for instance, the intense luminosity of the château corresponds to a destructive power and the shadow of the trenches to a spirit of resistance. And it has been noted[7] that the subtle use of candle lighting in *Barry Lyndon* for the film's warmer, more intimate scenes (conver-

Film noir . . .
1. *Jerry Jarret, full face* (Killer's Kiss)
2. *Jay C. Flippen, Sterling Hayden, Elisha Cook Jr., Ted de Corsia, Joe Sawyer, Marie Windsor* (The Killing)
. . . *and the influence of expressionistic lighting on Kubrick's other works:*
3. *James Mason, Sue Lyon* (Lolita)
4. *George C. Scott, Peter Bull* (Dr Strangelove)

In Barry Lyndon *candlelight creates softness and warmth, but invests the gaming sequences with a nightmarish quality*
1. *Ryan O'Neal*
2. *Patrick Magee, Ryan O'Neal*

sations with Captain Grogan and the young German woman) gradually begins, as we climb higher up the social ladder, to create a nightmarish vision of nobility on show at the gaming-tables, like so many sinister figures waiting for death.

15

The unfinished projects of great film-makers (Fellini's *Il viaggio di G. Mastorna*, Resnais' *Harry Dickson*, Losey's *A la recherche du temps perdu*) reveal both their chief concerns and indicate certain themes which, temporarily denied expression, were to be reinvested elsewhere. So it is with *Napoleon*, which Kubrick was supposed to direct for MGM after *2001* and which he had to abandon because of its immense budget and the crisis in Hollywood at the time. One is reminded of Hegel's letter to Niethammer: 'I saw the Emperor – that soul of the world – leave town on a reconnaissance mission: it is, indeed, a wonderful sensation to see such an individual who, concentrated here in one point, astride his horse, nevertheless bestraddles the world and dominates it' (13 October 1806).

After the Nietzschean tone of *2001* (with man's rebirth to the accompaniment of Richard Strauss's *Also Sprach Zarathustra*), it was natural for Kubrick to turn his attention to a man who was the personification of power and the inspiration for the philosopher's cult of the individual and theory of the Superman. It was also the Emperor who inspired the Promethean music of Beethoven, that same Ludwig Van to whom can be traced all the joys and sufferings of Alex, the perverted and Dionysian hero of *A Clockwork Orange*. In Napoleon there co-existed not only a gift for administration, a zeal for the passing of laws and decrees, a love of order and discipline, a genius for the invention of new strategies, a taste for harmony (expressed in the neo-classicism of his period's art), but also an insatiable appetite for power and an energy in wielding it which were to prove his downfall and play havoc with his most meticulously plotted calculations. In this he was undoubtedly a child of the eighteenth century and the French Revolution, when the goddess Reason was undone by her marriage to Passion. One wonders if what interested a political sceptic like Kubrick was the possibility of examining by what tragic irony a revolution that saw itself as liberating could have led, first to bloodthirsty terror and then to despotism (an experience repeated a century-and-a-half later in the second great revolution of modern history, that of 1917).

Barry Lyndon at last gratified Kubrick's long-repressed ambition to make a costume film, to recreate the past (a demiurgic yet childish dream which, I believe, every director has toyed with at some time). One can also see it as a reverse image, a more prosaic version of the Napoleonic saga: the story of a young islander, thirsting after power, who crosses oceans, fights a continental war, rises in society, then, defeated, returns to his island. Bonaparte married Josephine (who had two children from her first marriage), then Marie-Louise (without ever managing to make the courts of Europe accept him): Barry's marriage to Lady Lyndon recalls these two situations. His domestic problems are complicated by social difficulties (cf. the rebuffs of Lord Wendover and the king's sarcasm: he does not belong to their world). Finally, with the absence of the father, the mother's power – like that of Letizia – is exerted from the native isle to the vicissitudes of Barry's rise and fall. And his surname, after his marriage, will serve as a Christian name, just as, inversely, the Emperor's Christian name became a surname after his coronation.

16

Barry Lyndon is structured on the same principle of oppositions to be found in almost all of Kubrick's films, with *A Clockwork Orange* as the most perfect example. As the narrator says: 'Barry was one of those born clever enough at gaining a fortune but incapable of keeping one. For the qualities and energies which lead a man to achieve the first are often the very cause of his ruin in the latter case.' Alex's fate is governed by a similar symmetry. In *Dr Strangelove*, systems designed to protect man from destruction turn out to be the cause of his death. More generally, Kubrick's heroes advance the pawns of an unassailable strategy which nevertheless contrives to lead to their undoing. The minutely detailed plan of the gangsters in *The Killing* fails at the last minute and prevents them from enjoying the fruits of their hold-up. General Mireau, via a doomed offensive, a court-martial and three token executions, will still be denied the promotion he craves and be driven to suicide (*Paths of Glory*). No matter that he shadows Humbert and deceives him with Lolita, Quilty will die at his victim's hands. And, like Mireau, Jack D. Ripper will find himself checkmated by his own military gambit and trigger off a planetary holocaust (*Dr Strangelove*). In fact, the great calculators of Kubrick's films are also locked into their obsessions (including the paranoid HAL 9000). When describing Johnny Clay (Sterling Hayden), the commentary of *The Killing* provided an excellent definition of every Kubrickian character: 'He knew exactly how long it would take him to drive to the track, park his car and walk to the grandstand.' But logic and precision are thwarted by passion, by some 'emotional' error. Kubrick's love of machines perhaps derives from his suspicion of human weakness. The reasoning of the finest technological systems is always at the mercy of an operator's mistake; and if the computer in *2001* breaks down, the cause of its break-down must be ascribed to some human being on earth. Given what man is, Kubrick is forced to place his trust in machines; but given, too, that they depend on man, their power may well turn against him precisely because of his own fallibility. Hence the tragic element of this dialectic. As in Hegel, it designates a movement from one extreme to the other, from which all possibility of conciliation has been excluded. That there is no solution explains the troubled consciousness which inexorably casts man back into his misery, his mortality, the tragedy of his failure.

It is not difficult to explain the misunderstanding that caused Kubrick in the late fifties, after *Spartacus* (because of Trumbo's screenplay) and *Paths of Glory*, to be regarded as a socialist or liberal. To be sure, there was in both of these films a merciless indictment of the master-slave relationship, and therefore of all systems of oppression, but it gradually became clear that the director's pessimism, however lucidly and corrosively it dealt with the higher echelons of power, excluded any Marxist dialectic of progress. And though a synthesis seems to be offered in *A Clockwork Orange*, it in fact only brings the spectator to another impasse.

Alex's second cure (after that of the Ludovico treatment) reconverts him to his earlier nature, except that this time his destructive energies are placed at the service of authority. If the negation of a negation has brought him back to square one, it has been achieved with a cynicism worthy of Orwell's *1984*, in which 'freedom is slavery'.

There is no paradox in the fact of its being the technological reverie of *2001* that enabled Kubrick to escape from his pessimism. But it was achieved only through the creation of a Utopia. The limitations of machines and the reasoning processes are indicated by man's 'leap' into infinity and

accession to a higher plane of existence. One remembers Nietzsche's opposition to Hegelianism (with which Kubrick has certain affinities), to its ill-humour, its sense of guilt, its dialectical conception of man, its concept of negativity to which he responded with a Dionysian affirmation of life and passion, to its Christian nihilism which disparaged existence through faith in another world (note the echo of Bossuet or Donne in the concluding title of *Barry Lyndon*: 'It was in the reign of George III that the aforesaid personages lived and quarrelled. Good or bad, handsome or ugly, rich or poor, they are all equal now.').

In fact, Kubrick's vision of the future is not far from Orwell's negative Utopia. In *Dr Strangelove*, *A Clockwork Orange* and *2001*, the characters live in closed, isolated worlds, like hermits in non-communicating cells. This 'air-tightness' is precisely the principle on which *Dr Strangelove* is constructed, its three sets (the bomber, the base, the Pentagon) remaining so rigidly separate from one another that the precarious communications among them inevitably lead, first to misunderstanding, then to the ultimate tragedy. The décors of *2001* and *A Clockwork Orange* (the space station; the apartments of Mr Alexander and the Cat Lady) are so aseptic and sterile that they might have been dreamt up by General Ripper, with his fears for his vital fluids. They reflect a corresponding atrophy of emotions embodied in the soulless

routine of polite encounters and in the impoverished, cliché-ridden, terrifyingly banal language of social intercourse (the conversations between the Russian and American scientists in *2001*; the speeches of Alex's parents, etc.), as well as in the verbal delirium of *Dr Strangelove*, totally contradicting what we are given to see ('Peace is our profession' reads a signpost in the military camp around which a battle is raging; 'Gentlemen, you can't fight in here. This is the War Room' protests the President of the United States). And Alex has to invent another language, 'nadsat', through which he can express his rebellion (once cured, he drops it). The social conduct of *Barry Lyndon* and military conduct of *Paths of Glory* both lead to a Brave New World in which life is replaced by an empty ritual. While Alex's thirst for power is harnessed by a higher power, Dave Bowman's is given free rein in a utopian voyage to the stars, and will be eternally renewed. The final shot of *2001* is perhaps the only really peaceful image created by an artist more at ease in nightmare.

The sterility of the future:
1. Hilton Space Station (2001: A Space Odyssey)
2. Leonard Rossiter, William Sylvester, Margaret Tyzack (2001: A Space Odyssey)
3. David Prowse (A Clockwork Orange)

Wordplay in Dr Strangelove:
1. Keenan Wynn
2. Burpelson Base
3. Slim Pickens

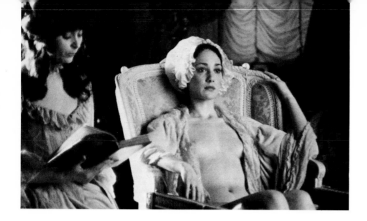

17

The French poem read by a companion to Lady Lyndon in her bath mixes science with metaphysics. In this story of Barry's opportunism and his wife's love for him being turned against themselves, it represents the reconciliation of reason and passion. An ironic counterpoint, perhaps, but also a moment of genuine emotion since it precedes Barry's entry, the apologies he tenders his wife, taking her hand in his and kneeling beside her, offering the only hint of affection to be found in the whole film.

Les coeurs l'un par l'autre
    attirés
  Se communiquent
    leur substance
  Tels deux miroirs ardents
Concentrent la lumière
    et se la réfléchissent
  Les rayons tour à tour
    recueillis
  ... divisés
  En se multipliant
S'accriossent, s'embellissent
  Et d'autant plus actifs
Qu'ils se sont plus croisés
Au même point se réunissent.

(Two hearts by each other
    attracted
  Communicate
    their substance
  Like two burning mirrors
Concentrating light
    and reflecting it back
  The beams collected
    each in turn
  ... divided
  By multiplying
Grow larger and more
    beautiful
  And becoming
    the more active
The more they intersect
Are at one and the same point
    reunited.)

The bath scene in Barry Lyndon: *Marisa Berenson and Ryan O'Neal*

A moment of stability which the director, fascinated by optics, offers as a brief respite from the increasingly rapid decline and fall of his protagonist. For what governs the visual style of Kubrick's films is rather the disruption of symmetry by violence – violence caused by resentment, revenge or sheer instinctive aggression. A smooth, symmetrical, well-composed shot is suddenly upset, thrown off balance by the movement of a hand-held camera. In *Barry Lyndon*, the orderliness of military life and the boxing match which interrupts it; or the concert at Hackton Castle and the blustering entrance of Bullingdon, who wrestles on the floor with his stepfather. In *A Clockwork Orange*, the cool elegance of Mr Alexander's home with its chequered floor and corridor of mirrors reflecting each other, befouled by the arrival of Alex and the rape of his wife; or again, in the Cat Lady's apartment, a shot composed with perfect symmetry, both in terms of the décor itself and the posture of the human body, followed by her murder.

In the 'Dawn of Man' section of *2001*, there are the imposing images of earth and sky, mountains and desert, and the fighting of the apes filmed with a mobile camera; and, in the same film, the computer's 'memory' with its Vasarely-like geometry through which Dave Bowman floats before lobotomizing HAL. In general, whether it be in the trenches in *Paths of Glory* or at Burpelson Base in *Dr Strangelove*, the hand-held camera suggests the confusion of a life-and-death struggle.

The sudden irruption of disorder is often expressed through hand-held camerawork:
1. The attack on Burpelson Base (Dr Strangelove)
2. Keir Dullea (2001: A Space Odyssey)
3. Marie Kean, Ryan O'Neal, Leon Vitali (Barry Lyndon)

Compensating for this loss of spatial control is one of Kubrick's favourite stylistic devices, a reverse tracking shot through a narrow corridor both mastering the space and conveying a sense of confinement within it: Dax and Mireau inspecting the trenches in *Paths of Glory*; the corridors of space and of the spacecraft in *2001*; the Minister's visit, the arrival of the psychiatrist and especially the stroll taken by Alex through the Drugstore in *A Clockwork Orange*, a scene mirrored in *Barry Lyndon* when Bullingdon dramatically bursts into the club to demand an apology from his stepfather (and Leon Vitali bears a strange resemblance to Malcolm McDowell, even in the way he is dressed). In *Barry Lyndon* Kubrick appropriates the filmic space more fully and clearly by the constant use of a slow reverse zoom which, moving out from a single character, enlarges the field of vision until its powerful scrutiny takes possession of the whole décor.

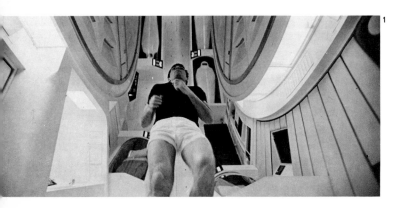

18

As we have seen, Kubrick learned his craft in the school of *film noir* (*Killer's Kiss*, *The Killing* and even *Lolita*) and the war movie (*Fear and Desire*, *Paths of Glory*). With the exception of *Paths of Glory*, they could even be said to represent his view of the present. The characteristics of the *noir* genre in particular must both have confirmed and heightened his fatalism, his sense of despair and his innate pessimism. The fear of failure, the paranoid vision of a hostile world, though they would be explored more fully in his subsequent work, were already coherently articulated in these early films. As Alexander Walker has pertinently remarked[6], the convergence in *film noir* of the visual experimentation of German Expressionism and the American tradition of realism (re-established after the war, one might add, through the influence of Italian neo-realism) coloured Kubrick's artistic vision – that integration of the idea with significant form which we have already noted. It also influenced his use of commentary, either in the form of a subjective account (as in private-eye movies) or in that of an impersonal narrator (as in the series of thrillers produced by Louis de Rochemont, whose documentary pretentions were inspired by the 'March of Time' newsreels). The protagonist tells his own story in *Killer's Kiss*, *Lolita* and *A Clockwork Orange*; an 'objective' commentary accompanies the images in *Fear and Desire*, *The Killing*, *Paths of Glory*, *Dr Strangelove* and *Barry Lyndon*. The sole exception is *2001* (for which Kubrick had nevertheless thought of a commentary, before dispensing with it); but we have seen to what extent that film was conceived as a Utopian response to the others, though retaining close links with them. Its style is poetic and

A favourite stylistic device: the reverse track
1. *Gary Lockwood* (2001: A Space Odyssey)
2. *Kirk Douglas* (Paths of Glory)
3. *Ryan O'Neal (left), Roger Booth (centre) partly concealing Anthony Sharp* (Barry Lyndon)
4. *Michael Gover, Anthony Sharp, Godfrey Quigley (in the background)* in A Clockwork Orange
5. *Shelley Duvall, Danny Lloyd, Scatman Crothers* (The Shining)

1

2

metaphoric, as against the irony and analysis which are otherwise the rule in Kubrick's art.

A commentary creates detachment, sets the narrative within the confines of fatality, constantly undermines and counterpoints the impression of reality and denies the characters all free-will. Kubrick has spoken of it merely as a practical means of avoiding lengthy exposition; but, particularly in *Barry Lyndon*, it subtly exploits a whole range of modulations in the film's point of view. It eliminates suspense and emphasizes the force of destiny by preparing the spectator in advance for Barry's fall and the loss of his son, as also for the death of Sir Charles Lyndon. It removes any potential aftertaste of romanticized tenderness in the scene with the young German peasant woman by informing us *afterwards* that, like cities in time of war, she had been taken more than once. It describes *beforehand* the emotion that will wring Barry's heart on meeting Balibari in order to insure that it will not wring ours. Like the film's music (about which Michel Sineux has written an important essay[39]), the commentary cannot be dissociated from the image which it suffuses. Its relation to it is either dialectical or emotional – in any event, never neutral.

19

Kubrick has frequently been criticized for having lost interest in mankind since *Dr Strangelove*, for having substituted fables, puppets and machines for the creation of real characters. *Barry Lyndon*, in its study of the family and purely human relationships, signalled the return of a 'domestic' Kubrick. On those rare occasions when he dealt with this theme in the past, it was to evoke Oedipal anxiety and the problem of substitution within the family unit. In *Barry Lyndon* as in *Lolita*, there is a character who takes the father's place, in the former case to satisfy a craving for position in society, in the latter to appease an 'abnormal' desire. Charlotte Haze and Lady Lyndon are seduced, but not for themselves. One will die as a result, the other will be profoundly hurt. Lolita sleeps with her stepfather; Bullingdon symbolically castrates his by having him physically mutilated; both destroy them. In *A Clockwork Orange*, the first ordeal which Alex has to face in the long series of punishments inflicted on him after he leaves prison will be to find his place at home taken by Joe, the lodger his parents have adopted as a son. In *Barry Lyndon*, Sir Charles Lyndon reproaches Barry for wishing to step into his shoes. Later, Bullingdon will put his half-brother into his own shoes – which are much too large for him – thereby signifying that he is taking his place and adding to Barry's usurpation. Even as early as *Killer's Kiss*, the heroine was jealous of a sister whom her father preferred.

In the first half of *Barry Lyndon* (which begins with the death of the father in a duel) we see the search for another father; in the second, the misfortune of becoming one oneself. Barry

(Left) the reverse track:
1. The dramatic entry of Bullingdon (Leon Vitali) into the club (Barry Lyndon) mirrors Alex's stroll through the Drugstore in A Clockwork Orange *(2)*
(Right) relationships within the family:
1. Gloria (Irene Kane) beside snapshots of her father and her sister Iris (a ballerina played by Ruth Sobotka, Stanley Kubrick's second wife) in Killer's Kiss
2. Philip Stone, Sheila Raynor, Malcolm McDowell (A Clockwork Orange)

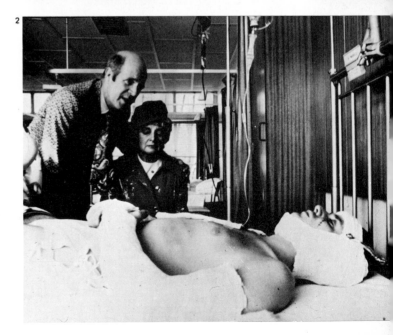

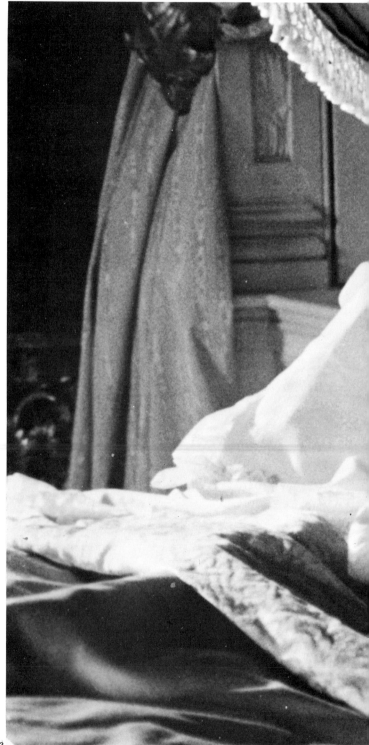

Relationships within the family:
1. James Mason and Shelley Winters beside Lolita's photograph
2. William Sylvester, Vivian Kubrick (the director's daughter) in 2001:
A Space Odyssey
3. Marisa Berenson and Ryan O'Neal (Barry Lyndon)

meets two benevolent fathers, Grogan and Balibari, who, before the death of his own son, are the only characters capable of moving him to tears; and two apparently affable fathers (Feeney the highwayman and Potzdorf, the Prussian officer), who seek only his downfall. The rivals directly involved in his attempts at seduction, Quint and Sir Charles Lyndon, are grotesque characters, the only ones treated caricaturally by Kubrick (as was, in *A Clockwork Orange*, Mr Alexander, whose wife is raped by Alex). Strange, too, is the obsession in Kubrick's work with a paralysed man in a wheelchair: Dr Strangelove, Mr Alexander and Sir Charles Lyndon, whose presence in each case presages some crucial transformation: the nuclear explosion, Alex's suicide attempt and subsequent 'cure', Barry's rise in society. Nor is there any real exchange of feeling in the male–female sexual relations. Lady Lyndon is attracted to Barry's good looks and he feels only indifference towards her; Humbert is madly in love with Lolita, who trifles with him. In *Barry Lyndon* there exists only homosexual love (the mutual tenderness of Jonathan and Freddy in the river), paternal love and friendship towards one's mentor. Here again, *2001* can be interpreted as a Utopian dream, in which the Superman gives birth to the astral foetus – auto-reproducing, so to speak – without the intervention of woman. The old man dies to make way for his son – another self. Against this futuristic Oedipus one might set the historical Oedipus suggested by the only two dates written down in Kubrick's work and which figure in the only two of his films (see footnote on page 59) dealing with consanguineous relations, *Lolita* and *Barry Lyndon*. The first, 1776, shortly after the scene in which Quilty dies; the second, 1789, on the promissory note which Lady Lyndon signs for her husband in exile; in both cases (the Declaration of Independence and the break with England; the French Revolution), a collective parricide.

The paralysed man in his wheelchair:
1. Marisa Berenson, Frank Middlemass, Dominic Savage, Murray Melvin (Barry Lyndon)
2. Patrick Magee (A Clockwork Orange)
3. Peter Sellers (Dr Strangelove)

20

What family life represents for Kubrick, then, is the continuation of war in society by other means (Barry birches Bullingdon, as soldiers are birched in the army). As is emphasized by the construction of *Barry Lyndon*, the domestic trials of the second half mirror the battlefields of the first. We have already noted the radical pessimism of Kubrick's political views. In *A Clockwork Orange*, the most complete portrait of a society which he has given us to date, Mr Alexander, a member of the left-wing opposition party, behaves at first like a gullible naif, allowing hooligans into his home and causing the death of his wife; then expresses his contempt for the people and resorts to the same scheming methods as the government. In that film, too, the low-angle slow-motion shot of Alex striking his droogs, Georgie and Dim, is a direct mirror image of a similar shot in the first section of *2001* when the ape turns a tool into a weapon. From prehistoric times to the society of the future, man is for Kubrick, as for any other disciple of Hobbes, a wolf to his fellow man. He does not change. As for progress, it is fuelled by bloodshed (the weapon-tool of *2001*). And in his opening sentence the commentator of Kubrick's first short, *Day of the Fight*, describes the public of boxing matches as 'wanting to see strength triumph over strength'. For Kubrick, 'Man isn't a noble savage. He is irrational, brutal, weak, unable to be objective about anything where his own interests are involved ... and any attempt to create social institutions to a false view of nature is probably doomed to failure[1].' In the pessimism of his films there is what might be termed the hygiene of a *tabula rasa*. And his interest in the eighteenth century stems from an endeavour to understand how any belief in the perfectability of man could ever have arisen (precisely with its theory of the noble savage). Not that one can find on Kubrick's part any defence of the old order, but since all social systems are oppressive, the notion of revolution appears less urgent, perhaps even useless, given how rapidly it degenerates into oppression; and the 'Marseillaise', a revolutionary hymn, acts as an ironic accompaniment to the credit-titles of *Paths of Glory*, providing a republican alibi for executions '*pour encourager les autres*' in a class society.

The word 'fascism' has sometimes been used in connection with *A Clockwork Orange*. The accusation is unfounded in that Kubrick is in no sense promoting another kind of society; he is denouncing brainwashing of every kind and making a plea for free-will. His spokesman is undoubtedly the prison chaplain who demands that Alex be allowed freedom of choice. Here, too, Kubrick seems torn between acceptance of a rational order, a stable society which could control man's errors and his egotism, and the irrepressible urge for freedom, the exaltation of individual passion and energy – the classic conflict of Hegel and Nietzsche. One can detect the same tension between his Romantic irony which affirms the vanity of all things, the meaninglessness of values, and on the other hand the cult of the ego, the search for something tangible and essential – something that only artistic creation can achieve. The century of enlightenment bequeathed to Romanticism a view of the work of art as 'the quintessential act of a free conscience. The artist becomes the chosen depositary and on occasion the prophet of freedom as a value which everywhere else is compromised[241].'

Nietzsche – who, because he rejected socialism no less than bourgeois democracy, was later to be accused of an alleged pre-Nazism! – would develop the idea of the artist as Superman in his own writings. In the Nietzschean Utopia, the creator is the incarnation of power and he alone can reconcile passion with reason. In his heroically Romantic conception of the artist he resembled Alex's own favourite Ludwig Van and also Balzac. Such, then, is the contradictory and troubled situation of the sceptic, conscious of the void yet obstinately investing all his Promethean energies in a work which he is determined will last. Art is the only means by which he can flee the emptiness and boredom surrounding him and affirm his existence and his grandeur in a tireless and eternally renewed effort. Thus one of the major obsessions of Kubrick's films – the desire for absolute power over people and things and its inevitable correlative, the terror of losing control – informs the very practice of his craft. Anxiety, even despair, are at the core of Kubrick's work; they are also the driving force of his creative activity.

The low-angle, slow-motion shot of Alex (Malcolm McDowell) in A Clockwork Orange *recalls the destructive gesture of the ape (Daniel Richter) in* 2001: A Space Odyssey *(2 and 3)*

2

3

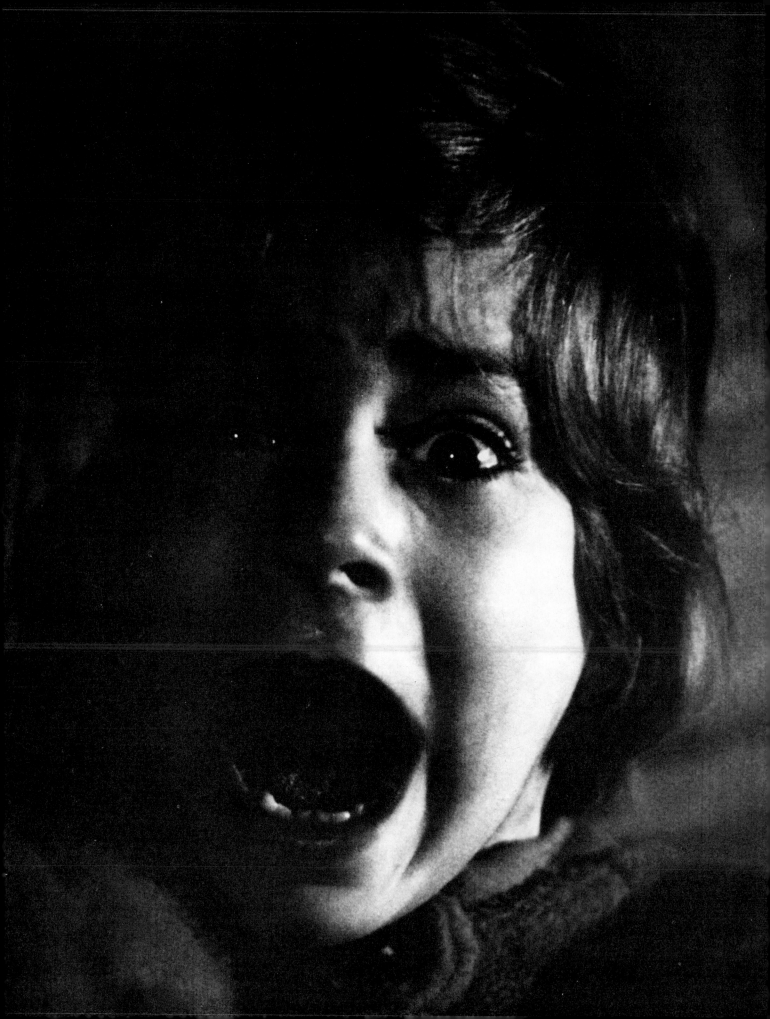

Kubrick and the fantastic

'Science has not yet taught us if madness is or is not the sublimity of the intelligence.'

Edgar Allan Poe

For over twenty years, Stanley Kubrick's films – with the exception of *Barry Lyndon*, a demiurgic work which claims nothing less than to have reconstituted a whole world – have tended to transcend the limits of the cinematic 'realism' (however flexibly one cares to define the term) by which *Lolita*, his war movies and thrillers were bound. *Dr Strangelove* (1963) and *A Clockwork Orange* (1971) belong less to science-fiction proper than to political-fiction (international politics and nuclear war; the workings of the internal political system), their action being situated in the near future; and they derive, in the first instance, from burlesque farce, in the second, from the philosophical and satirical fable. It is here that Kubrick's comic genius – present in all his films – can be given free rein, with his sense of sarcasm and derision, of caricature and humour. *Dr Strangelove* (in the character of the Doctor himself and the Doomsday Device) and *A Clockwork Orange* (in the Ludovico treatment) bear at least a tangential relation to the genre of the fantastic. But they impress us above all as 'one-off' films, without any real precursors or progeny, whereas *2001: A Space Odyssey* and *The Shining* seem on the contrary to belong wholly to the genre, the first in terms of science-fiction, the second of the horror movie. Notwithstanding their evident differences of approach, such theorists as Roger Caillois, Gérard Lenne and Tzvetan Todorov concur in the opinion that the fantastic represents a breach in the recognized order of things so scandalous that neither experience nor reason dares admit its existence.

'The fantastic is the hesitation experienced by a being cognizant only of the laws of nature when confronted with an apparently supernatural phenomenon[242].' It therefore constitutes the shock between what is real and what is imaginary, excluding forms of pure fantasy in which nothing surprises us, nothing astounds us since, in the realm of the subconscious, anything can happen. It is easy to see how Kubrick might have been attracted to such a transgression of codified normality, such a defiance of reason. The apparitions of the monolith in *2001*, those of the ghosts in *The Shining*, the arrival of the astronaut Dave Bowman in the Louis XVI room and the presence of Jack at the July 4 party held in the Overlook Hotel in 1921 are all instances of the incomprehensible, or even the unthinkable. In either film, the spectator is incapable of supplying a rational explanation for what he has witnessed and ends up by accepting the supernatural. This form of the fantastic therefore tends towards sheer fantasy (without coinciding with it), if one accepts Todorov's definition: 'Either the reader (spectator) admits that a rational explanation can be found for apparently supernatural events and we then switch from the fantastic to the merely strange; or else he concedes their existence as such and we find ourselves in fantasy[242].'

But, as we have seen, the fantastic can only originate from a background of strongly defined 'realism'. For there to exist an opposition between the real and the imaginary, and conceivably a fusion between the two, the framework of reality must be scrupulously respected. The whole tradition of fantastic literature was founded in the century of enlightenment (a period which Kubrick regards as the representation of all our current problems), from the English Gothic novel to German Romanticism. Its development in the nineteenth century ran parallel to that of science and positivism (of which it may be considered the shadowy underside); and it is instructive to note that, from Hoffmann to Gogol, from Balzac to Maupassant, the greatest authors of the fantastic were also adepts of realism, even naturalism – before Jules Verne and H. G. Wells used science-fiction to illustrate the encounter between technology and magic.

Finally, *2001: A Space Odyssey* and *The Shining* explore the two orientations of the fantastic, as they were defined by Lenne in his remarkable essay[238]. In the first, the danger comes from man. One recognizes the schema of the sorcerer's apprentice to which the myth of Frankenstein belongs. Out of a wish to dominate the universe, man creates a machine which places him in jeopardy: this is one of the themes of *2001*, in which the real becomes imaginary. In the second, however, the danger comes from elsewhere, as illustrated by the myth of Dracula: this time man is dominated, metamorphosed and himself becomes the danger. *The Shining*, in which the imaginary becomes real, conforms to such a definition. But, as Lenne very clearly demonstrates, these oppositions – awe of the hyper-rational/awe of the irrational, uncertainty of matter/uncertainty of mind – operate only on the explicit narrative level. 'It is man, in fact, who is the source of every superstition and every danger.'

2001: A Space Odyssey and *The Shining* can be compared in the way they expose these threats from within. The fact that one of them is the most audacious film ever made by Kubrick and the other is the one most subservient to the laws of a genre (as if he realized that he could not afford to disregard the inflexible codes of cinematic horror) should not disguise what the two have in common. From the macrocosm of *2001* to the microcosm of *The Shining*, the quest has remained the same: to search through the fantastic and its myths for the *reason* behind the *irrational* terrors which govern human beings.

To search for the reason *behind* irrational *terrors (Danny Lloyd in* The Shining*)*

2001: A Space Odyssey

'Eternity is in love with the productions of time.'

William Blake

The opening shots of *Dr Strangelove* revealed an unknown, threatening terrain at the extremity of the earth and the cosmos; at the end of the film we were shown the whole planet exploding. These shots anticipated *2001: A Space Odyssey*. Every Utopia contains an element of intellectual speculation, the kind of mind-boggling calculation that is

Poole (Gary Lockwood) falling into the void (2001: A Space Odyssey)

bound to attract Kubrick. And by setting the action in the year 2001 (in Arabia 1000 signifies the uncountable and 1001 conjures up infinity, as witness the tales of Scheherazade; 2001 is also the date at which Ray Bradbury set part of his *Martian Chronicles* and Arno Schmidt's *The Republic of Scientists* takes place), Kubrick was setting himself beyond the breakup of civilization which he had already illustrated in the most sombre tones. Aurel David has shown how 'the balance between the living and inert parts of the world has now been upset by a continual loss of the living substance. Life is slipping out of the biologist's hands into those of the physicist[235].' The aim of cybernetics is the substitution of the machine for man in every menial task, in everything that is mechanical and mediatory. If it is impossible to isolate what is specifically human, one can reabsorb or destroy what is non-human and replaceable by technology, perhaps even down to the ultimate 0·01%, the intellectual proportion of a human being. Man would then be wholly mechanizable and cease to exist. Such speculations are not far removed from those of Arthur C. Clarke, the film's co-scenarist, who envisions a world peopled by robots, in which machines will prevail simply because their potential is infinitely greater than man's[239]. Aurel

David has noted how this search for the ultimate resorts of life is tinged with the fascination of disaster, a dark Romanticism well-attuned to this age of ours and which is expressed in a phrase of the great cybernetician Norbert Wiener: 'We are castaways on a planet that is condemned to death.'

The world of *2001* is ready to die, ripe for destruction as is suggested by the intensely melancholic music by Khatchaturian that accompanies the empty, monotonous existence of the astronauts inside the *Discovery*. The science of cybernetics could not fail to intrigue Kubrick, obsessed as he always has been with the idea of remote-controlled action and the mechanization of living organisms. The word, moreover, was already used by Ampère when referring to the art of politics (taken from the Greek *kubernésis*, meaning 'pilot'), so linking the workings of power as analysed by Kubrick with those of the most futuristic science. But such action, however efficient, has no power to determine the final goal. Man at that point is alone and machinery cannot help him. This is what *2001* is about: man, who transcended the animal condition by means of technology, must free himself of that same technology to arrive at a superhuman condition.

In the film can be found again Kubrick's despair when confronted with the fundamental question posed by Pascal's free-thinker: 'By whose order and bidding has this place and this time been made my destiny?' The anthropomorphic vision of the classical period and the Renaissance was succeeded by the hegemony of science, which restored man to his rightful place in the universe without ever relinquishing the age-old dream of overcoming all natural obstacles, even to the point of thrilling nineteenth-century man with the notion of absolute knowledge through scientific progress. But modern science has taught us that we can no longer consider nature as a thing in itself, as the ultimate objective reality. 'The subject of research is therefore no longer nature in itself, but nature given over to human interrogation and to this extent all man will encounter there is himself yet again[237].' It was the eternally tormenting trio of questions – Where do I come from? Who am I? Where am I going? – which prompted Kubrick to compose the visual symphony of *2001*. And it offers conclusive refutation of Heisenberg's belief that the image of the universe given us by the natural sciences has had no direct influence on the dialogue of the modern artist with nature itself. Taking as his point of departure a thought

expressed by Arthur Clarke which he admits to sharing: 'Sometimes I think we are alone in the universe and sometimes I think we aren't: in both cases, the idea makes me dizzy', he conceived a film which overnight made all other cinematic science-fiction look stale, even if it disappointed the 'specialists', who were lost without their favourite extra-terrestrial being, and baffled 'laymen' with its radically unconventional narrative.

In effect, one of the traps awaiting authors of science-fiction is their frequent inability to rise above an anthropomorphic view of the universe. There are ten billion stars in a galaxy and ten billion galaxies in the known universe, and one of the principal themes of the genre is undoubtedly that of 'other' civilizations. But it is hard to imagine these different worlds without having recourse to human 'standards' and thereby rendering them ridiculous. Kubrick himself has pointed out how impotent human thought becomes in such a context. 'Such cosmic intelligence growing in knowledge over the aeons would be as far removed from man as we are from the ants. They could be in instantaneous telepathic communication throughout the universe; they might have achieved total mastery over matter; in their ultimate form, they might exist as a disembodied immortal consciousness throughout the universe. Once you begin discussing such possibilities you realize that the religious implications are inevitable

2001: A Space Odyssey
1. *The spacecraft* Orion
2. *Aboard the* Discovery
3. *In the lunar bus (William Sylvester, Robert Beatty, Sean Sullivan)*

because all the essential attributes of such extra-terrestrial intelligence are the attributes we give to God. What we're dealing with here is, in fact, a scientific definition of God[14].' The strength of *2001* is that it confronts our civilization with another without ever dissipating the mystery of the encounter. The black monolith appears both as a threat and as a sign of hope at four decisive moments in human evolution: first of all, it is the ape which approaches it with respect, then shortly after hits upon the use of a bone as a weapon, the first stage in a *technical* domination of the world. But this discovery, which was made in a state of terror, causes it to use the bone to kill another ape. (What Kubrick seems to be suggesting is that all human progress is linked to the satisfying of instincts. When these are deadened or repressed, as in the society of 2001, man wastes away. It is only by killing HAL 9000 that Bowman accedes to a higher level.) Thus the relation between fear and aggression, present in all of Kubrick's films, is vividly depicted in *2001*. The bone cast into the air by the ape (now

become a man) is transformed at the other extreme of civilization, by one of those abrupt ellipses characteristic of the director, into a spacecraft on its way to the moon. The mysterious slab reappears on the moon, the eerie signals which it emits being the object of much study by the astronauts, and this time it precedes the immense vault into the unknown represented by the journey to Jupiter. It is in Jupiter's sky that the monolith materializes for the third time, before Bowman plunges 'beyond infinity'. It is finally in another spatio–temporal dimension altogether that it rears up yet again, as an old man points a finger at it, his gesture presaging the birth of another man. *2001* thus takes on the aspect of a quest, reminiscent of that other great documentary voyage, that other interrogation into the meaning of life, *Moby Dick* (in which Melville proved that he was no less well-

informed and accurate on whale-fishing than Kubrick on astronautics).

The monolith – whether it be an image of God, of extra-terrestrial beings or of some cosmic force – is another manifestation of the determinism which has tended to govern Kubrick's view of the world. Since the dawn of man, the ape then man himself have been passive servants. They represent a higher authority which manipulates them as the soldiers in *Paths of Glory* were manipulated, or Alex undergoing the Ludovico treatment, or Jack by the inhabitants of the Overlook Hotel. But it is also possible for the monolith to escape from this symbolic reduction and become one with the vital impulse that drives man on to transcend himself.

The oratorio by György Ligeti which acts as a musical leitmotif for the presence of the monolith coincides with Arthur C. Clarke's idea that all technology, if sufficiently advanced, is touched with magic and a certain irrationality. Its choral accompaniment leads us onto the threshold of the unknown, just as Kubrick's use of the opening bars of *Also Sprach Zarathustra* prepared us for the profundity of his intentions. Nietzsche's vision is no more 'illustrated' by Richard Strauss's symphonic poem than by Kubrick's own symphonic film-poem: rather, it echoes through what are two totally autonomous artistic recreations. *2001* postulates the same progression as in Nietzsche's work, from the ape to man, then from man to the superman ('What is the ape to man? a mockery or a painful humiliation. And that is what man must be to the superman: a mockery or a painful humiliation.') The title given to the first section of the film, 'The Dawn of Man',

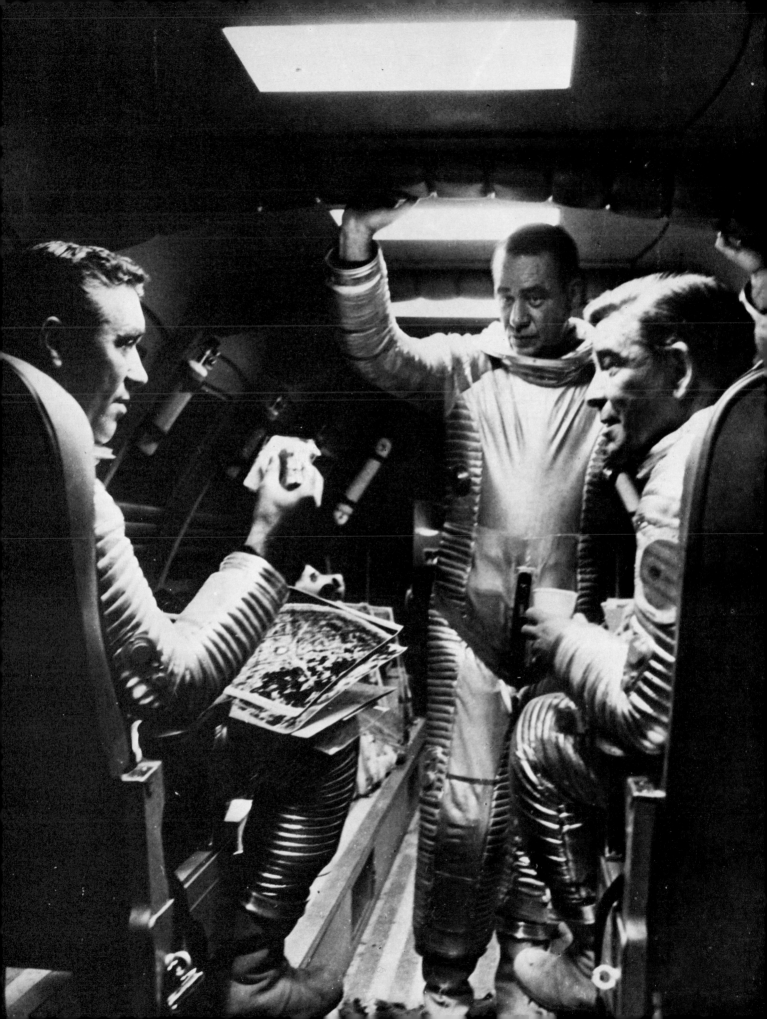

applies equally to the whole work. The foetus which appears at the end to form a second globe opposite the earth, this new being on the threshold of a new dawn, is the expression of an eternal return. We have seen how Kubrick would strip man of every shred of individuality. What is most extraordinary about *2001* is that, at the precise moment when he poses the fundamental human question, he deprives his universe of characters. The metaphysical quest is accomplished by David Bowman alone after the death of his friend Frank Poole and the three scientists in hibernation. Though we saw Dr Floyd's little daughter on television, though we were shown Poole's parents, we know nothing of Bowman, his tastes or his past. He is abstract man, man as Nietzsche conceived him, a means rather than an end, like 'a rope stretched between the beast and the superman, a rope over an abyss'. Richard Strauss's theme, sometimes known as the 'World Riddle' theme, is introduced by an ascending line of three notes, do-sol-do, the same number three which is embodied in the presence of three spheres after the credit titles, the moon, the earth and the sun; a magical number which is also that of the known dimensions and which is finally abolished by the transition into the fourth dimension anticipated by the apparition of the monolith among the three globes.

For *2001* – a poem, as it has often been described – is also so rigorously articulated as to have inspired the only outstanding work of structural analysis devoted to a film[107]. For her part, Carolyn Geduld[108] has demonstrated the importance of the number four in relation to the work: four years in the making, four episodes, a four million years time-span, four heroes (ape, scientist, computer, astronaut), four evolutions (man, machine, extra-terrestrial, universe), four composers, a four-sided rectangle which appears four times on the screen. Pursuing her insight even further, in each of the four sections the same *leitmotiven* recur, assuring the continuity of human evolution, its permanence beyond the variations of civilization. Eating (the apes' meals, at first vegetarian, then carnivorous; Dr Floyd's automat meal in plastic sachets; the meals eaten by Poole and Bowman aboard the *Discovery*; Bowman's last meal in the Louis XVI room); bodily cares (the apes delousing each other; Floyd in the zero gravity toilet; Poole sunbathing; Bowman in the Louis XVI bathroom); and conflict (the apes' squabble over the water-hole; the latent rivalry between the Russian and American scientists on the space station; the life-or-death struggle between the computer and the astronauts; Bowman's conflict with himself before his final transformation).

His move into the fourth dimension is for David Bowman a moment of confrontation facing all of Kubrick's characters. Suddenly aged, Bowman encounters his double (HAL, too, had a twin computer), then another, even older form of himself lying in bed and breathing heavily (and there one recognizes two of the director's obsessions). The death of man is a new beginning; and the immense eyes of the foetus revolving in space present the same anguished gaze as that of the ape in the first section contemplating the moon, or of Goya's *Colossus* 'whose unquiet features dream among the stars', in Malraux's expression.

2001, like every true odyssey, is a journey out into the external world which also becomes one of self-discovery. From being objective, the narrative becomes subjective and, by penetrating into the memory bank of HAL 9000, Bowman undertakes an expedition into the labyrinth of his own consciousness. The spacecraft *Discovery* draws him on to a revelation of his own destiny; and if Kubrick's film recalls the Homeric myths evoked in its title (the fight between the navigator Bowman – literally 'bow-man' or 'archer', like Ulysses – and the computer-Cyclops which he defeats by cunning), it represents, in the manner of the Greek epic, an inner exploration.

But the ambition and seriousness of *2001* should not disguise its essential humour, an aspect of the film which has been little remarked on (that of *The Shining* would prove more obvious, with Jack Nicholson's performance recalling the acerbic brio of Peter Sellers in *Lolita* or George C. Scott in *Dr Strangelove*). In the imposing opening section, with its vast

1

desert landscapes where a leopard attacks a colony of apes then keeps watch at night over the corpse of a zebra, there gradually emerges an undercurrent of irony (one close to Swift and his Yahoos) which, though remaining in the most remote prehistorical period, contrives to offer a reasonably fruitful summary of the evolution of humanity. It would have served no purpose for Kubrick to have traced the millions of years separating the origin of the species from the discovery of the cosmos: in a series of stages leading from ape to man (signalled by fadeouts to black) we see unfold the conflict of the weak against the strong, the organization of rival groups, the territorial imperative and the search for food. In the

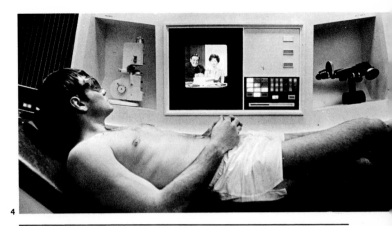

2001: A Space Odyssey
1. Bowman (Keir Dullea) journeys towards infinity and his own death

Humour in 2001: A Space Odyssey
3. The souvenir snapshot on the moon
4. Poole's parents sing 'Happy Birthday' to him (Gary Lockwood)

orbiting Hilton Hotel or aboard the *Discovery*, man is viewed with the same sardonic detachment: the exchange of banalities, outmoded forms of politeness, hollow speechifying, reciprocal suspicion, the Howard Johnson lounge, the souvenir snapshots taken by the moon explorers, the ridiculous 'Happy Birthday' intoned thousands of miles away by parents proud of their astronaut offspring, the father who no longer knows how to talk to his little girl, the jokes about eating and the gravity-free toilets. The fantastic progress of technology has not been accompanied by any comparable moral or emotional evolution, and this disparity seems all the greater between these men living in glacial solitude and the world which they have fabricated. The brilliant idea of using 'The Blue Danube' not only evokes the music of the spheres with a deliciously buoyant humour but adds a dash of Kubrick's characteristic nostalgia for a period when Johann Strauss's melody cradled revellers on board the Big Wheel in Vienna's Prater.

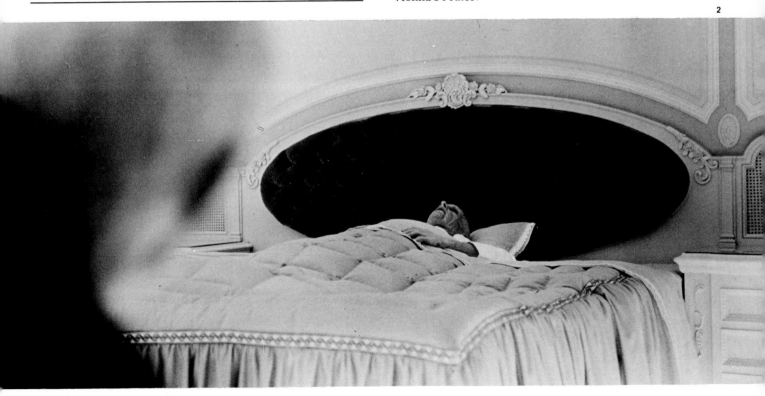

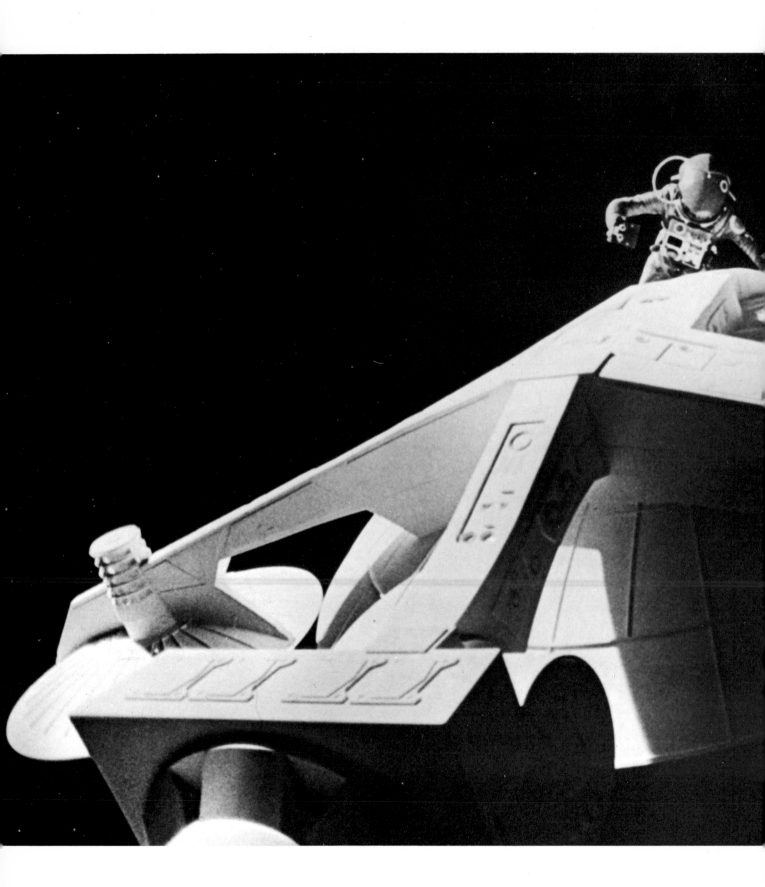

Bowman (Keir Dullea) and the antenna of the Discovery (2001: A Space Odyssey)

Thus we can see the series of equations by which Kubrick makes ape equal to man, and man to machine, the better to undermine the complacency of his audience. If, in his preceding film, Dr Strangelove became a sinister robot governed by conditioned reflexes, here it is the machine that becomes human – too human – both eager to serve and wishing to dominate, incapable of assuming the conflict between truth and lies. HAL 9000, in control of the journey to Jupiter, alone informed of the destination planned by the scientists, is a touching, oddly asexual creature with a soft, wheedling voice (it was originally to have a feminine voice and be named Athena, who, one recalls, was born straight out of Jupiter's brain), a chess fan, of course, who ends by snapping the fragile thread on which the success of the expedition depends. In *2001*, too, a crack appears in the system and creates havoc, except that this time the vertiginous free fall through time and space is the prelude to a regeneration. It is HAL who is responsible, not a man but a machine; one which, rebelling against its mission, falling prey to anxiety and the fear of death, wreaks vengeance on those who no longer have confidence in it by finally sinking into criminal madness. HAL's death, a lobotomy performed by Bowman on its reasoning circuits, is one of the most poignant sequences in Kubrick's work; with its entreaties, 'I'm afraid, Dave. My mind is going. I can feel it. My mind is going – there's no question about it,' then the nostalgic song of its youth 'Daisy, Daisy, give me your answer do . . .', and its voice slowly fading away, becoming deeper and deeper, until it expires in an endless death rattle. By maintaining a precise balance between the two, Kubrick prevents the underlying humour from weakening the emotion generated by the paranoid computer and its death agony. Paradoxically, HAL is the only genuine character in the film, the only one whose anxiety and schizophrenia

can be compared to those of Kubrick's protagonists. As for the astronauts, they are prisoners in their spacecraft, scrutinized by HAL's omniscient 'eye'; even in space they can be considered captives, as when Bowman finds himself outside the *Discovery*. Breaking in again through one of the craft's portholes, he sets about freeing himself of HAL's oppressive dominance and, alone, goes to face his destiny.

As we have seen, this destiny culminates in renaissance as a foetus – a renaissance which was foreshadowed by an earlier 'delivery' when he 'expelled' himself from space into the vessel, as also by his dramatic passage through the stellar entry with its erotic and genital visions. In effect, *2001* is full of sexual imagery – uterine, ovular and phallic – from the arrow-shaped spacecraft *Orion* landing inside the celestial wheel to the *Aries* sphere alighting on a circular base. A film of metamorphoses, fertilizations and births, *A Space Odyssey* ends with an autoreproduction. It is possible to interpret this conclusion, as does Jacques Goimard[120], as yet another representation of the Oedipal drama: in this reading, the monolith would not only be a symbol of God but of authority in general, therefore of the father, whom the child dreams of killing in order to take his place. The old man dies and the astral foetus succeeds him, as in primitive societies the king must be killed to allow his successor to mount the throne. On a cosmic scale, *2001* allegorizes the family drama which has always fascinated Kubrick and which was to form the essence of his latest film to date, *The Shining*.

The same polite affability, the same social relations:
1. On the moon, before the astronauts' mission (2001: A Space Odyssey)
2. In the Overlook Hotel, before Jack Torrance's mission (Barry Dennen, Barry Nelson, Jack Nicholson) in The Shining

1

The Shining

'Je est un autre'
Arthur Rimbaud

It is not surprising – quite the reverse, in fact – that, in *The Shining*, Kubrick should present us with the antithesis of the film which preceded it, *Barry Lyndon*. Such a succession only confirms his habit over the last twenty years of alternating between deliberately slow-paced, meditative, even melancholic works and others with a taut, staccato rhythm, generated by a dynamism which can occasionally be frenetic (*Dr Strangelove* following *Lolita*, *A Clockwork Orange* following *2001*) – like the systolic and diastolic movements of the human heart. It is also likely that Kubrick hoped to achieve one of those enormous popular successes which had always eluded him and which have become almost a prerequisite since the

2

Movie Brats took Hollywood by storm. (In its first few weeks on the North American market alone, *The Shining* earned forty-seven million dollars, the highest gross of any of Kubrick's films!) It has reinstated the director in a position of strength which had been slightly impaired by the commercial failure of *Barry Lyndon*, just as *A Clockwork Orange* and its more immediate fascination followed *2001*, whose success was slow and gradual. But if Kubrick has not forgotten the need for strategy, he also realizes – even if he pretends not to – that mental demons may be lurking behind the most meticulously rational of calculations. In this respect, *The Shining* reprises – though, as always, with new inflections – his most fundamental obsessions and preoccupations.

Though they belong to the same genre of the fantastic, *The Shining* clearly differs in many respects from *2001*. Yet it presents disturbing analogies with the earlier work. Thus its narrative construction is also based on the number four, even if the temporal relationship between the sections is conspicuously different. The first movement reveals a magnificent landscape of mountains, forests and lakes, one in which the characters are lost, crushed, dominated (cf. 'The Dawn of Man'). The second movement, in the Overlook Hotel, finds the

manager entrusting Jack with a mission, that of safeguarding his establishment for several months. Here one sees the same polite affability, the same stereotyped social relations as in the scenes on the moon preceding the *Discovery's* departure. The third movement confines our three passengers within an enclosed space, cut off from the rest of the world, where they have to handle machinery and communicate with the outside by telephone, then radio, until the transmission system is put out of order. Like the spacecraft, the Overlook enables Kubrick to combine the contradictory sensations of agoraphobia and claustrophobia, and his characters to indulge in games and sports (Danny with his tricycle and his darts, Jack with his ball), before the person ostensibly in charge sinks into homicidal madness.

And this immense set must have demanded the director's constant attention (one thinks again of Stroheim having the Grand Hôtel de Monte-Carlo reconstructed in Hollywood for *Foolish Wives*), as well as swallowing up the greater part of his budget. No less than the *Discovery*, it becomes one of the film's characters, its role being to diminish the importance of man, now fallen victim to his fate and his instincts. As for the fourth movement – wordless like the first (in a symmetry similar to that governing *2001*) – it constitutes an initiatory journey of death and transfiguration, this time inside a labyrinth, which terminates in the past to the accompaniment of nostalgic twenties music. The final song recalls the Fitzgeraldian atmosphere in which the alcoholic writer wallows, just as the Johann Strauss waltz over the end titles of *2001* evoked the vanished era of a Vienna that was light-hearted, intoxicating and perched on the brink of an abyss. *The Shining* (whose running time is virtually identical to that of *2001*, even if its 'subjective' time-span seems shorter) is also the only one of Kubrick's films, with *A Space Odyssey*, to dispense with a 'voice-off' text (either first-person narration or objective commentary) in favour of title cards punctuating the narrative progression. Finally, both films make use of contemporary and consciously 'modern' music (Ligeti in *2001*; Ligeti again, Penderecki and Bartók in *The Shining*) mingled with extracts from Romantic works (in this case a *Dies Irae* inspired by the final 'Witches Sabbath' movement of Berlioz's *Symphonie fantastique*) which act as a prelude to some violent and total mental breakdown.

The narrative development of *The Shining* is particularly radical. The gradual compression of 'objective' space and time (from the mountains to the hotel, from the hotel to the labyrinth; from months to days, from days to hours) is allied to a corresponding expansion of 'inner' time and space. Here the response to the cosmic fusion that formed the epilogue to *2001* is that transgression of the boundaries between mind and matter which can be seen as one of the first symptoms of madness. One thinks of the passage from Gérard de Nerval's *Aurélia*, quoted by Todorov[242], in which the narrator confesses: 'We live in our race and our race lives in us. This *idea* I immediately felt as *perceptible* and, as if the walls of the room had opened on to infinite perspectives, I seemed to see an uninterrupted chain of men and women in whom I was and who were in me.' The gradual erosion of the frontier between the ego and the world, the real and the imaginary, characteristic of schizophrenia, is visible in *The Shining* – at first stimulated by the special 'gift' possessed by both Danny and Hallorann then, by a process of contamination, affecting Jack and eventually Wendy, who also enter into contact with the ghosts. This personality splitting is accompanied, as often in Kubrick's work, by double images: Danny and his double Tony, the apparitions of the twins, the Overlook's lounges with their symmetrical decoration, the labyrinth with its

---

1This essay is based on the original running time (146mn) of the film as screened in the United States.

perverse symmetry, which is revealed as a miniaturized double of the hotel and is doubled in its turn in the form of a model and a map. The camera itself – with its forward, lateral and reverse tracking shots no longer sweeping the space in baroque spirals as was the case in *Paths of Glory* and *Lolita* but following a rigorously geometric circuit – adds further to the sense of implacable logic and an almost mathematical progression.

The most perfect expression of this generalized determinism is the hotel whose very name (meaning both 'to survey' and, in an archaic usage, 'to cast a spell') indicates its manipulative function. If in Kubrick's films, as we have noted, puppets, robots, dolls and statues connote a world in which man has become no more than a docile machine, a toy in a society of empty forms, a servile being in a universe of semblances (and in *The Shining* the quasi-mechanical gestures of both Lloyd the barman and Grady the attendant conform to the rule), we can find in *2001* and *The Shining* an even more powerful evocation of the world as shadow-theatre, with extra-terrestrial spirits guiding the evolution of mankind (*2001*) and the evil entity represented by the hotel (*The Shining*). Kubrick's latest film lends even greater force to the thesis of Carolyn Geduld[108], for whom *2001* embodied a vision of cosmic design as the work of Satan, depriving man of all free-will, from the 'Genesis' of the Prologue to the 'Cana' of the Epilogue, by way of the Black Mass celebrated in the Tycho crater on the moon. The whisperings in the corridors of the Overlook Hotel are not unlike those which greet Dave Bowman in his Louis XVI suite, and the shots of blood seeping through the elevator gates, like the apparitions of the monolith, posit the existence of a higher order.

Fascinated by the theme of immortality, Kubrick wanted to accord it even more importance in *2001*, if we are to believe Arthur C. Clarke. At an advanced stage of the screenplay, the director could not resign himself to letting one of his astronauts, Frank Poole, disappear into space after being killed by HAL 9000; he wished to have him return from the dead. Speaking of his co-scenarist, Clarke said: 'I'm afraid his obsession with immortality has got the better of his artistic instincts[105].' The child and the Negro in *The Shining*, along with certain topographical elements (the hotel had been built on a former Indian burial ground), relate the ordeals undergone by the characters to magic, animism, to a primitive conception of the universe of spirits. Like some primitive being, the child is closer to those psychic activities which characterized humanity at an earlier stage of its development. This proximity to death is no less strongly present in the adult, except that it is masked, 'censored' by the process of civilization. For Freud, 'the proposition "all men are mortal" is to be found in every treatise on logic, but it is actually a given for no one and our subconscious has as little room today as in the past for the representation of our own mortality[236].'

But Kubrick proceeds with the greatest caution when manipulating his fantastic themes. He insures that they have a completely realistic foundation, makes very sparing use of expressionistic lighting and plays on the ambiguous relation between imagination and reality almost to the end of the film. Are they authentic ghosts or the characters' mental projections? Evidence of supernatural forces or signs of oncoming madness in the protagonist? Perhaps even a form of interaction whereby Jack's psychic condition ends with him investing his spectres with physical existence? One ought, like Jean-Loup Bourget[183], to enumerate the motifs of the fantastic in *The Shining*: reincarnation or metempsychosis (the final shot); vampirism (the scar on Danny's neck); second sight; telepathy; a pact with the devil (the barman Lloyd); the

Shelley Duvall (The Shining)

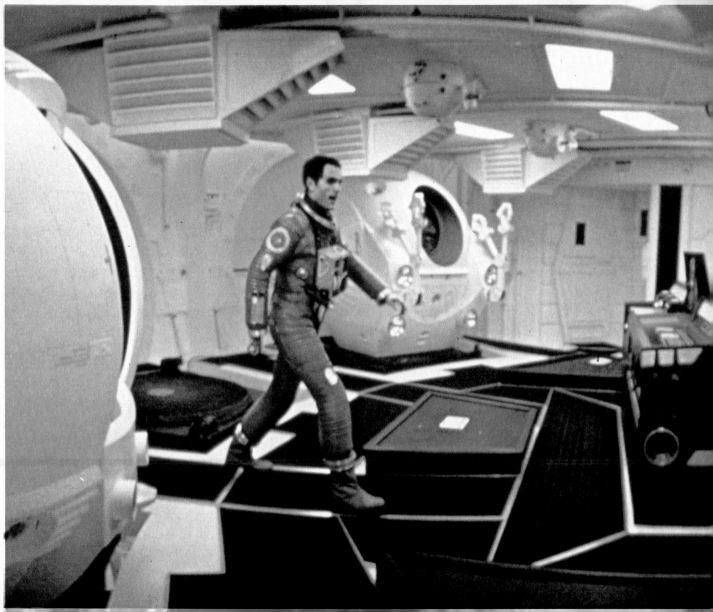

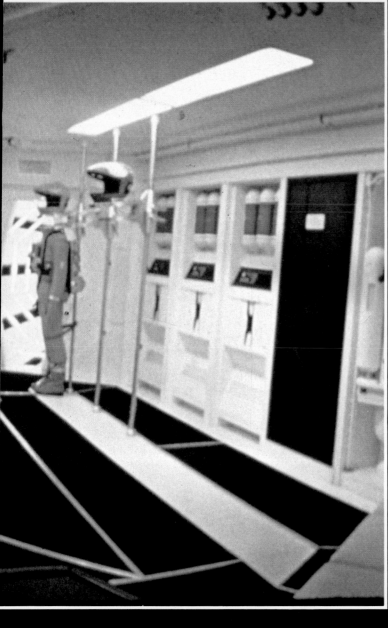

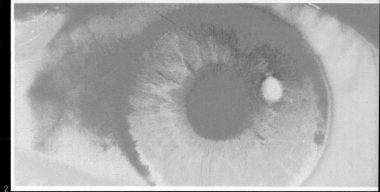

2001: A Space Odyssey
1. The interior of the Discovery
2. and 3. Bowman's visions beyond infinity
4. The lunar landscape

Jack's nightmare (Jack Nicholson, Shelley Duvall) in The Shining
2. Wendy (Shelley Duvall) flees from the Overlook Hotel (The Shining)

2

The nocturnal 'return of the repressed'
*1. The journey of Alex and his droogs through the English
countryside (in the foreground Malcolm McDowell and Michael Tarn,
behind James Marcus and Warren Clarke) in* A Clockwork Orange
2. Dave Bowman's journey beyond infinity (Keir Dullea in 2001:
A Space Odyssey)
3. Jack Torrance's journey through the labyrinth (Jack Nicholson in
The Shining)

materialization of ghosts (to which, with the encounter in Room 237, might be added necrophilia, the union of love and death common in Kubrick's work). There are also borrowings from fairy-tales (the forbidden room in which lurks a sexual secret; Jack as the Big Bad Wolf ready to devour the little pigs Danny and Wendy; the wiles of Hop O' My Thumb in the labyrinth, etc.), but it should be emphasized that the director is just as concerned to play down the effects of the uncanny that Freud associates with the pure fantastic. In his essay on *Das Unheimliche*, he demonstrates those processes which lead to an explanation for something that ought to have remained hidden, secret, and how what was once pleasant and familiar (*heimlich*) becomes disturbing and sinister (*unheimlich*). And what is latent is precisely everything connected with death, corpses and ghosts. When Jack arrives at the Overlook, he describes this sensation of familiarity, of well-being ('It's very homey'), he would 'like to stay here forever', he confesses even to having 'never been this happy, or comfortable anywhere', refers to a sense of *déjà vu* and has the feeling that he has 'been here before'. 'When someone dreams of a locality or a landscape,' according to Freud, 'and

common to dreams, fantasies and myths, between the eyes and the penis? If, as Freud believed, fear for one's eyes is a frequent substitute for the fear of castration, is second sight not then the expression of some hyper-virility which will oppose the father's destructive will and lead him, by an infernal cycle, towards an even more pronounced annihilatory rage?

In Kubrick's films, the eye has always played an essential role; and, particularly in *2001*, it united instinct with intelligence and was linked with the presence of the monolith (the eye of the ape, of the leopard, of HAL 9000, of the astronaut, of the foetus) preceding each of mankind's advances. As with every great film-maker who has reflected on the very nature of *mise en scène* (Lang, Boorman, Hitchcock, etc.), sight and its faculties are called into question by Kubrick. By abolishing time and space, by creating a parallel world to replace the real one, Danny assumes the same 'imagining' function as any director. He also represents the victory of the visual over the written word, the fertility of the child as against the sterility of the father.

Emotional family relationships are therefore a central

while dreaming thinks "I know this, I've been here before", one is authorized to interpret that place as substituting for the genital organs and the maternal body.' And Jack takes possession of the immense womb which the Overlook represents by a regressive involution which makes him withdraw from his wife and cultivate his own narcissism.

The relationships within the Torrance family illustrate the classic development of the Oedipal triangle. A few years earlier, Jack, disturbed in his work by Danny, had dislocated the boy's shoulder in a fit of rage. This castratory gesture – the father's Oedipal act always preceding that of the child – caused Danny to invent for himself a double who speaks out of his own mouth. 'The double was in primitive terms an insurance against the destruction of the *ego*, a radical denial of the power of death.' (Freud[236]) But if, for the child, the double is a protector and guarantor of survival, it becomes for the adult (as witness Jack's gradual schizophrenia, accentuated by the film's mirror images of him) a terrifying harbinger of death. To take the analysis even further, might not the gift of second sight which Danny has possessed for some time be another instance of the substitutive relation,

The look of despair:
1. The Dawn of Man (2001: A Space Odyssey)
2. Malcolm McDowell (A Clockwork Orange)
3. Scatman Crothers (The Shining)

concern of *The Shining*. Home and hearth, attacked from outside in *A Clockwork Orange* (the writer Mr Alexander, a victim of his double, Alex), become with *Barry Lyndon* and especially *The Shining* the private arena of every conflict. And it is finally within Jack himself that the real battle is fought. Since *Lolita* Kubrick's work has been suffused with the Oedipal theme – even if this has attracted little critical attention – and it was pivotal in *Barry Lyndon*. We know that prior to *Lolita* Kubrick wanted to adapt Stefan Zweig's *The Burning Secret*, a novel which is almost the inverted double of Nabokov's: a man befriends a young boy the better to seduce his mother. Similarly, his unfulfilled ambition (dating from the early seventies) of filming Arthur Schnitzler's *Rhapsody: A Dream Novel* found an outlet in *The Shining*. Schnitzler's tale deals with the relation between the real and the unreal through the story of a husband, the father of a little seven-

year-old girl, who spends a night in Vienna during which reality is coloured by his imagination. The mutual infidelities of the parent couple – whether dreamt or fantasized – reveal the psychic urges of their inner life. In *The Shining* Jack, haunted by his obsession with the rivalry of his son (as always, more attached to the mother, despite recurrent bouts of affection for the father), will be driven to madness and death; and the child, however threatening seems the father, will once more end victorious. As in *Lolita* and *Barry Lyndon*, the defeat of authority is sanctioned by a date (here 4 July, Independence Day in the United States, in the earlier films 1776 and 1789) which is also, as we have already noted, that of an Oedipal juncture in history.

In the extensive adaptation which Stephen King's novel underwent at the hands of Kubrick and Diane Johnson, their concern being for ever greater precision in order to pare the work down to its essentials and allow the power of its themes and situations to emerge more clearly, the most remarkable idea was undoubtedly the final one of the labyrinth. It enriched the plot with a new mythic dimension and fully responded to the needs of a director for whom – as he has often insisted – the truth of anything in the cinema is to be found in the sensation of that thing rather than in its conceptualization. It is his belief that film communicates, not with the intellect, but with the emotions and subconscious. The labyrinth, which is both a spatial and temporal expression, would seem to be the ideal terminus for a Kubrickian journey. If it is, as has been noted by Paolo Santarcangeli[240], a symbol for the maternal belly, for the intestines, it is also the extension of the objective correlative to Jack's psychism, already represented by the Overlook Hotel. Finally, combining two motifs linked to the concept of infinity – one of which, the intertwining, is closed, evil and pessimistic (the eternal return associated with Jack), the other, the spiral, is positive, open and optimistic (the perpetual evolution associated with Danny) – it signifies the definitive victory of the son over the father, of the 'child of light' over the forces of darkness, of intelligence over instinct, of Theseus, the solar hero, over the Minotaur. Jack, penetrating ever further along its serpentine snow-blanketed paths beneath a bluish night sky, returns to the animal condition, with the low-hung forehead and panting breath of the bull. Armed with his axe (traditionally associated with the myth of the labyrinth), he recalls the great shedders of blood in Kubrick's universe: *2001*'s Moonwatcher with his bone, *A Clockwork Orange*'s Alex with his truncheon, *Barry Lyndon*'s Bullingdon with his pistol, all of them living symbols of the bestial instinct (one thinks, too, of the hallucinated 'trip' which Dave Bowman takes beyond infinity). In the labyrinth and its initiatory circuit is played out the struggle of life and death. As in *2001*, the death of the father, both necessary and unjust – whence the tragic sentiment – precedes the son's rebirth. And one can see how this 'mental theme, in which hope and anxiety are intermingled, capable of fostering a kind of intellectual nightmare which comes close to madness[240]' would have fascinated Kubrick.

In many respects, *The Shining* is one of his most intimate works. Isolated, hemmed in, beset by a siege mentality, an intellectual (a former teacher) sees himself as an artist but cannot manage to create. The anguish of the white page culminates in one disturbing sentence typed out *ad infinitum*: 'All work and no play makes Jack a dull boy'. By choosing an artist for the first time as the protagonist of one of his stories (a theme prefigured in *Lolita* by the character of Humbert) and making him a failure, Kubrick exorcises his own demons and demonstrates – by default, as it were – the exalting supremacy of artistic creation. If Jack has given reality to his nightmares (he admits to Wendy that, in his dreams, he killed both her and Danny), it is undoubtedly because he has proved incapable of sublimating his instincts by writing his novel. Artistic creation has, after all, a genuine cathartic

value. Just as myths do, Kubrick appears to be telling us, which is why he has always wished to identify his films with the collective subconscious. Modern civilization and science have divested our conception of the world of all its mythologies, and are exclusively bound by the principle of reality and the death instinct. It therefore befits the film-maker to create for the largest possible numbers – with no distinction of class or society – archetypal, mythopoeic works in which the spectator will find a balm for his torments and his desires.

So it is, perhaps, that Kubrick, a disillusioned romantic become a 'disillusionist' in his turn, rejecting lies and subterfuges, regarding life as either a tragedy or a grotesque farce, and often accused for just those reasons of being a nihilist, is in reality a great liberator. Helping us to know ourselves better is the same thing as allowing us to gain our independence. The contradiction which he has been exploring – that of admitting the importance and legitimacy of the instincts and the subconscious, while at the same time regarding reason as the only solution for both the individual and mankind as a whole – is one that confronts us all. Kubrick does not know the answer, even if the artist in him seems to have found it, but he poses the question with a magnificent and endlessly renewed invention of forms.

Oedipal relations:
1. *Jack Nicholson and Danny Lloyd (The Shining)*
2. *David Morley and Ryan O'Neal (Barry Lyndon)*
3. *Marisa Berenson and Dominic Savage (Barry Lyndon)*
4. *Shelley Duvall and Danny Lloyd (The Shining)*

3

4

First Interview

Stanley Kubrick (filming A Clockwork Orange)

A Clockwork Orange

Since so many different interpretations have been offered about A Clockwork Orange, *how do you see your own film?*

The central idea of the film has to do with the question of free-will. Do we lose our humanity if we are deprived of the choice between good and evil? Do we become, as the title suggests, A Clockwork Orange? Recent experiments in conditioning and mind control on volunteer prisoners in America have taken this question out of the realm of science-fiction. At the same time, I think the dramatic impact of the film has principally to do with the extraordinary character of Alex, as conceived by Anthony Burgess in his brilliant and original novel. Aaron Stern, the former head of the MPAA rating board in America, who is also a practising psychiatrist, has suggested that Alex represents the unconscious; man in his *natural* state. After he is given the Ludovico *cure* he has been *civilized*, and the sickness that follows may be viewed as the neurosis imposed by society.

The chaplain is a central character in the film.

Although he is partially concealed behind a satirical disguise, the prison chaplain, played by Godfrey Quigley, is the moral voice of the film. He challenges the ruthless opportunism of the state in pursuing its programme to reform criminals through psychological conditioning. A very delicate balance had to be achieved in Godfrey's performance between his somewhat comical image and the important ideas he is called upon to express.

On a political level the end of the film shows an alliance between the hoodlum and the authorities.

The government eventually resorts to the employment of the cruellest and most violent members of the society to control everyone else – not an altogether new or untried idea. In this sense, Alex's last line, 'I was cured all right,' might be seen in the same light as Dr Strangelove's exit line, 'Mein Führer, I can walk.' The final images of Alex as the spoon-fed child of a corrupt, totalitarian society, and Strangelove's rebirth after his miraculous recovery from a crippling disease, seem to work well both dramatically and as expressions of an idea.

What amuses me is that many reviewers speak of this society as a communist one, whereas there is no reason to think it is.

The Minister, played by Anthony Sharp, is clearly a figure of the Right. The writer, Patrick Magee, is a lunatic of the Left. 'The common people must be led, driven, pushed!' he pants into the telephone. 'They will sell their liberty for an easier life!'

But these could be the very words of a Fascist.

Yes, of course. They differ only in their dogma. Their means and ends are hardly distinguishable.

You deal with the violence in a way that appears to distance it.

If this occurs it may be because the story both in the novel and the film is told by Alex, and everything that happens is seen through his eyes. Since he has his own rather special way of seeing what he does, this may have some effect in distancing the violence. Some people have asserted that this made the violence attractive. I think this view is totally incorrect.

The Cat Lady was much older in the book. Why did you change her age?

She fulfils the same purpose as she did in the novel, but I think she may be a little more interesting in the film. She is younger, it is true, but she is just as unsympathetic and unwisely aggressive.

You also eliminated the murder that Alex committed in prison.

That had to do entirely with the problem of length. The film is, anyway, about two hours and seventeen minutes long, and it didn't seem to be a necessary scene.

Alex is no longer a teenager in the film.

Malcolm McDowell's age is not that easy to judge in the film, and he was, without the slightest doubt, the best actor for the part. It might have been nicer if Malcolm had been seventeen, but another seventeen-year-old actor without Malcolm's extraordinary talent would not have been better.

Somehow the prison is the most acceptable place in the whole movie. And the warder, who is a typical British figure, is more appealing than a lot of other characters.

The prison warder, played by the late Michael Bates, is an obsolete servant of the new order. He copes very poorly with the problems around him, understanding neither the criminals nor the reformers. For all his shouting and bullying, though, he is less of a villain than his trendier and more sophisticated masters.

In your films the State is worse than the criminals but the scientists are worse than the State.

I wouldn't put it that way. Modern science seems to be very dangerous because it has given us the power to destroy ourselves before we know how to handle it. On the other hand, it is foolish to blame science for its discoveries, and in any case, we cannot control science. Who would do it, anyway? Politicians are certainly not qualified to make the necessary technical decisions. Prior to the first atomic bomb tests at Los Alamos, a small group of physicists working on the project argued against the test because they thought there was a possibility that the detonation of the bomb might cause a chain reaction which would destroy the entire planet. But the majority of the physicists disagreed with them and recommended that the test be carried out. The decision to ignore this dire warning and proceed with the test was made by political and military minds who could certainly not understand the physics involved in either side of the argument. One would have thought that if even a minority of the physicists thought the test might destroy the Earth no sane men would decide to carry it out. The fact that the Earth is still here doesn't alter the mind-boggling decision which was made at that time.

Alex has a close relationship with art (Beethoven) which the other characters do not have. The Cat Lady seems interested in modern art but, in fact, is indifferent. What is your own attitude towards modern art?

I think modern art's almost total pre-occupation with subjectivism has led to anarchy and sterility in the arts. The notion that reality exists only in the artist's mind, and that the thing which simpler souls had for so long believed to be

reality is only an illusion, was initially an invigorating force, but it eventually led to a lot of highly original, very personal and extremely uninteresting work.

In Cocteau's film *Orpheus*, the poet asks what he should do. 'Astonish me', he is told. Very little of modern art does that – certainly not in the sense that a great work of art can make you wonder how its creation was accomplished by a mere mortal. Be that as it may, films, unfortunately, don't have this problem at all. From the start, they have played it as safe as possible, and no one can blame the generally dull state of the movies on too much originality and subjectivism.

Well, don't you think that your films might be called original?

I'm talking about major innovations in form, not about quality, content, or ideas, and in this respect I think my films are still not very far from the traditional form and structure which has moved sideways since the beginning of sound.

The film makes a reference to Christ.

Alex brutally fantasizes about being a Roman guard at the Crucifixion while he feigns Bible study in the prison library. A few moments later, he tells the prison chaplain that he wants to be good. The chaplain, who is the only decent man in the story, is taken in by Alex's phoney contrition. The scene is still another example of the blackness of Alex's soul.

But why did you shoot this crucifixion scene like a bad Hollywood movie?

I thought Alex would have imagined it that way. That's why he uses the American accent we've heard so many times before in biblical movies when he shouts, 'Move on there!'

Do you think there is any relationship between this and your interpretation of antiquity in Spartacus?

None at all. In *Spartacus* I tried with only limited success to make the film as real as possible but I was up against a pretty dumb script which was rarely faithful to what is known about Spartacus. History tells us he twice led his victorious slave army to the northern borders of Italy, and could quite easily have gotten out of the country. But he didn't, and instead he led his army back to pillage Roman cities. What the reasons were for this would have been the most interesting question the film might have pondered. Did the intentions of the rebellion change? Did Spartacus lose control of his leaders who by now may have been more interested in the spoils of war than in freedom? In the film, Spartacus was prevented from escape by the silly contrivance of a pirate leader who reneged on a deal to take the slave army away in his ships. If I ever needed any convincing of the limits of persuasion a director can have on a film where someone else is the producer and he is merely the highest-paid member of the crew, *Spartacus* provided proof to last a lifetime.

You use technical devices which break the narrative fluidity, and the illusion of reality: accelerated action, slow motion, and an unusual reliance on ultra-wide angle lenses.

I tried to find something like a cinematic equivalent of Burgess's literary style, and Alex's highly subjective view of things. But the style of any film has to do more with intuition than with analysis. I think there is a great deal of over-simplified over-conceptualizing by some film-makers which is encouraged by the way interviewers formulate their questions, and it passes for serious and useful thought and seems to inspire confidence in every direction.

Why did you shoot the orgy in skip-frame high-speed motion?

It seemed to me a good way to satirize what had become the fairly common use of slow-motion to solemnize this sort of

---

The prison warder: 'less of a villain than his masters' (Michael Bates and Malcolm McDowell in A Clockwork Orange)

thing, and turn it into 'art'. The William Tell Overture also seemed a good musical joke to counter the standard Bach accompaniment.

The first three sequences are very striking, employing the same zoom pull-back shots, starting from a close-up and ending on the whole set. How do you prepare this kind of shot?

There was no special preparation. I find that, with very few exceptions, it's important to save your cinematic ideas until you have rehearsed the scene in the actual place you're going to film it. The first thing to do is to rehearse the scene until something happens that is worth putting on film – only then should you worry about *how* to film it. The *what* must always precede the *how*.

No matter how carefully you have pre-planned a scene, when you actually come to the time of shooting, and you have

camera operator and show him the composition that you want at each point in the take. But you can't do this when the camera is hand-held. Sometimes there are certain effects which can only be achieved with a hand-held camera, and sometimes you hand hold it because there's no other way to move through a confined space or over obstacles.

Most of the shooting was done on location.

The entire film was shot on location with the exception of four sets which were built in a small factory which we rented for the production. Nothing was filmed in a studio. The four sets we had to build were the Korova Milk Bar, the Prison Check-in, the Writer's Bathroom, and the Entrance Hall to his house. In the latter case, we built this small set in a tent in the back garden of the house in which we filmed the interiors of the writer's house. The locations were supposed to look a bit futuristic, and we did our preliminary location search by

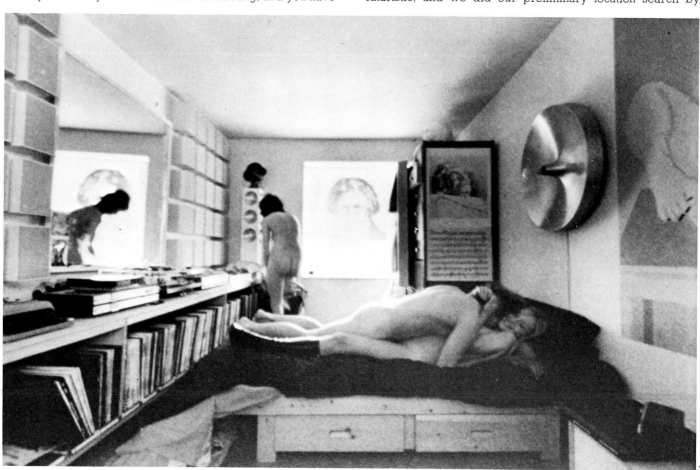

the actors on the set, having learned their lines, dressed in the right clothes, and you have the benefit of knowing what you have already got on film, there is usually some adjustment that has to be made to the scene in order to achieve the best result.

There are many sequences – for example Alex's return to his parents' house or the prison – in which the camera is very still and the editing reduced to a minimum.

I think there should always be a reason for making a cut. If a scene plays well in one camera set up and there is no reason to cut, then I don't cut. I try to avoid a mechanical cutting rhythm which dissipates much of the effect of editing.

You did a lot of hand-held camera work yourself, especially for the action scenes.

I like to do hand-held shooting myself. When the camera is on a dolly you can go over the action of the scene with the

looking through back issues of several British architectural magazines, getting our leads for most of the locations that way.

Was the idea of the Milk Bar yours?

Part of it was. I had seen an exhibition of sculpture which displayed female figures as furniture. From this came the idea for the fibreglass nude figures which were used as tables in the Milk Bar. The late John Barry, who was the film's Production Designer, designed the set. To get the poses right for the sculptress who modelled the figures, John photographed a nude model in as many positions as he could imagine would make a table. There are fewer positions than you might think.

It was with Dr Strangelove *that you really started to use music as a cultural reference. What is your attitude to film music in general?*

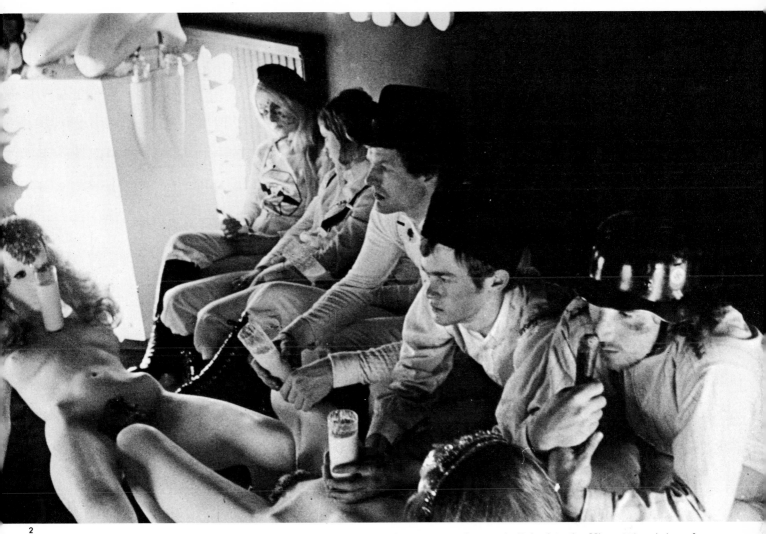

2

'A good way to satirize the common use of slow-motion' (Malcolm McDowell, Gillian Hills and, in the background, Barbara Scott in A Clockwork Orange)
2. 'Female figures as sculpture': The Korova Milk Bar (A Clockwork Orange)

Unless you want a pop score, I don't see any reason not to avail yourself of the great orchestral music of the past and present. This music may be used in its correct form or synthesized, as was done with the Beethoven for some scenes in A Clockwork Orange. But there doesn't seem to be much point in hiring a composer who, however good he may be, is not a Mozart or a Beethoven, when you have such a vast choice of existing orchestral music which includes contemporary and avant-garde work. Doing it this way gives you the opportunity to experiment with the music early in the editing phase, and in some instances to cut the scene to the music. This is not something you can easily do in the normal sequence of events.

Was the music chosen after the film was completed? And on which grounds?
Most of it was, but I had some of it in mind from the start. It is a bit difficult to say why you choose a piece of music. Ideas occur to you, you try them out, and at some point you decide that you're doing the right thing. It's a matter of taste, luck and imagination, as is virtually everything else connected with making a film.

Is your taste for music linked to the Viennese origins of your father?
My father was born in America, and he is a doctor living in California. His mother was Rumanian, and his father came from a place which today is in Poland. So I think my musical tastes were probably acquired not inherited.

It would appear that you intended to make a trilogy about the future in your last three films. Have you thought about this?
There is no deliberate pattern to the stories that I have chosen to make into films. About the only factor at work each time is that I try not to repeat myself. Since you can't be systematic about finding a story to film, I read anything. In addition to books which sound interesting, I rely on luck and accident to eventually bring me together with *the book*. I read as unselfconsciously as I can to avoid interfering with the story's emotional impact. If the book proves to be exciting and suggests itself as a possible choice, subsequent readings are done much more carefully, usually with notes taken at the same time. Should the book finally be what I want, it is very important for me to retain, during the subsequent phases of making the film, my impressions of the first reading. After you've been working on a film, perhaps for more than a year, everything about it tends to become so familiar that you are in danger of not seeing the forest for the trees. That's why it's so important to be able to use this first impression as the criterion for making decisions about the story much later on. Whoever the director may be, and however perceptively he has filmed and edited his movie, he can never have the same experience that the audience has when it sees the film for the

first time. The director's *first time* is the first reading of the story, and the impressions and excitement of this event have to last through to the final work on the movie. Fortunately I've never chosen a story where the excitement hasn't gone the distance. It would be a terrible thing if it didn't.

What were the various projects that you have dropped?

One was a screenplay of Stefan Zweig's story, *The Burning Secret*, which Calder Willingham and I wrote in the middle fifties, for Dore Schary at MGM, after I made *The Killing*. The story is about a mother who goes away on vacation without her husband but accompanied by her young son. At the resort hotel where they are staying, she is seduced by an attractive gentleman she meets there. Her son discovers this but when mother and son eventually return home the boy lies at a crucial moment to prevent his father from discovering the truth. It's a good story but I don't know how good the screenplay was. A few years later, I wrote an incomplete screenplay about Mosby's Rangers, a Southern guerilla force in the American Civil War.

Around that time I also wrote a screenplay called *I Stole 16 Million Dollars*, based on the autobiography of Herbert Emmerson Wilson, a famous safe-cracker. It was written for Kirk Douglas who didn't like it, and that was the end of it. I must confess I have never subsequently been interested in any of these sceenplays.

In Mr Alexander's House (A Clockwork Orange)
1. *Malcolm McDowell, Michael Tarn, James Marcus, Patrick Magee, Adrienne Corri, Warren Clarke*
2. *Michael Tarn*
3. *Malcolm McDowell, James Marcus, Adrienne Corri*

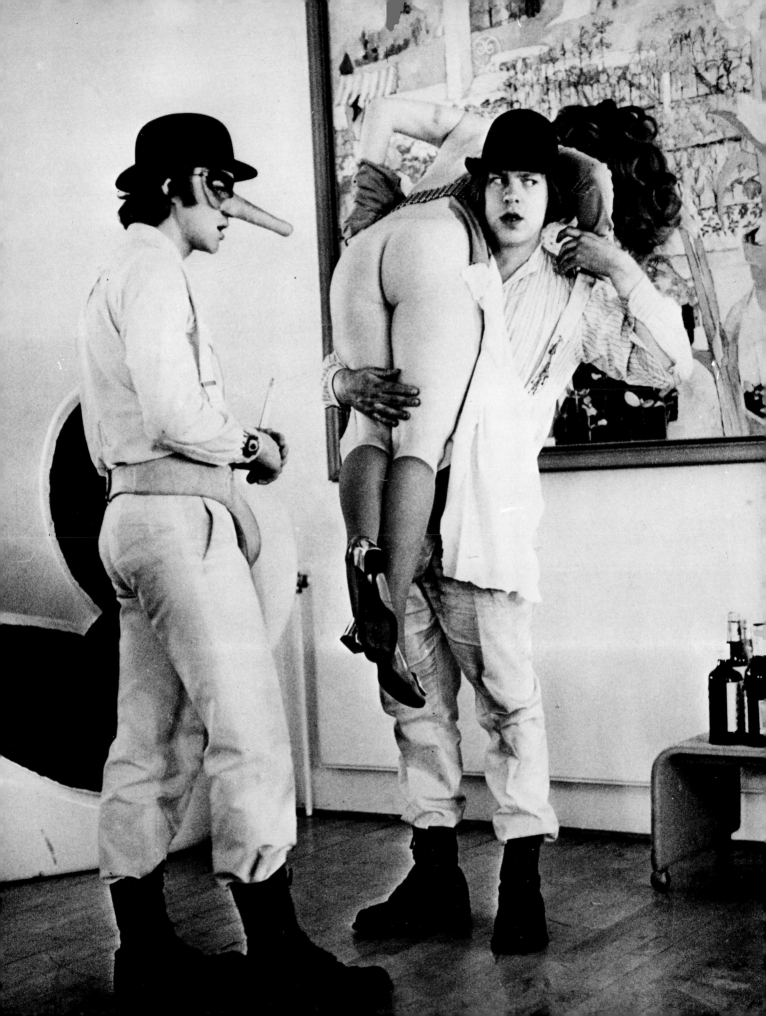

There is also a novel by Arthur Schnitzler, *Rhapsody: A Dream Novel*, which I intend to do but on which I have not yet started to work. It's a difficult book to describe – what good book isn't? It explores the sexual ambivalence of a *happy marriage*, and tries to equate the importance of sexual dreams and *might-have-beens* with reality. All of Schnitzler's work is psychologically brilliant, and he was greatly admired by Freud, who once wrote to him apologizing for having always avoided a personal meeting. Making a joke (a joke?), Freud said this was because he was afraid of the popular superstition that if you meet your Doppleganger (double) you would die.

Did you make a film for American television around 1960 about Lincoln?

It was in the early fifties, and I only worked for about a week doing some second unit shots in Kentucky for the producer, Richard de Rochemont.

Your films seem to show an attraction for Germany: the German music, the characters of Dr Strangelove, Professor Zempf in Lolita.

I wouldn't include German music as a relevant part of that group, nor would I say that I'm attracted but, rather, that I share the fairly widespread fascination with the horror of the Nazi period. Strangelove and Zempf are just parodies of movie clichés about Nazis.

You seem to be very interested in language. Lolita *and A* Clockwork Orange *are two films where the manipulation of words play an essential role*

Yes, of course I am. But my principal interest in *A Clockwork Orange* wasn't the language, however brilliant it was, but rather, the story, the characters and the ideas. Of course the language is a very important part of the novel, and it contributed a lot to the film, too. I think *A Clockwork Orange* is one of the very few books where a writer has played with syntax and introduced new words where it worked.

In a film, however, I think the images, the music, the editing and the emotions of the actors are the principal tools you have to work with. Language is important but I would put it after those elements. It should even be possible to do a film which isn't gimmicky without using any dialogue at all. Unfortunately, there has been very little experimentation with the form of film stories, except in avant-garde cinema where, unfortunately, there is too little technique and expertise present to show very much.

As far as I'm concerned, the most memorable scenes in the best films are those which are built predominantly of images and music.

We could find that kind of attempt in some underground American films.

Yes, of course, but, as I said, they lack the technique to prove very much.

The powerful things that you remember may be the images but perhaps their strength comes from the words that precede them. Alex's first-person narration at the beginning of the film increases the power of the images.

You can't make a rule that says that words are *never more*

The Ludovico treatment (Malcolm McDowell in A Clockwork Orange)

2. *Alex and his drocgs (James Marcus, Warren Clarke, Malcolm McDowell in* A Clockwork Orange)

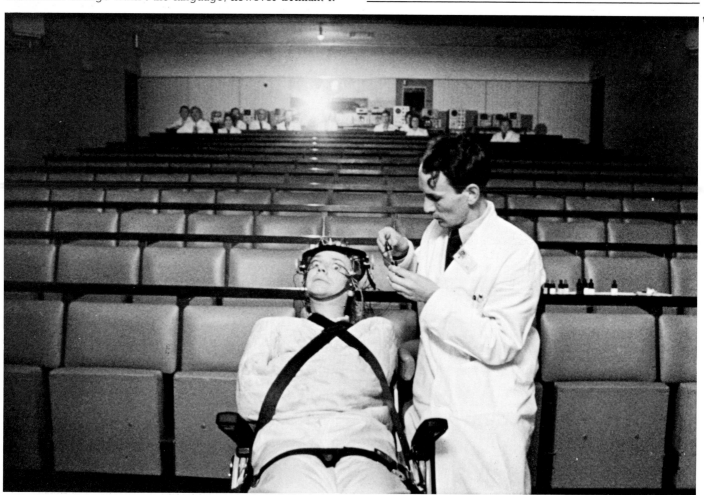

useful than images. And, of course, in the scene you refer to, it would be rather difficult to do without words to express Alex's thoughts. There is an old screenplay adage that says if you have to use voice-over it means there's something wrong with the script. I'm quite certain this is not true, and when thoughts are to be conveyed, especially when they are of a nature which one would not say to another person, there is no other good alternative.

This time you wrote your script alone. How would you equate the problems of writing a screenplay to writing a novel.?

Writing a screenplay is a very different thing than writing a novel or an original story. A good story is a kind of a miracle, and I think that is the way I would describe Burgess's achievement with the novel. *A Clockwork Orange* has a wonderful plot, strong characters and clear philosophy.

Peter George, a former RAF navigator. The ideas of the story and all its suspense were still there even when it was completely changed into black comedy.

The end of A Clockwork Orange *is different from the one in the Burgess book.*

There are two different versions of the novel. One has an extra chapter. I had not read this version until I had virtually finished the screenplay. This extra chapter depicts the rehabilitation of Alex. But it is, as far as I am concerned, unconvincing and inconsistent with the style and intent of the book. I wouldn't be surprised to learn that the publisher had somehow prevailed upon Burgess to tack on the extra chapter against his better judgement, so the book would end on a more positive note. I certainly never gave any serious consideration to using it.

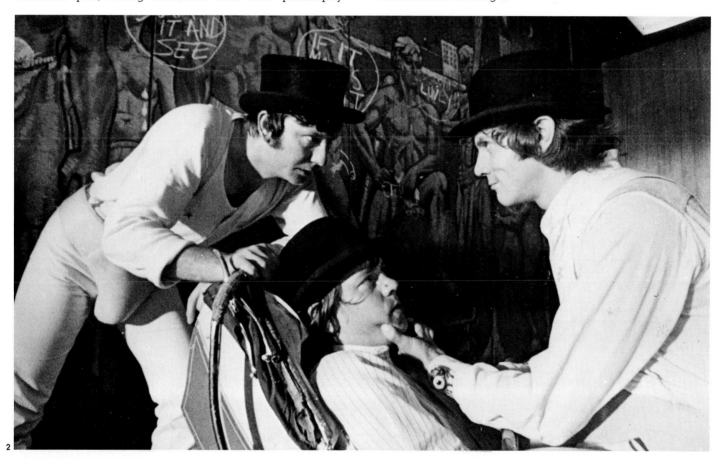

2

When you can write a book like that, you've really done something. On the other hand, writing the screenplay of the book is much more of a logical process – something between writing and breaking a code. It does not require the inspiration or the invention of the novelist. I'm not saying it's easy to write a good screenplay. It certainly isn't, and a lot of fine novels have been ruined in the process.

However serious your intentions may be, and however important you think are the ideas of the story, the enormous cost of a movie makes it necessary to reach the largest potential audience for that story, in order to give your backers their best chance to get their money back and hopefully make a profit. No one will disagree that a good story is an essential starting point for accomplishing this. But another thing, too, the stronger the story, the more chances you can take with everything else.

I think *Dr Strangelove* is a good example of this. It was based on a very good suspense novel, *Red Alert*, written by

In A Clockwork Orange, *Alex is an evil character, as Strangelove was, but Alex somehow seems less repellent.*

Alex has vitality, courage and intelligence, but you cannot fail to see that he is thoroughly evil. At the same time, there is a strange kind of psychological identification with him which gradually occurs, however much you may be repelled by his behaviour. I think this happens for a couple of reasons. First of all, Alex is always completely honest in his first-person narrative, perhaps even painfully so. Secondly, because on the unconscious level I suspect we all share certain aspects of Alex's personality.

Are you attracted by evil characters?

Of course I'm not, but they are good for stories. More people read books about the Nazis than about the UN. Newspapers headline bad news. The bad characters in a story can often be more interesting than the good ones.

How do you explain the kind of fascination that Alex exercises on the audience?

I think that it's probably because we can identify with Alex on the unconscious level. The psychiatrists tell us the unconscious has no conscience – and perhaps in our unconscious we are all potential Alexes. It may be that only as a result of morality, the law and sometimes our own innate character that we do not become like him. Perhaps this makes some people feel uncomfortable and partly explains some of the controversy which has arisen over the film. Perhaps they are unable to accept this view of human nature. But I think you find much the same psychological phenomena at work in Shakespeare's *Richard III*. You should feel nothing but dislike towards Richard, and yet when the role is well played, with a bit of humour and charm, you find yourself gradually making a similar kind of identification with him. Not because you sympathize with Richard's ambition or his actions, or that you like him or think people should behave like him but, as you watch the play, because he gradually works himself into your unconscious, and recognition occurs in the recesses of the mind. At the same time, I don't believe anyone leaves the theatre thinking Richard III or Alex are the sort of people one admires and would wish to be like.

Some people have criticized the possible dangers of such an admiration.

But it's not admiration one feels, and I think that anyone who says so is completely wrong. I think this view tends to come from people who, however well meaning and intelligent, hold committed positions in favour of broader and stricter censorship. No one is corrupted watching *A Clockwork Orange* any more than they are by watching *Richard III*. *A Clockwork*

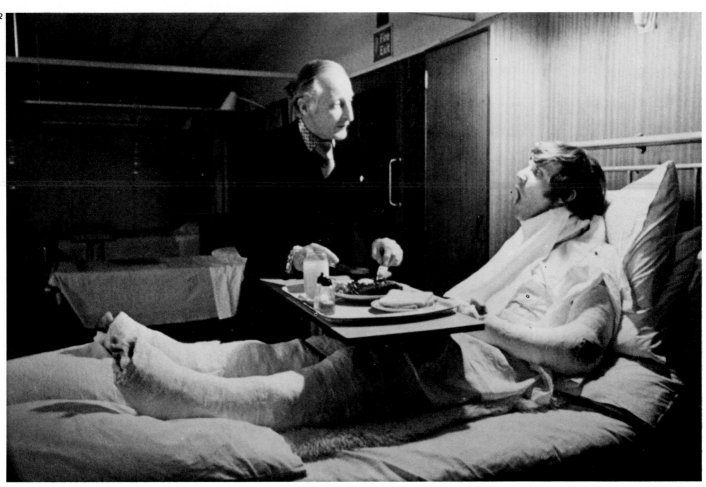

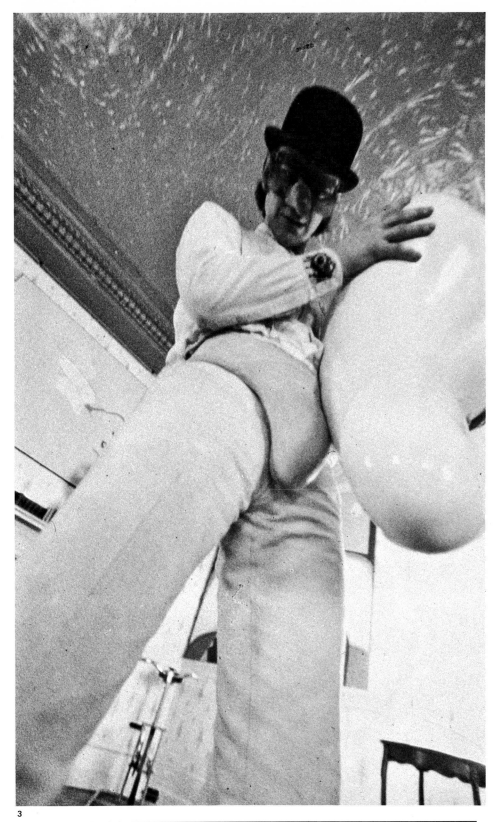

3

1. 'Mein Führer, I can walk.' (George C. Scott and Peter Sellers in
Dr Strangelove)
2. 'I was cured all right.' (Anthony Sharp, Malcolm McDowell in
A Clockwork Orange)
3. Alex in the house of the Cat Lady (Malcolm McDowell in
A Clockwork Orange)

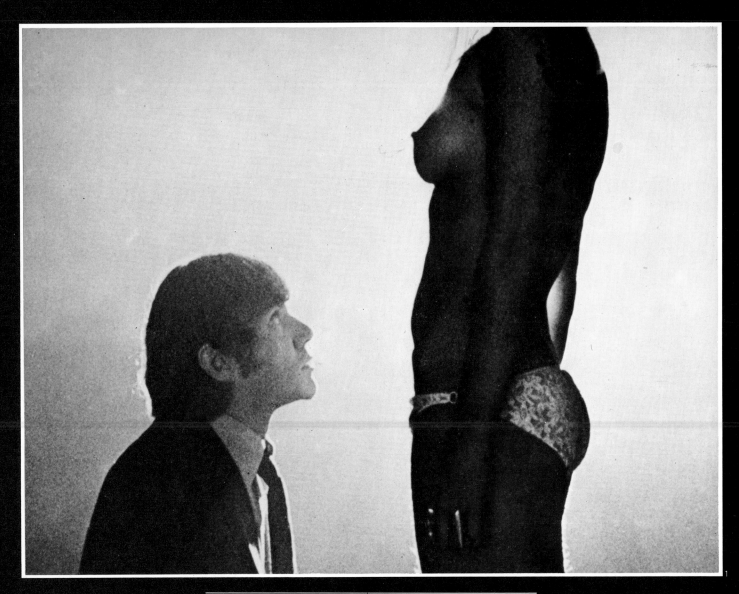

Sexuality as will and representation (A Clockwork Orange)
1. After the Ludovico treatment (Malcolm McDowell and Virginia Weatherell)
2. Alex and 'the very important work of art' (Malcolm McDowell)
3. In the Drugstore: Alex and Lolitaesque, lollipop-sucking friends (Gillian Hills, Malcolm McDowell and Barbara Scott)

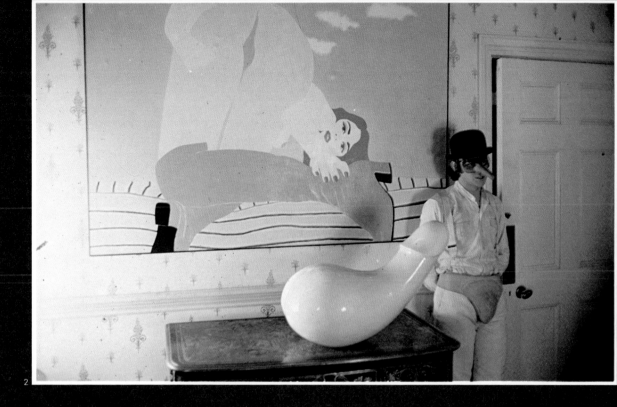

Orange has received world-wide acclaim as an important work of art. It was chosen by the New York Film Critics as the Best Film of the year, and I received the Best Director award. It won the Italian David Donatello award. The Belgian film critics gave it their award. It won the German Spotlight award. It received four USA Oscar nominations, and seven British Academy Award nominations. It won the Hugo award for the Best Science-Fiction movie.

It was highly praised by Fellini, Buñuel and Kurosawa. It has also received favourable comment from educational, scientific, political, religious and even law-enforcement groups. I could go on. But the point I want to make is that the film has been accepted as a work of art, and no work of art has ever done social harm, though a great deal of social harm has been done by those who have sought to protect society against works of art which they regarded as dangerous.

What was your attitude towards violence and eroticism in your film?

The erotic decor in the film suggests a slightly futuristic period for the story. The assumption being that erotic art will eventually become popular art, and just as you now buy African wildlife paintings in Woolworth's, you may one day buy erotica. The violence in the story has to be given sufficient dramatic weight so that the moral dilemma it poses can be seen in the right context. It is absolutely essential that Alex is seen to be guilty of a terrible violence against society, so that when he is eventually transformed by the state into a harmless zombie you can reach a meaningful conclusion about the relative rights and wrongs. If we did not see Alex first as a brutal and merciless thug it would be too easy to

'It is wrong to turn even unforgiveably vicious criminals into vegetables.' (A Clockwork Orange)
1. Paul Farrell
2. Patrick Magee (from behind), Malcolm McDowell, David Prowse
3. Malcolm McDowell

2

agree that the state is involved in a worse evil in depriving him of his freedom to choose between good and evil. It must be clear that it is wrong to turn even unforgiveably vicious criminals into vegetables, otherwise the story would fall into the same logical trap as did the old, anti-lynching Hollywood Westerns which always nullified their theme by lynching an innocent person. Of course no one will disagree that you shouldn't lynch an innocent person – but will they agree that it's just as bad to lynch a guilty person, perhaps even someone guilty of a horrible crime? And so it is with conditioning Alex.

What is your opinion about the increasing presence of violence on the screen in recent years?

There has always been violence in art. There is violence in the Bible, violence in Homer, violence in Shakespeare, and many psychiatrists believe that it serves as a catharsis rather than a model. I think the question of whether there has been an increase in screen violence and, if so, what effect this has had, is to a very great extent a media-defined issue. I know there are well-intentioned people who sincerely believe that

films and TV contribute to violence, but almost all of the official studies of this question have concluded that there is no evidence to support this view. At the same time, I think the media tend to exploit the issue because it allows them to display and discuss the so-called harmful things from a lofty position of moral superiority. But the people who commit violent crime are not ordinary people who are transformed into vicious thugs by the wrong diet of films or TV. Rather, it is a fact that violent crime is invariably committed by people with a long record of anti-social behaviour, or by the unexpected blossoming of a psychopath who is described afterward as having been '… such a nice, quiet boy,' but whose entire life, it is later realized, has been leading him inexorably to the terrible moment, and who would have found the final ostensible reason for his action if not in one thing then in another. In both instances immensely complicated social, economic and psychological forces are involved in the individual's criminal behaviour. The simplistic notion that films and TV can transform an otherwise innocent and good

person into a criminal has strong overtones of the Salem witch trials. This notion is further encouraged by the criminals and their lawyers who hope for mitigation through this excuse. I am also surprised at the extremely illogical distinction that is so often drawn between *harmful* violence and the so-called *harmless* violence of, say, *Tom and Jerry* cartoons or James Bond movies, where often sadistic violence is presented as unadulterated fun. I hasten to say, I don't think that they contribute to violence either. Films and TV are also convenient whipping boys for politicians because they allow them to look away from the social and economic causes of crime, about which they are either unwilling or unable to do anything.

Alex loves rape and Beethoven: what do you think this implies?

I think this suggests the failure of culture to have any morally refining effect on society. Hitler loved good music and many top Nazis were cultured and sophisticated men but it didn't do them, or anyone else, much good.

Contrary to Rousseau, do you believe that man is born bad and that society makes him worse?

I wouldn't put it like that. I think that when Rousseau transferred the concept of original sin from man to society, he was responsible for a lot of misguided social thinking which followed. I don't think that man is what he is because of an imperfectly structured society, but rather that society is imperfectly structured because of the nature of man. No philosophy based on an incorrect view of the nature of man is likely to produce social good.

Your film deals with the limits of power and freedom.

The film explores the difficulties of reconciling the conflict between individual freedom and social order. Alex exercises his freedom to be a vicious thug until the State turns him into a harmless zombie no longer able to choose between good and evil. One of the conclusions of the film is, of course, that there are limits to which society should go in maintaining law and order. Society should not do the wrong thing for the right reason, even though it frequently does the right thing for the wrong reason.

What attracted you in Burgess's novel?

Everything. The plot, the characters, the ideas. I was also interested in how close the story was to fairy tales and myths, particularly in its deliberately heavy use of coincidence and plot symmetry.

In your films, you seem to be critical of all political factions. Would you define yourself as a pessimist or anarchist?

I am certainly not an anarchist, and I don't think of myself as a pessimist. I believe very strongly in parliamentary democracy, and I am of the opinion that the power and authority of the State should be optimized and exercised only to the extent that is required to keep things *civilized*. History has shown us what happens when you try to make society too civilized, or do too good a job of eliminating undesirable elements. It also shows the tragic fallacy in the belief that the destruction of democratic institutions will cause better ones to arise in their place.

Certainly one of the most challenging and difficult social problems we face today is, how can the State maintain the necessary degree of control over society without becoming repressive, and how can it achieve this in the face of an increasingly impatient electorate who are beginning to regard legal and political solutions as too slow? The State sees the spectre looming ahead of terrorism and anarchy, and this increases the risk of its over-reaction and a reduction in our freedom. As with everything else in life, it is a matter of groping for the right balance, and a certain amount of luck.

3

The décors of A Clockwork Orange:
1. At home with Alex's parents (Philip Stone, Malcolm McDowell,
Clive Francis, Sheila Raynor)
2. Alex's room (Malcolm McDowell)
3. The Korova Milk Bar

Second Interview

1. *Stanley Kubrick (filming* Barry Lyndon)
2. *'It isn't likely that he is the only soldier she has brought home.'*
(Ryan O'Neal and Diana Koerner in Barry Lyndon)

Barry Lyndon

You have given almost no interviews on Barry Lyndon. *Does this decision relate to this film particularly, or is it because you are reluctant to speak about your work?*

I suppose my excuse is that the picture was ready only a few weeks before it opened and I really had no time to do any interviews. But if I'm to be completely honest, it's probably due more to the fact that I don't like doing interviews. There is always the problem of being misquoted or, what's even worse, of being quoted exactly, and having to see what you've said in print. Then there are the mandatory – 'How did you get along with actor X, Y or Z?' – 'Who really thought of good idea A, B or C?' I think Nabokov may have had the right approach to interviews. He would only agree to write down the answers and then send them on to the interviewer who would then write the questions.

Do you feel that Barry Lyndon *is a more secret film, more difficult to talk about?*

Not really. I've always found it difficult to talk about any of my films. What I generally manage to do is to discuss the background information connected with the story, or perhaps some of the interesting facts which might be associated with it. This approach often allows me to avoid the 'What does it mean? Why did you do it?' questions. For example, with *Dr Strangelove* I could talk about the spectrum of bizarre ideas connected with the possibilities of accidental or unintentional nuclear warfare. *2001: A Space Odyssey* allowed speculation about ultra-intelligent computers, life in the universe, and a whole range of science-fiction ideas. *A Clockwork Orange* involved law and order, criminal violence, authority versus freedom, etc. With *Barry Lyndon* you haven't got these topical issues to talk around, so I suppose that does make it a bit more difficult.

Your last three films were set in the future. What led you to make an historical film?

I can't honestly say what led me to make any of my films. The best I can do is to say I just fell in love with the stories. Going beyond that is a bit like trying to explain why you fell in love with your wife: she's intelligent, has brown eyes, a good figure. Have you really said anything? Since I am currently going through the process of trying to decide what film to make next, I realize just how uncontrollable is the business of finding a story, and how very much it depends on chance and spontaneous reaction. You can say a lot of 'architectural' things about what a film story should have: a strong plot, interesting characters, possibilities for cinematic development, good opportunities for the actors to display emotion, and the presentation of its thematic ideas truthfully and intelligently. But, of course, that still doesn't really explain why you finally chose something, nor does it lead you to a story. You can only say that you probably wouldn't choose a story that doesn't have most of those qualities.

2

Since you are completely free in your choice of story material, how did you come to pick up a book by Thackeray, almost forgotten and hardly republished since the nineteenth century?

I have had a complete set of Thackeray sitting on my bookshelf at home for years, and I had read several of his novels before reading *Barry Lyndon*. At one time, *Vanity Fair* interested me as a possible film but, in the end, I decided the story could not be successfully compressed into the relatively short time-span of a feature film. This problem of length, by the way, is now wonderfully accommodated for by the television mini-series which, with its ten- to twelve-hour length, presented on consecutive nights, has created a completely different dramatic form. Anyway, as soon as I read *Barry Lyndon* I became very excited about it. I loved the story and the characters, and it seemed possible to make the transition from novel to film without destroying it in the process. It also offered the opportunity to do one of the things that movies can do better than any other art form, and that is to present historical subject matter. Description is not one of the things that novels do best but it is something that movies do effortlessly, at least with respect to the effort required of the audience. This is equally true for science-fiction and fantasy, which offer visual challenges and possibilities you don't find in contemporary stories.

Barry Lyndon's *Ireland:*
1. *Gay Hamilton, Leonard Rossiter*
2. *Ryan O'Neal, Marie Kean*
3. *Gay Hamilton, Ryan O'Neal*

How did you come to adopt a third-person commentary instead of the first-person narrative which is found in the book?

I believe Thackeray used Redmond Barry to tell his own story in a deliberately distorted way because it made it more interesting. Instead of the omniscient author, Thackeray used the imperfect observer, or perhaps it would be more accurate to say the dishonest observer, thus allowing the reader to judge for himself, with little difficulty, the probable truth in Redmond Barry's view of his life. This technique worked extremely well in the novel but, of course, in a film you have objective reality in front of you all of the time, so the effect of Thackeray's first-person story-teller could not be repeated on the screen. It might have worked as comedy by the juxtaposition of Barry's version of the truth with the reality on the screen, but I don't think that *Barry Lyndon* should have been done as a comedy.

You didn't think of having no commentary?

There is too much story to tell. A voice-over spares you the cumbersome business of telling the necessary facts of the story through expositional dialogue scenes which can become very tiresome and frequently unconvincing: 'Curse the blasted storm that's wrecked our blessed ship!' Voice-over, on the other hand, is a perfectly legitimate and economical way of conveying story information which does not need dramatic weight and which would otherwise be too bulky to dramatize.

But you use it in other ways – to cool down the emotion of a scene, and to anticipate the story. For instance, just after the meeting with the German peasant girl – a very moving scene – the voice-over compares her to a town having been often conquered by siege.

In the scene that you're referring to, the voice-over works as an ironic counterpoint to what you see portrayed by the actors on the screen. This is only a minor sequence in the story and has to be presented with economy. Barry is tender and romantic with the girl but all he really wants is to get her into bed. The girl is lonely and Barry is attractive and attentive. If you think about it, it isn't likely that he is the only soldier she has brought home while her husband has been away to the wars. You could have had Barry give signals to the audience, through his performance, indicating that he is really insincere and opportunistic, but this would be unreal. When we try to deceive we are as convincing as we can be, aren't we?

The film's commentary also serves another purpose, but this time in much the same manner it did in the novel. The story has many twists and turns, and Thackeray uses Barry to give you hints in advance of most of the important plot developments, thus lessening the risk of their seeming contrived.

When he is going to meet the Chevalier Balibari, the commentary anticipates the emotions we are about to see, thus possibly lessening their effect.

Barry Lyndon is a story which does not depend upon surprise. What is important is not *what* is going to happen next, but *how* it will happen. I think Thackeray trades off the advantage of surprise to gain a greater sense of inevitability and a better integration of what might otherwise seem melodramatic or contrived. In the scene you refer to where Barry meets the Chevalier, the film's voice-over establishes the necessary groundwork for the important new relationship which is rapidly to develop between the two men. By talking about Barry's loneliness being so far from home, his sense of isolation as an exile, and his joy at meeting a fellow country-man in a foreign land, the commentary prepares the way for the scenes which are quickly to follow showing his close attachment to the Chevalier. Another place in the story where I think this technique works particularly well is where we are told that Barry's young son, Bryan, is going to die at the same

time we watch the two of them playing happily together. In this case, I think the commentary creates the same dramatic effect as, for example, the knowledge that the *Titanic* is doomed while you watch the carefree scenes of preparation and departure. These early scenes would be inexplicably dull if you didn't know about the ship's appointment with the iceberg. Being told in advance of the impending disaster gives away surprise but creates suspense.

There is very little introspection in the film. Barry is open about his feelings at the beginning of the film, but then he becomes less so.

At the beginning of the story, Barry has more people around him to whom he can express his feelings. As the story progresses, and particularly after his marriage, he becomes more and more isolated. There is finally no one who loves him, or with whom he can talk freely, with the possible exception of his young son, who is too young to be of much help. At the same time I don't think that the lack of introspective dialogue scenes are any loss to the story. Barry's feelings are there to be seen as he reacts to the increasingly difficult circumstances of his life. I think this is equally true for the other characters in the story. In any event, scenes of people talking about themselves are often very dull.

In contrast to films which are preoccupied with analyzing the psychology of the characters, yours tend to maintain a mystery around them. Reverend Runt, for instance, is a very opaque person. You don't know exactly what his motivations are.

But you know a lot about Reverend Runt, certainly all that is necessary. He dislikes Barry. He is secretly in love with Lady Lyndon, in his own prim, repressed, little way. His little smile of triumph, in the scene in the coach, near the end of the film, tells you all you need to know regarding the way he feels about Barry's misfortune, and the way things have worked out. You certainly don't have the time in a film to develop the motivations of minor characters.

Lady Lyndon is even more opaque.

Thackeray doesn't tell you a great deal about her in the novel. I found that very strange. He doesn't give you a lot to go on. There are, in fact, very few dialogue scenes with her in the book. Perhaps he meant her to be something of a mystery. But the film gives you a sufficient understanding of her, anyway.

You made important changes in your adaptation, such as the invention of the last duel, and the ending itself.

Yes, I did, but I was satisfied that they were consistent with the spirit of the novel and brought the story to about the same place the novel did, but in less time. In the book, Barry is pensioned off by Lady Lyndon. Lord Bullingdon, having been believed dead, returns from America. He finds Barry and gives him a beating. Barry, tended by his mother, subsequently dies in prison, a drunk. This, and everything that went along with it in the novel to make it credible would have taken too much time on the screen. In the film, Bullingdon gets his revenge and Barry is totally defeated, destined, one can assume, for a fate not unlike that which awaited him in the novel.

And the scene of the two homosexuals in the lake was not in the book either.

The problem here was how to get Barry out of the British Army. The section of the book dealing with this is also fairly lengthy and complicated. The function of the scene between the two gay officers was to provide a simpler way for Barry to escape. Again, it leads to the same end result as the novel but by a different route. Barry steals the papers and uniform of a

Barry Lyndon: *'the empty attraction they have for each other'*
1. Marisa Berenson
2. Ryan O'Neal, Marisa Berenson

British officer which allow him to make his way to freedom. Since the scene is purely expositional, the comic situation helps to mask your intentions.

Were you aware of the multiple echoes that are found in the film: flogging in the army, flogging at home, the duels, etc, and the narrative structure resembling that of A Clockwork Orange? *Does this geometrical pattern attract you?*

The narrative symmetry arose primarily out of the needs of telling the story rather than as part of a conscious design. The artistic process you go through in making a film is as much a matter of discovery as it is the execution of a plan. Your first responsibility in writing a screenplay is to pay the closest possible attention to the author's ideas and make sure you really understand *what* he has written and *why* he has written it. I know this sounds pretty obvious but you'd be surprised how often this is not done. There is a tendency for the screenplay writer to be 'creative' too quickly. The next thing is to make sure that the story survives the selection and compression which has to occur in order to tell it in a maximum of three hours, and preferably two. This phase usually seals the fate of most major novels, which really need the large canvas upon which they are presented.

In the first part of A Clockwork Orange, *we were against Alex. In the second part, we were on his side. In this film, the attraction/repulsion feeling towards Barry is present throughout.*

Thackeray referred to it as 'a novel without a hero'. Barry is naïve and uneducated. He is driven by a relentless ambition for wealth and social position. This proves to be an unfortunate combination of qualities which eventually lead to great misfortune and unhappiness for himself and those around him. Your feelings about Barry are mixed but he has charm and courage, and it is impossible not to like him despite his vanity, his insensitivity and his weaknesses. He is a very real character who is neither a conventional hero nor a conventional villain.

The feeling that we have at the end is one of utter waste.

Perhaps more a sense of tragedy, and because of this the story can assimilate the twists and turns of the plot without

From innocence to . . . experience (Barry Lyndon):
1. Ryan O'Neal, Gay Hamilton
2. André Morell, Marisa Berenson, Ryan O'Neal, Anthony Sharp

becoming melodrama. Melodrama uses all the problems of the world, and the difficulties and disasters which befall the characters, to demonstrate that the world is, after all, a benevolent and just place.

The last sentence which says that all the characters are now equal can be taken as a nihilistic or religious statement. From your films, one has the feeling that you are a nihilist who would like to believe.

I think you'll find that it is merely an ironic postscript taken from the novel. Its meaning seems quite clear to me and, as far as I am concerned, it has nothing to do with nihilism or religion.

One has the feeling in your films that the world is in a constant state of war. The apes are fighting in 2001. There is fighting,

In many ways, the film reminds us of silent movies. I am thinking particularly of the seduction of Lady Lyndon by Barry at the gambling table.

That's good. I think that silent films got a lot more things right than talkies. Barry and Lady Lyndon sit at the gaming table and exchange lingering looks They do not say a word. Lady Lyndon goes out on the balcony for some air. Barry follows her outside. They gaze longingly into each other's eyes and kiss. Still not a word is spoken. It's very romantic, but at the same time, I think it suggests the empty attraction they have for each other that is to disappear as quickly as it arose. It sets the stage for everything that is to follow in their relationship. The actors, the images and the Schubert worked well together, I think.

1

too, in Paths of Glory, *and* Dr Strangelove. *In* Barry Lyndon, *you have a war in the first part, and then in the second part we find the home is a battleground, too.*

Drama is conflict, and violent conflict does not find its exclusive domain in my films. Nor is it uncommon for a film to be built around a situation where violent conflict is the driving force. With respect to *Barry Lyndon*, after his successful struggle to achieve wealth and social position, Barry proves to be badly unsuited to this role. He has clawed his way into a gilded cage, and once inside his life goes really bad. The violent conflicts which subsequently arise come inevitably as a result of the characters and their relationships. Barry's early conflicts carry him forth into life and they bring him adventure and happiness, but those in later life lead only to pain and eventually to tragedy.

Did you have Schubert's Trio in mind while preparing and shooting this particular scene?

No, I decided on it while we were editing. Initially, I thought it was right to use only eighteenth-century music. But sometimes you can make ground-rules for yourself which prove unnecessary and counter-productive. I think I must have listened to every LP you can buy of eighteenth-century music. One of the problems which soon became apparent is that there are no tragic love-themes in eighteenth-century music. So eventually I decided to use Schubert's Trio in E Flat, Opus 100, written in 1828. It's a magnificent piece of music and it has just the right restrained balance between the tragic and the romantic without getting into the headier stuff of later Romanticism.

You also cheated in another way by having Leonard Rosenman orchestrate Handel's Sarabande in a more dramatic style than you would find in eighteenth-century composition.

This arose from another problem about eighteenth-century music – it isn't very dramatic, either. I first came across the Handel theme played on a guitar and, strangely enough, it made me think of Ennio Morricone. I think it worked very well in the film, and the very simple orchestration kept it from sounding out of place.

It also accompanies the last duel – not present in the novel – which is one of the most striking scenes in the film and set in a dovecote.

The setting was a tithe barn which also happened to have a

depending on where the ball bounces and where the other side happens to be, opportunities and problems arise which can only be effectively dealt with at that very moment.

In *2001: A Space Odyssey*, for example, there seemed no clever way for HAL to learn that the two astronauts distrusted him and were planning to disconnect his brain. It would have been irritatingly careless of them to talk aloud, knowing that HAL would hear and understand them. Then the perfect solution suggested itself from the actual physical layout of the space pod in the pod bay. The two men went into the pod and turned off every switch to make them safe from HAL's microphones. They sat in the pod facing each other and in the centre of the shot, visible through the sound-proof glass port, you could plainly see the red glow of HAL's bug-eye lens,

2

lot of pigeons nesting in the rafters. We've seen many duels before in films, and I wanted to find a different and interesting way to present the scene. The sound of the pigeons added something to this, and, if it were a comedy, we could have had further evidence of the pigeons. Anyway, you tend to expect movie duels to be fought outdoors, possibly in a misty grove of trees at dawn. I thought the idea of placing the duel in a barn gave it an interesting difference. This idea came quite by accident when one of the location scouts returned with some photographs of the barn. I think it was Joyce who observed that accidents are the portals to discovery. Well, that's certainly true in making films. And perhaps in much the same way, there is an aspect of film-making which can be compared to a sporting contest. You can start with a game plan but

some fifteen feet away. What the conspirators didn't think of was that HAL would be able to read their lips.

Did you find it more constricting, less free, making an historical film where we all have precise conceptions of a period? Was it more of a challenge?

No, because at least you know what everything looked like. In *2001: A Space Odyssey* everything had to be designed. But neither type of film is easy to do. In historical and futuristic films, there is an inverse relationship between the ease the audience has taking in at a glance the sets, costumes and decor, and the film-maker's problems in creating it. When everything you see has to be designed and constructed, you greatly increase the cost of the film, add tremendously to all the normal problems of film-making, making it virtually impossible to have the flexibility of last-minute changes which you can manage in a contemporary film.

You are well-known for the thoroughness with which you accumulate information and do research when you work on a project. Is it for you the thrill of being a reporter or a detective?

I suppose you *could* say it is a bit like being a detective. On *Barry Lyndon*, I accumulated a very large picture file of drawings and paintings taken from art books. These pictures served as the reference for everything we needed to make – clothes, furniture, hand props, architecture, vehicles, etc. Unfortunately, the pictures would have been too awkward to use while they were still in the books, and I'm afraid we finally had very guiltily to tear up a lot of beautiful art books. They were all, fortunately, still in print which made it seem a little less sinful. Good research is an absolute necessity and I enjoy doing it. You have an important reason to study a subject in much greater depth than you would ever have done otherwise, and then you have the satisfaction of putting the knowledge to immediate good use.

The designs for the clothes were all copied from drawings and paintings of the period. None of them were *designed* in the normal sense. This is the best way, in my opinion, to make historical costumes. It doesn't seem sensible to have a designer interpret – say – the eighteenth century, using the same picture sources from which you could faithfully copy the clothes. Neither is there much point sketching the costumes again when they are already beautifully represented in the paintings and drawings of the period. What is very important is to get some actual clothes of the period to learn how they were originally made. To get them to look right, you really have to make them the same way. Consider also the problem of taste in designing clothes, even for today. Only a handful of designers seem to have a sense of what is striking and beautiful. How can a designer, however brilliant, have a feeling for the clothes of another period which is equal to that of the people and the designers of the period itself, as recorded in their pictures? I spent a year preparing *Barry Lyndon* before the shooting began and I think this time was very well spent. The starting point and *sine qua non* of any historical or futuristic story is to make you believe what you see.

The trials of Redmond Barry:
1. Ryan O'Neal
Preceding pages:
1. Ryan O'Neal, Leonard Rossiter
2. Ryan O'Neal, Arthur O'Sullivan

The danger in an historical film is that you lose yourself in details, and become decorative.

The danger connected with any multi-faceted problem is that you might pay too much attention to some of the problems to the detriment of others, but I am very conscious of this and I make sure I don't do that.

Why do you prefer natural lighting?

Because it's the way we see things. I have always tried to light my films to simulate natural light; in the daytime using the windows actually to light the set, and in night scenes the practical lights you see in the set. This approach has its problems when you can use bright electric light sources, but when candelabras and oil lamps are the brightest light sources which can be in the set, the difficulties are vastly increased. Prior to *Barry Lyndon*, the problem has never been properly solved. Even if the director and cameraman had the desire to light with practical light sources, the film and the lenses were not fast enough to get an exposure. A 35mm movie camera shutter exposes at about 1/50 of a second, and a useable exposure was only possible with a lens at least 100% faster than any which had ever been used on a movie camera. Fortunately, I found just such a lens, one of a group of ten which Zeiss had specially manufactured for NASA satellite photography. The lens had a speed of FO.7, and it was 100% faster than the fastest movie lens. A lot of work still had to be done to it and to the camera to make it useable. For one thing, the rear element of the lens had to be 2·5mm away from the film plane, requiring special modification to the rotating camera shutter. But with this lens it was now possible to shoot in light conditions so dim that it was difficult to read. For the day interior scenes, we used either the real daylight from the windows, or simulated daylight by banking lights outside the windows and diffusing them with tracing paper taped on the glass. In addition to the very beautiful lighting you can achieve this way, it is also a very practical way to work. You don't have to worry about shooting into your lighting equipment. All your lighting is outside the window behind tracing paper, and if you shoot towards the window you get a very beautiful and realistic flare effect.

How did you decide on Ryan O'Neal?

He was the best actor for the part. He looked right and I was confident that he possessed much greater acting ability than he had been allowed to show in many of the films he had previously done. In retrospect, I think my confidence in him was fully justified by his performance, and I still can't think of anyone who would have been better for the part. The personal qualities of an actor, as they relate to the role, are almost as important as his ability, and other actors, say, like Al Pacino, Jack Nicholson or Dustin Hoffman, just to name a few, who are great actors, would nevertheless have been wrong to play Barry Lyndon. I liked Ryan and we got along very well together. In this regard, the only difficulties I have ever had with actors happened when their acting technique wasn't good enough to do something you asked of them. One way an actor deals with this difficulty is to invent a lot of excuses that have nothing to do with the real problem. This was very well represented in Truffaut's *Day for Night* when Valentina Cortesa, the star of the film within the film, hadn't bothered to learn her lines and claimed that her dialogue fluffs were due to the confusion created by the script girl playing a bit part in the scene.

How do you explain some of the misunderstandings about the film by the American press and the English press?

The American press was predominantly enthusiastic about the film, and *Time* magazine ran a cover story about it. The international press was even more enthusiastic. It is true that the English press was badly split. But from the very beginning, all of my films have divided the critics. Some have thought them wonderful, and others found very little good to say. But subsequent critical opinion has always resulted in a very remarkable shift to the favourable. In one instance, the same critic who originally rapped the film has several years later put it on an All-time-best list. But, of course, the lasting and ultimately most important reputation of a film is not based on reviews, but on what, if anything, people say about it over the years, and on how much affection for it they have.

You are an innovator, but at the same time you are very conscious of tradition.

I try to be, anyway. I think that one of the problems with twentieth-century art is its preoccupation with subjectivity and originality at the expense of everything else. This has been especially true in painting and music. Though initially stimulating, this soon impeded the full development of any particular style, and rewarded uninteresting and sterile originality. At the same time, it is very sad to say, films have had the opposite problem – they have consistently tried to formalize and repeat success, and they have clung to a form and style introduced in their infancy. The *sure thing* is what everyone wants, and *originality* is not a nice word in this context. This is true despite the repeated example that nothing is as dangerous as a sure thing.

You have abandoned original film music in your last three films.

Exclude a pop music score from what I am about to say. However good our best film composers may be, they are not a Beethoven, a Mozart or a Brahms. Why use music which is less good when there is such a multitude of great orchestral music available from the past and from our own time? When you're editing a film, it's very helpful to be able to try out different pieces of music to see how they work with the scene. This is not at all an uncommon practice. Well, with a little more care and thought, these *temporary* music tracks can become the final score. When I had completed the editing of *2001: A Space Odyssey,* I had laid in *temporary* music tracks for almost all of the music which was eventually used in the film. Then, in the normal way, I engaged the services of a distinguished film composer to write the score. Although he and I went over the picture very carefully, and he listened to these *temporary* tracks (Strauss, Ligeti, Khatchaturian) and agreed that they worked fine and would serve as a guide for the musical objectives of each sequence he, nevertheless, wrote and recorded a score which could not have been more alien to the music we had listened to, and much more serious than that, a score which, in my opinion, was completely inadequate for the film. With the premiere looming up, I had no time left even to think about another score being written, and had I not been able to use the music I had already selected for the *temporary* tracks I don't know what I would have done. The composer's agent phoned Robert O'Brien, the then head of MGM, to warn him that if I didn't use his client's score the film would not make its premiere date. But in that instance, as in all others, O'Brien trusted my judgement. He is a wonderful man, and one of the very few film bosses able to inspire genuine loyalty and affection from his film-makers.

Why did you choose to have only one flashback in the film: the child falling from the horse?

I didn't want to spend the time which would have been required to show the entire story action of young Bryan sneaking away from the house, taking the horse, falling, being found, etc. Nor did I want to learn about the accident solely through the dialogue scene in which the farm workers, carrying the injured boy, tell Barry. Putting the flashback fragment in the middle of the dialogue scene seemed to be the right thing to do.

Are your camera movements planned before?

Very rarely. I think there is virtually no point putting camera instructions into a screenplay, and only if some really important camera idea occurs to me, do I write it down. When you rehearse a scene, it is usually best not to think about the camera at all. If you do, I have found that it invariably interferes with the fullest exploration of the ideas of the scene. When, at last, something happens which you know is worth filming, that is the time to decide how to shoot it. It is *almost* but not quite true to say that when something really exciting and worthwhile is happening, it doesn't matter how you shoot it. In any event, it never takes me long to decide on set-ups, lighting or camera movements. The visual part of film making has always come easiest to me, and that is why I am careful to subordinate it to the story and the performances.

Do you like writing alone or would you like to work with a script writer?

I enjoy working with someone I find stimulating. One of the most fruitful and enjoyable collaborations I have had was with Arthur C. Clarke in writing the story of *2001: A Space Odyssey.* One of the paradoxes of movie writing is that, with a few notable exceptions, writers who can really write are not interested in working on film scripts. They quite correctly regard their important work as being done for publication. I wrote the screenplay for *Barry Lyndon* alone. The first draft took three or four months but, as with all my films, the subsequent writing process never really stopped. What you have written and is yet unfilmed is inevitably affected by what has been filmed. New problems of content or dramatic weight reveal themselves. Rehearsing a scene can also cause script changes. However carefully you think about a scene, and however clearly you believe you have visualized it, it's never the same when you finally see it played. Sometimes a totally new idea comes up out of the blue, during a rehearsal, or even during actual shooting, which is simply too good to ignore. This can necessitate the new scene being worked out with the actors right then and there. As long as the actors know the objectives of the scene, and understand their characters, this is less difficult and much quicker to do than you might imagine.

Marriage, maternity, pageantry and prayer: four moments in the life of Lady Lyndon:
1. Ryan O'Neal, Marisa Berenson
2. and 3. Marisa Berenson
4. Murray Melvin, Marisa Berenson

Third interview

The Shining

In several of your previous films you seem to have had a prior interest in the facts and problems which surround the story – the nuclear threat, space travel, the relationship between violence and the State – which led you to Dr Strangelove, 2001: A Space Odyssey, A Clockwork Orange. *In the case of* The Shining, *were you attracted first by the subject of ESP, or just by Stephen King's novel?*

I've always been interested in ESP and the paranormal. In addition to the scientific experiments which have been conducted suggesting that we are just short of conclusive proof of its existence, I'm sure we've all had the experience of opening a book at the exact page we're looking for, or thinking of a friend a moment before they ring on the telephone. But *The Shining* didn't originate from any particular desire to do a film about this. The manuscript of the novel was sent to me by John Calley, of Warner Bros. I thought it was one of the most ingenious and exciting stories of the genre I had read. It seemed to strike an extraordinary balance between the psychological and the supernatural in such a way as to lead you to think that the supernatural would eventually be explained by the psychological: 'Jack must be imagining these things because he's crazy'. This allowed you to suspend your doubt of the supernatural until you were so thoroughly into the story that you could accept it almost without noticing.

Do you think this was an important factor in the success of the novel?

Yes, I do. It's what I found so particularly clever about the way the novel was written. As the supernatural events occurred you searched for an explanation, and the most likely one seemed to be that the strange things that were happening would finally be explained as the products of Jack's imagination. It's not until Grady, the ghost of the former caretaker who axed to death his family, slides open the bolt of the larder door, allowing Jack to escape, that you are left with no other explanation but the supernatural.

The novel is by no means a serious literary work, but the plot is for the most part extremely well worked out, and for a film that is often all that really matters.

Don't you think that today it is in this sort of popular literature that you find strong archetypes, symbolic images which have vanished somehow from the more highbrow literary works?

Yes, I do, and I think that it's part of their often phenomenal success. There is no doubt that a good story has always mattered, and the great novelists have generally built their work around strong plots. But I've never been able to decide whether the plot is just a way of keeping people's attention while you do everything else, or whether the plot is really more important than anything else, perhaps communicating with us on an unconscious level which affects us in the way that myths once did.

Stanley Kubrick (filming The Shining*)*

I think, in some ways, the conventions of realistic fiction and drama may impose serious limitations on a story. For one thing, if you play by the rules and respect the preparation and pace required to establish realism, it takes a lot longer to make a point than it does, say, in fantasy. At the same time, it is possible that this very work that contributes to a story's realism may weaken its grip on the unconscious. Realism is probably the best way to dramatize argument and ideas. Fantasy may deal best with themes which lie primarily in the unconscious. I think the unconscious appeal of a ghost story, for instance, lies in its promise of immortality. If you can be frightened by a ghost story, then you must accept the possibility that supernatural beings exist. If they do, then there is more than just oblivion waiting beyond the grave.

This kind of implication is present in much of the fantastic literature.

I believe fantasy stories at their best serve the same function for us that fairy tales and mythology formerly did. The current popularity of fantasy, particularly in films, suggests that popular culture, at least, isn't getting what it wants from realism. The nineteenth century was the golden age of realistic fiction. The twentieth century may be the golden age of fantasy.

After Barry Lyndon *did you begin work straight away on* The Shining?

When I finished *Barry Lyndon* I spent most of my time reading. Months went by and I hadn't found anything very exciting. It's intimidating, especially at a time like this, to think of how many books you should read and never will. Because of this, I try to avoid any systematic approach to reading, pursuing instead a random method, one which depends as much on luck and accident as on design. I find this is also the only way to deal with the newspapers and magazines which proliferate in great piles around the house – some of the most interesting articles turn up on the reverse side of pages I've torn out for something else.

Did you do research on ESP?

There really wasn't any research that was necessary to do. The story didn't require any and, since I have always been interested in the topic, I think I was as well informed as I needed to be. I hope that ESP and related psychic phenomena will eventually find general scientific proof of their existence. There are certainly a fair number of scientists who are sufficiently impressed with the evidence to spend their time working in the field. If conclusive proof is ever found it won't be quite as exciting as, say, the discovery of alien intelligence in the universe, but it will definitely be a mind expander. In addition to the great variety of unexplainable psychic experiences we can all probably recount, I think I can see behaviour in animals which strongly suggests something like ESP. I have a long-haired cat, named Polly, who regularly gets knots in her coat which I have to comb or scissor out. She hates this, and on dozens of occasions while I have been stroking her and *thinking* that the knots have got bad enough

The inhabitants of the Overlook Hotel: the double, death and love the wound, symmetry, the mask (The Shining)
1. Lisa and Louise Burns
2. Joe Turkel
3. Jack Nicholson, Lia Beldam
4. Norman Gay
5. Philip Stone, Jack Nicholson
6. Anon

to do something about them, she has suddenly dived under the bed before I have made the slightest move to get a comb or scissors. I have obviously considered the possibility that she can tell when I plan to use the comb because of some special way I feel the knots when I have decided to comb them, but I'm quite sure that isn't how she does it. She almost always has knots, and I stroke her innumerable times every day, but it's only when I have actually decided to do something about them that she ever runs away and hides. Ever since I have become aware of this possibility, I am particularly careful not to feel the knots any differently whether or not I think they need combing. But most of the time she still seems to know the difference.

Who is Diane Johnson who wrote the screenplay with you?

Diane is an American novelist who has published a number of extremely good novels which have received serious and important attention. I was interested in several of her books and in talking to her about them I was surprised to learn that she was giving a course at the University of California at Berkeley on the Gothic novel. When *The Shining* came up she seemed to be the ideal collaborator, which, indeed, she proved to be. I had already been working on the treatment of the book, prior to her starting, but I hadn't actually begun the screenplay. With *The Shining*, the problem was to extract the essential plot and to re-invent the sections of the story that were weak. The characters needed to be developed a bit differently than they were in the novel. It is in the pruning down phase that the undoing of great novels usually occurs because so much of what is good about them has to do with the fineness of the writing, the insight of the author and often the density of the story. But *The Shining* was a different matter. Its virtues lay almost entirely in the plot, and it didn't prove to be very much of a problem to adapt it into the screenplay form. Diane and I talked a lot about the book and then we made an outline of the scenes we thought should be included in the film. This list of scenes was shuffled and reshuffled until we thought it was right, and then we began to write. We did several drafts of the screenplay, which was subsequently revised at different stages before and during shooting.

It is strange that you emphasize the supernatural aspect since one could say that in the film you give a lot of weight to an apparently rational explanation of Jack's behaviour: altitude, claustrophobia, solitude, lack of booze.

Stephen Crane wrote a story called *The Blue Hotel.* In it you quickly learn that the central character is a paranoid. He gets involved in a poker game, decides someone is cheating him, makes an accusation, starts a fight and gets killed. You think the point of the story is that his death was inevitable because a paranoid poker player would ultimately get involved in a fatal gunfight. But, in the end, you find out that the man he accused *was* actually cheating him. I think *The Shining* uses a similar kind of psychological misdirection to forestall the realization that the supernatural events are actually happening.

Why did you change the end and dispense with the destruction of the hotel?

To be honest, the end of the book seemed a bit hackneyed to me and not very interesting. I wanted an ending which the audience could not anticipate. In the film, they think Hallorann is going to save Wendy and Danny. When he is killed they fear the worst. Surely, they fear, there is no way now for Wendy and Danny to escape. The maze ending may have suggested itself from the animal topiary scenes in the novel. I don't actually remember how the idea first came about.

Jack Nicholson (The Shining)

Why did the room number switch from 217 in the novel to 237 in the film?

The exterior of the hotel was filmed at the Timberline Lodge, near Mount Hood, in Oregon. It had a room 217 but no room 237, so the hotel management asked me to change the room number because they were afraid their guests might not want to stay in room 217 after seeing the film. There is, however, a genuinely frightening thing about this hotel which nestles high up on the slopes of Mount Hood. Mount Hood, as it happens, is a dormant volcano, but it has quite recently experienced pre-eruption seismic rumbles similar to the ones that a few months earlier preceded the gigantic eruption of Mount St Helens, less than sixty miles away. If Mount Hood

ings. From these, small models of all the sets were built. I wanted the hotel to look authentic rather than like the traditionally spooky movie hotel. The hotel's labyrinthine layout and huge rooms, I believed, would alone provide an eerie enough atmosphere. This *realistic* approach was also followed in the lighting, and in every aspect of the decor. It seemed to me that the perfect guide for this approach could be found in Kafka's writing style. His stories are fantastic and allegorical, but his writing is simple and straightforward, almost journalistic. On the other hand, all the films that have been made of his work seem to have ignored this completely, making everything look as weird and dreamlike as possible. The final details for the different rooms of the hotel came from

should ever erupt like Mount St Helens, then the Timberline Hotel may indeed share the fiery fate of the novel's Overlook Hotel.

How did you conceive the hotel with your Art Director, Roy Walker?

The first step was for Roy to go around America photographing hotels which might be suitable for the story. Then we spent weeks going through his photographs making selections for the different rooms. Using the details in the photographs, our draughtsmen did proper working draw-

a number of different hotels. The red mens-room, for example, where Jack meets Grady, the ghost of the former caretaker, was inspired by a Frank Lloyd Wright mens-room in an hotel in Arizona. The models of the different sets were lit, photographed, tinkered with and revised. This process continued, altering and adding elements to each room, until we were all happy with what we had.

There are similar movie clichés about apparitions.

From the more convincing accounts I have read of people who have reported seeing ghosts, they are invariably described as being as solid and as real as someone actually standing in the room. The movie convention of the see-through ghost, shrouded in white, seems to exist only in the province of art.

You have not included the scene from the novel which took place in the elevator, but have only used it for the recurring shot of blood coming out of the doors.

The length of a movie imposes considerable restrictions on how much story you can put into it, especially if the story is told in a conventional way.

Which conventions are you referring to?

The convention of telling the story primarily through a series of dialogue scenes. Most films are really little more

economy of statement gave silent movies a much greater narrative scope and flexibility than we have today. In my view, there are very few sound films, including those regarded as masterpieces, which could not be presented almost as effectively on the stage, assuming a good set, the same cast and quality of performances. You couldn't do that with a great silent movie.

But surely you could not put 2001: A Space Odyssey *on the stage?*

True enough. I know I've tried to move in this direction in all of my films but never to an extent which has satisfied me. By the way, I should include the best TV commercials along

1. and 2. 'Danny has had a frightening and disturbing childhood'; *Danny Lloyd* (The Shining)

than stage plays with more atmosphere and action. I think that the scope and flexibility of movie stories would be greatly enhanced by borrowing something from the structure of silent movies where points that didn't require weight could be presented by a shot and a title card. Something like: *Title: 'Billy's uncle'. Picture: Uncle giving Billy ice cream.* In a few seconds, you could introduce Billy's uncle and say something about him without being burdened with a scene. This

with silent films, as another example of how you might better tell a film story. In thirty seconds, characters are introduced, and sometimes a surprisingly involved situation is set up and resolved.

When you shoot these scenes which you find theatrical, you do it in a way that emphasizes their ordinariness. The scenes with Ullman or the visit of the doctor in The Shining, *like the conference with the astronauts in* 2001, *are characterized by their social conventions, their mechanical aspect.*

Well, as I've said, in fantasy you want things to have the appearance of being as realistic as possible. People should behave in the mundane way they normally do. You have to be especially careful about this in the scenes which deal with the bizarre or fantastic details of the story.

You also decided to show few visions and make them very short.

If Danny had perfect ESP, there could be no story. He would anticipate everything, warn everybody and solve every problem. So his perception of the paranormal must be imperfect and fragmentary. This also happens to be consistent with most of the reports of telepathic experiences. The same applies to Hallorann. One of the ironies in the story is that you have people who can see the past and the future and have telepathic contact, but the telephone and the short-wave radio don't work, and the snowbound mountain roads are impassable. Failure of communication is a theme which runs through a number of my films.

You use technology a lot but seem to be afraid of it.

I'm not afraid of technology. I am afraid of aeroplanes. I've been able to avoid flying for some time but, I suppose, if I had to I would. Perhaps it's a case of a little knowledge being a dangerous thing. At one time, I had a pilot's licence and 160 hours of solo time on single-engine light aircraft. Unfortunately, all that seemed to do was make me mistrust large airplanes.

Did you think right away of Jack Nicholson for the role?

Yes, I did. I believe that Jack is one of the best actors in Hollywood, perhaps on a par with the greatest stars of the past like Spencer Tracy and Jimmy Cagney. I should think that he is on almost everyone's first-choice list for any role which suits him. His work is always interesting, clearly conceived and has the X-factor, *magic*. Jack is particularly suited for roles which require intelligence. He is an intelligent and literate man, and these are qualities almost impossible to act. In *The Shining*, you believe he's a writer, failed or otherwise.

Did the scene where he fights with Shelley Duvall on the stairs require many rehearsals?

Yes, it did. It was only with the greatest difficulty that Shelley was able to create and sustain for the length of the scene an authentic sense of hysteria. It took her a long time to achieve this and when she did we didn't shoot the scene too many times. I think there were five takes favouring Shelley, and only the last two were really good. When I have to shoot a very large number of takes it's invariably because the actors don't know their lines, or don't know them well enough. An actor can only do one thing at a time, and when he has learned his lines only well enough to say them while he's thinking about them, he will always have trouble as soon as he has to work on the emotions of the scene or find camera marks. In a strong emotional scene, it is always best to be able to shoot in complete takes to allow the actor a continuity of emotion, and it is rare for most actors to reach their peak more than once or twice. There are, occasionally, scenes which benefit from extra takes, but even then, I'm not sure that the early takes aren't just glorified rehearsals with the added adrenalin of film running through the camera. In *The Shining*, the scene in the ballroom where Jack talks to Lloyd, the sinister apparition of a former bartender, belongs to this category. Jack's performance here is incredibly intricate, with sudden changes of thought and mood – all grace notes. It's a very difficult scene to do because the emotional flow is so mercurial. It demands knife-edged changes of direction and a tremendous concentration to keep things sharp and economical. In this particular scene Jack produced his best takes near the highest numbers.

1. and 2. Shelley Duvall, Jack Nicholson (The Shining)

He is just as good when he walks down the corridor making wild movements before meeting the barman.

I asked Jack to remember the rumpled characters you see lunging down the streets of New York, waving their arms about and hissing to themselves.

Did you choose Shelley Duvall after seeing her in Three Women?

I had seen all of her films and greatly admired her work. I think she brought an instantly believable characterization to her part. The novel pictures her as a much more self-reliant and attractive woman, but these qualities make you wonder why she has put up with Jack for so long. Shelley seemed to be exactly the kind of woman that would marry Jack and be stuck with him. The wonderful thing about Shelley is her eccentric quality – the way she talks, the way she moves, the way her nervous system is put together. I think that most interesting actors have physical eccentricities about them which make their performances more interesting and, if they don't, they work hard to find them.

How did you find the boy?

About 5000 boys were interviewed in America over a period of six months. This number eventually narrowed down to five boys who could have played the part. That worked out to about one child in a thousand who could act – actually not a bad average. The interviews were done in Chicago, Denver and Cincinnati by my assistant, Leon Vitali, the actor who played the older Lord Bullingdon in *Barry Lyndon*, and his wife, Kersti. I chose those three cities because I wanted the child to have an accent which would fall somewhere between the way Jack and Shelley speak. The local Warner Bros. office placed newspaper ads inviting parents to make applications with photographs for the part. From the photographs a list was made of the boys who looked right. Leon interviewed everyone in this group, subsequently doing small acting improvisations which he recorded on video tape with those who seemed to have a little something. Further video work was done with the boys who were good. I looked at the tapes.

Where does Danny Lloyd come from?

He comes from a small town in Illinois. His father is a railway engineer. Danny was about five-and-a-half when we cast him. We had certain problems shooting with him in England because children are only allowed to work for three hours a day, and may only work a certain number of days in a calendar year. But, fortunately, rehearsal days on which you do not shoot are not counted in this total. So we rehearsed with him one day and shot on the next. I think his performance was wonderful – everything you could want from the role. He was a terrific boy. He had instinctive taste. He was very smart, very talented and very sensible. His parents, Jim and Ann, were very sensitive to his problems and very supportive, and he had a great time. Danny always knew his lines, and despite the inevitable pampering which occurred on the set, he was always reasonable and well behaved.

What did the Steadicam achieve for you in the film?

The Steadicam allows one man to move the camera any place he can walk – into small spaces where a dolly won't fit, and up and down staircases. We used an Arriflex BL camera, which is silent and allows you to shoot sound. You can walk or run with the camera, and the Steadicam smooths out any unsteadiness. It's like a magic carpet. The fast, flowing camera movements in the maze would have been impossible to do without the Steadicam. You couldn't lay down dolly tracks without the camera seeing them and, in any case, a dolly couldn't go around the right-angled corners of the maze pathways. Without a Steadicam you could have done your best with the normal hand-held camera but the running movements would have made it extremely unsteady. The only problem with the Steadicam is that it requires training, skill and a certain amount of fitness on the part of the operator. You can't just pick it up and use it. But any good camera operator can do useful work even after a few days' training. He won't be an ace but he'll still be able to do much more than he could without it. I used Garrett Brown as the Steadicam operator. He probably has more experience than anyone with the Steadicam because he also happened to invent it. The camera is mounted on to a spring-loaded arm, which is attached to a frame, which is in turn strapped to the operator's shoulders, chest and hips. This, in effect, makes the camera weightless.

The tricky part is that the operator has to control the camera movements in every axis with his wrist. He watches the framing on a very small television monitor which is mounted on his rig. It takes skill while you are walking or running to keep the horizon of the camera frame parallel to the ground, and pan and tilt just using your wrist. A further problem is caused by inertia, which makes it difficult to stop a movement smoothly and exactly where you want it. In order to stop on a predetermined composition you have to anticipate the stop and keep your fingers crossed.

The Steadicam allowed you to do even more of those long-tracking shots you have done in all your films.

Most of the hotel set was built as a composite, so that you could go up a flight of stairs, turn down a corridor, travel its length and find your way to still another part of the hotel. It mirrored the kind of camera movements which took place in the maze. In order to fully exploit this layout it was necessary to have moving camera shots without cuts, and of course the Steadicam made that much easier to do.

In the normal scenes you used dissolves and many camera movements. On the other hand, the paranormal visions are static and the cuts abrupt.

I don't particularly likes dissolves and I try not to use them, but when one scene follows another in the same place, and you want to make it clear that time has passed, a dissolve is often the simplest way to convey this. On the other hand, the paranormal visions are momentary glimpses into the past and the future, and must be short, even abrupt. With respect to the camera movements, I've always liked moving the camera. It's one of the basic elements of film grammar. When you have the means to do it and the set to do it in, it not only adds visual interest but it also permits the actors to work in longer, possibly complete, takes. This makes it easier for them to maintain their concentration and emotional level in the scene.

Did you always plan to use the helicopter shots of the mountains as the main-title background?

Yes I did. But the location, in Glacier National Park, Montana, wasn't chosen until very near the end of principal shooting. It was important to establish an ominous mood during Jack's first drive up to the hotel – the vast isolation and eerie splendour of high mountains, and the narrow, winding roads which would become impassable after heavy snow. In fact, the roads we filmed for the title sequence *are* closed throughout the winter and only negotiable by tracked vehicles. I sent a second-unit camera crew to Glacier National Park to shoot the title backgrounds but they reported that the place wasn't interesting. When we saw the test shots they sent back we were staggered. It was plain that the location was perfect but the crew had to be replaced. I hired Greg McGillivray, who is noted for his helicopter work, and he spent several weeks filming some of the most beautiful mountain helicopter shots I've seen.

Did you have all those extras pose for the last shot?

No, they were in a photograph taken in 1921 which we found in a picture library. I originally planned to use extras, but it proved impossible to make them look as good as the people in the photograph. So I very carefully photographed

Scatman Crothers (The Shining)

Jack, matching the angle and the lighting of the 1921 photograph, and shooting him from different distances too, so that his face would be larger and smaller on the negative. This allowed the choice of an image size which when enlarged would match the grain structure in the original photograph. The photograph of Jack's face was then air-brushed in to the main photograph, and I think the result looked perfect. Every face around Jack is an archetype of the period.

What type of music did you use?

The title music was based on the Dies Irae theme which has been used by many composers since the Middle Ages. It was re-orchestrated for synthesizer and voices by Wendy Carlos and Rachel Elkind, who did most of the synthesizer music for *A Clockwork Orange*. Bartók's *Music for Strings, Percussion and Celesta* was used for several other scenes. One com-

How do you see the character of Hallorann?

Hallorann is a simple, rustic type who talks about telepathy in a disarmingly unscientific way. His folksy character and naïve attempts to explain telepathy to Danny make what he has to say dramatically more acceptable than a standard pseudo-scientific explanation. He and Danny make a good pair.

The child creates a double to protect himself, whereas his father conjures up beings from the past who are also anticipations of his death.

A story of the supernatural cannot be taken apart and analysed too closely. The ultimate test of its rationale is whether it is good enough to raise the hairs on the back of your neck. If you submit it to a completely logical and detailed analysis it will eventually appear absurd. In his essay on the uncanny (*Das Unheimliche*), Freud said that the uncanny is the

position by Ligeti was used. But most of the music in the film came from the Polish composer Penderecki. One work titled 'Jakob's Dream' was used in the scene when Jack wakes up from his nightmare, a strange coincidence. Actually there were a number of other coincidences, particularly with names. The character that Jack Nicholson plays is called Jack in the novel. His son is called Danny in the novel and is played by Danny Lloyd. The ghost bartender in the book is called Lloyd.

What music did you use at the end?

It is a popular English dance tune of the twenties, 'Midnight, the Stars and You', played by Ray Noble's band with an Al Bowly vocal.

only feeling which is more powerfully experienced in art than in life.

If the genre required any justification, I should think this alone would serve as its credentials.

How do you see Danny's evolution?

Danny has had a frightening and disturbing childhood. Brutalized by his father and haunted by his paranormal visions, he has to find some psychological mechanism within himself to manage these powerful and dangerous forces. To do this, he creates his imaginary friend, Tony, through whom Danny can rationalise his visions and survive.

Some people criticized you a few years ago because you were making films that did not deal with the private problems of characters. With Barry Lyndon *and now with* The Shining, *you seem to be dealing more with personal relationships.*

If this is true it is certainly not as a result of any deliberate effort on my part. There is no useful way to explain how you decide what film to make. In addition to the initial problem of finding an exciting story which fulfils the elusively intangible requirements for a film, you have the added problem of its being sufficiently different from the films you have already done. Obviously the more films you make, the more this choice is narrowed down.

If you read a story which someone else has written you have the irreplaceable experience of reading it for the first time. This is something which you obviously cannot have if you write an original story. Reading someone else's story for the first time allows you a more accurate judgement of the

reading. But, not to put too fine a point on it, you can never again have that first, virginal experience with the plot.

It seems that you want to achieve a balance between rationality and irrationality, that for you man should acknowledge the presence of irrational forces in him rather than trying to repress them.

I think we tend to be a bit hypocritical about ourselves. We find it very easy not to see our own faults, and I don't just mean minor faults. I suspect there have been very few people who have done serious wrong who have not rationalized away what they've done, shifting the blame to those they have injured. We are capable of the greatest good and the greatest evil, and the problem is that we often can't distinguish between them when it suits our purpose.

2

1. *and 2. 'The emotional flow is so mercurial': Jack Nicholson* (The Shining)

narrative and helps you to be more objective than you might otherwise be with an original story. Another important thing is that while you're making a film, and you get deeper and deeper into it, you find that in a certain sense you know less and less about it. You get too close to it. When you reach that point, it's essential to rely on your original feelings about the story.

Of course, at the same time, because you know so much more about it, you can also make a great many other judgements far better than you could have after the first

Failing to understand this leads to some misunderstanding of A Clockwork Orange.

I have always found it difficult to understand how anyone could decide that the film presented violence sympathetically. I can only explain this as a view which arises from a prejudiced assessment of the film, ignoring everything else in the story but a few scenes. The distinguished film director Luis Buñuel suggested this in a way when he said in the *New York Times*: '*A Clockwork Orange* is my current favourite. I was very predisposed against the film. After seeing it, I realized it is the only movie about what the modern world really means.' *A Clockwork Orange* has been widely acclaimed throughout the world as an important work of art.

I don't believe that anyone really sympathizes with Alex, and there is absolutely no evidence that anyone does. Alex clashes with some authority figures in the story who seem as bad as he is, if not worse in a different way. But this doesn't excuse him. The story is satirical, and it is in the nature of satire to state the opposite of the truth as if it were the truth. I suppose you could misinterpret the film on this count, if you were determined to do so.

How do you see the main character of Jack in The Shining?

Jack comes to the hotel psychologically prepared to do its murderous bidding. He doesn't have very much further to go for his anger and frustration to become completely uncontrollable. He is bitter about his failure as a writer. He is married to a woman for whom he has only contempt. He hates his son. In the hotel, at the mercy of its powerful evil, he is quickly ready to fulfil his dark role.

So you don't regard the apparitions as merely a projection of his mental state?

For the purposes of telling the story, my view is that the paranormal is genuine. Jack's mental state serves only to prepare him for the murder, and to temporarily mislead the audience.

And when the film has finished? What then?

I hope the audience has had a good fright, has believed the film while they were watching it, and retains some sense of it. The ballroom photograph at the very end suggests the reincarnation of Jack.

You are a person who uses his rationality, who enjoys understanding things, but in 2001: A Space Odyssey *and* The Shining *you demonstrate the limits of intellectual knowledge. Is this an acknowledgement of what William James called the unexplained residues of human experience?*

Obviously, science-fiction and the supernatural bring you very quickly to the limits of knowledge and rational explanation. But from a dramatic point of view, you must ask yourself: 'If all of this were unquestionably true, how would it really happen?' You can't go much further than that. I like the regions of fantasy where reason is used primarily to undermine incredulity. Reason can take you to the border of these areas, but from there on you can be guided only by your

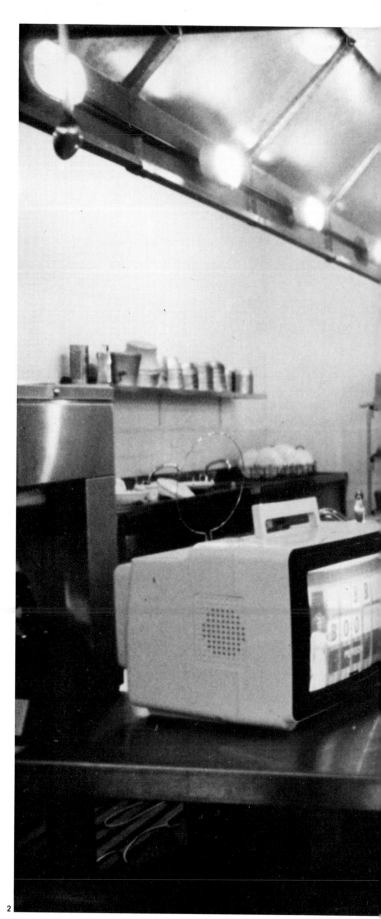

1. and 2. 'The wonderful thing about Shelley is her eccentric quality': *Shelley Duvall* (The Shining)

194

imagination. I think we strain at the limits of reason and enjoy the temporary sense of freedom which we gain by such exercises of our imagination.

Of course there is a danger that some audiences may misunderstand what you say and think that one can dispense altogether with reason, falling into the clouded mysticism which is currently so popular in America.

People can misinterpret almost anything so that it coincides with views they already hold. They take from art what they already believe, and I wonder how many people have ever had their views about anything important changed by a work of art?

Did you have a religious upbringing?

No, not at all.

You are a chess-player and I wonder if chess-playing and its logic have parallels with what you are saying?

First of all, even the greatest International Grandmasters, however deeply they analyse a position, can seldom see to the end of the game. So their decision about each move is partly based on intuition. I was a pretty good chess-player but, of course, not in that class. Before I had anything better to do (making movies) I played in chess tournaments at the Marshall and Manhattan Chess Clubs in New York, and for money in parks and elsewhere. Among a great many other things that chess teaches you is to control the initial excitement you feel when you see something that looks good. It trains you to think before grabbing, and to think just as objectively when you're in trouble. When you're making a film you have to make most of your decisions on the run, and there is a tendency to *always* shoot from the hip. It takes more discipline than you might imagine to think, even for thirty seconds, in the noisy, confusing, high-pressure atmosphere of a film set. But a few seconds' thought can often prevent a serious mistake being made about something that looks good at first glance. With respect to films, chess is more useful preventing you from making mistakes than giving you ideas. Ideas come spontaneously and the discipline required to evaluate and put them to use tends to be the real work.

Did you play chess on the set of The Shining *as you did on* Dr Strangelove *(with George C. Scott) and on* 2001?

I played a few games with Tony Burton, one of the actors in the film. He's a very good chess-player. It was very near the end of the picture and things had gotten to a fairly simple stage. I played quite a lot with George C. Scott during the making of *Dr Strangelove*. George is a good player, too, but if I recall correctly he didn't win many games from me. This gave me a certain edge with him on everything else. If you fancy yourself as a good chess-player, you have an inordinate respect for people who can beat you.

You also used to be a very good photographer. How do you think this helped you as a film-maker?

There is a much quoted aphorism that when a director dies he becomes a photographer. It's a clever remark but it'a bit glib, and usually comes from the kind of critic who will complain that a film has been too beautifully photographed. Anyway, I started out as a photographer. I worked for *Look* magazine from the age of seventeen to twenty-one. It was a miraculous break for me to get this job after graduation from high-school. I owe a lot to the then picture editor, Helen O'Brian, and the managing editor, Jack Guenther. This experience was invaluable to me, not only because I learned a lot about photography, but also because it gave me a quick education in how things happened in the world.

To have been a professional photographer was obviously a great advantage for me, though not everyone I subsequently worked with thought so. When I was directing *Spartacus*, Russel Metty, the cameraman, found it very amusing that I picked the camera set-ups myself and told him what I wanted in the way of lighting. When he was in particularly high-

spirits, he would crouch behind me as I looked through my viewfinder, holding his Zippo cigarette lighter up to his eye, as if it were a viewfinder. He also volunteered that the top directors just pointed in the direction of the shot, said something like, 'Russ, a tight 3-shot', and went back to their trailer.

What kind of photography were you doing at Look?

The normal kind of photo-journalism. It was tremendous fun for me at that age but eventually it began to wear thin, especially since my ultimate ambition had always been to make movies. The subject matter of my *Look* assignments was generally pretty dumb. I would do stories like: *'Is an Athlete Stronger Than a Baby?'*, photographing a college football player emulating the 'cute' positions an 18-month-old child would get into. Occasionally, I had a chance to do an interesting personality story. One of these was about Montgomery Clift, who was at the start of his brilliant career. Photography certainly gave me the first step up to movies. To make a film entirely by yourself, which initially I did, you may not have to know very much about anything else, but you must know about photography.

Do you have a preference for shooting in a studio or in real locations?

If the real locations exist, and if it's practical getting your crew there, it is a lot easier and cheaper to work on location. But sometimes going away on location is more expensive than building sets. It costs a lot of money today to keep a crew away from home.

Why did you do The Killing *in a studio?*

Because the sets were fairly cheap to build and the script let you spend a good chunk of time in each of them. Also, at that time, it was much more difficult to shoot in location interiors. There were no neck mikes or radio transmitters, and the cameras were big and the film slow.

Things have changed a lot since then. But I remember having an argument at the time with a cameraman who refused to shoot a scene with a 25mm lens, insisting that the lens was too wide-angled to pan or move the camera without distorting everything. Today, people think of a 25mm almost as a normal lens, and a wide-angle lens goes down to 9·8mm, which gives you about a 90° horizontal viewing angle. *The Shining* could not have had the same lighting if it had been filmed on location, and because of the snow effects it would have been extremely impractical to do that way. We would have been far too much of a nuisance in a real hotel, and in the case of those which were shut in the winter, they were closed because they really were inaccessible.

What kind of horror films did you like? Did you see Rosemary's Baby?

It was one of the best of the genre. I liked *The Exorcist* too.

And John Boorman's The Heretic?

I haven't seen it, but I like his work. *Deliverance* is an extremely good film. One of the things that amazes me about some directors (not Boorman) who have had great financial successes, is that they seem eager to give up directing to become film moguls. If you care about films, I don't see how you could want someone else to direct for you.

Perhaps they don't like the actual shooting.

It's true – shooting isn't always fun. But if you care about the film it doesn't matter. It's a little like changing your baby's diapers. It is true that while you're filming you are almost always in conflict with someone. Woody Allen, talking about directing *Interiors*, said that no matter how pleasant and relaxed everything seemed on the surface he felt his actors always resented being told anything. There are actors, however, with whom communication and co-operation is so good that the work really becomes exciting and satisfying. I find writing and editing very enjoyable, and almost completely lacking in this kind of tension.

Today it is more and more difficult for a film to get its money back. The film rental can be three times the cost of the film.

Much more than that. Take a film that costs $10 million. Today it's not unusual to spend $8 million on USA advertising, and $4 million on international advertising. On a big film, add $2 million for release-prints. Say there is a 20% studio overhead on the budget: that's $2 million more. Interest on the $10 million production cost, currently at 20% a year, would add an additional $2 million a year, say, for two years – that's another $4 million. So a $10 million film already costs $30 million. Now you have to get it back. Let's say an actor takes 10% of the gross, and the distributor takes a world-wide average of a 35% distribution fee. To roughly calculate the break-even figure, you have to divide the $30 million by 55%, the percentage left after the actor's 10% and the 35% distribution fee. That comes to $54 million of distributor's film rental. So a $10 million film may not break even, as far as the producer's share of the profits is concerned, until 5·4 times its negative cost. Obviously the *actual* break-even figure for the distributor is lower since he is taking a 35% distribution fee and has charged overheads.

But you came to realise very early in your career that if you didn't have the control of the production you couldn't have the artistic freedom.

There is no doubt that the more legal control you have over things, the less interference you have. This, in itself, doesn't guarantee you're going to get it right, but it gives you your best chance. But the more freedom you have the greater is your responsibility, and this includes the logistical side of film-making. I suppose you could make some kind of military analogy here. Napoleon, about whom I still intend to do a film, personally worked out the laborious arithmetic of the complicated timetables which were necessary for the co-ordinated arrival on the battlefield of the different elements of his army, which sometimes were scattered all over Europe.

His genius on the battlefield might have been of little use if large formations of his army failed to arrive on the day.

Of course, I'm not making a serious comparison between the burdens and the genius of L'Empereur and any film director, but the point is that if Napoleon believed it was necessary to go to all that trouble, then a comparative involvement in the logistical side of film-making should be a normal responsibility for any director who wants to ensure he gets what he wants when he wants it.

In a more fanciful vein, and perhaps stretching the analogy a bit, I suspect that for Napoleon, his military campaigns provided him with at least all of the excitement and satisfaction of making a film and, equally so, I would imagine everything in between must have seemed pretty dull by comparison. Of course this is not an explanation of the Napoleonic wars, but perhaps it suggests some part of the explanation for Napoleon's apparently irrepressible desire for still one more campaign. What must it be like to realize that you are perhaps the greatest military commander in history, have marshals like Ney, Murat, Davout, the finest army in Europe, and have no place to go and nothing to do?

Then, continuing with this by now overstretched analogy, there is the big-budgeted disaster – the Russian Campaign, in which, from the start, Napoleon ignored the evidence which suggested the campaign would be such a costly disaster. And, finally, before his first exile, after fighting a series of brilliant battles against the Allies' superior numbers, Napoleon still had a final opportunity for compromise, but he over-negotiated, gambled on his military magic, and lost.

In your screenplay about Napoleon, did you adopt a chronological approach?

Yes, I did. Napoleon, himself, once remarked what a great novel his life would be. I'm sure he would have said 'movie' if he had known about them. His entire life is the story, and it works perfectly well in the order it happened. It would also be nice to do it as a twenty hour TV series, but there is, as yet, not enough money available in TV properly to budget such a venture. Of course, there is the tremendous problem of the actor to play Napoleon. Al Pacino comes quickly to mind. And there is always the possibility of shooting the twenty episodes in such a way that he would be fifty by the time he got to St Helena. Al, I'm joking! I'm joking!

These three interviews were given in 1972, 1974 and 1980 and were corrected and approved by Stanley Kubrick for incomplete publication in magazines at those times. A complete version was published in the French edition of this work in 1980. In July 1981, Stanley Kubrick expressed a desire to revise these texts for all foreign editions of the book. It is this new expanded version which we are offering the reader here.

Interviews
with
colleagues

Stanley Kubrick (filming The Shining*)*

James B. Harris, producer

Did your career in the movies begin when you met Kubrick?

No, but that was when I made my first features. At seventeen, I had started on the distribution side. In the army, as I had already worked in the cinema, I was assigned to the film unit, where I met one of Kubrick's friends, the future director Alexander Singer. It was there that I learned how movies were made. In our spare time, Singer and I would make experimental films, and I got to know Kubrick when he came to see Alex. It was in 1953 and he had just directed *Fear and Desire*. He had brought his camera with him and photographed us at work. Naturally, I was impressed by someone who had already made an independent feature on his own.

When I was demobilised, I went back into distribution and got involved with the sale of films to TV; then I produced and directed a TV series on baseball combining interviews with newsreel footage. Kubrick invited me to a screening of his new film, *Killer's Kiss*, and also asked my help in trying to sell *Fear and Desire* to TV. We began to talk together. Since he had no money, he was unable to set up any new project. After seeing *Killer's Kiss*, I told him he had it in him to become one of the world's best directors. But he was only twenty-five, after all, and I told him he needed someone to raise financing, find a good story, professional actors and writers; so I suggested we become partners. And that's how I became his producer; except that we had nothing to film! I would hunt through bookstores and I came across Lionel White's *Clean Break*. After reading it, I thought it would make a first-rate movie. Stanley agreed and it turned into *The Killing*.

We went to Hollywood in 1955; together we made *Paths of Glory* in Germany and *Lolita* in England. I was executive administrator on these films, my role being to deal with practical problems, everything from financing to distribution, so that Kubrick could be left in peace to create. But at the same time I was learning about cinema and developing my own tastes. Stanley had an enormous influence on me. When it came to the preparation of *Lolita*, I was able to contribute much more to the film, to the development of the storyline. On our arrival in London, we weren't satisfied with the lengthy screenplay that Nabokov had written. We shut ourselves in one room for a month and rewrote it scene by scene. Of course, when shooting got under way, Stanley gave each scene a new dimension, as for example in a few improvised exchanges between Sellers and Mason. But I felt I had participated in the shaping of a movie and my one idea at that point was to become a director myself. I had the bug.

Then Stanley became interested in the question of nuclear weaponry which at that period really didn't interest me. He taught me a lot about the problem and we set up *Dr Strangelove*. But the question had been raised: was I going to continue as a producer or shift to direction? And Stanley, after long conversations together, encouraged me to become a director. He said to me: 'You ought to be a good director, but

2

1. *Emile Meyer, Timothy Carey* (Paths of Glory)
2. *Joe Turkel, Vince Edwards* (The Killing)

you'll never know if you don't try. It's a lonely job. We've enjoyed working together, we've never made a bad movie, even if we could have done better; there are no money problems, since we've earned a lot. You'll never know complete satisfaction until you've tried your hand at directing.' It was the kind of encouragement I needed.

How did Kubrick influence you?

Above all, in his way of narrating a scene or a plot. He would constantly emphasize the way people behaved. He advised me to read Freud's *Introduction to Psychoanalysis* and also Stanislavsky's works, in particular *Stanislavsky Directs*. I found all kinds of valuable suggestions in it. Firstly, that one must sense if a scene is working or not and be prepared to correct it. There are three possible reasons: 1) The actor is not prepared; 2) The actor hasn't understood the scene; 3) The scene hasn't been written properly. For Kubrick, technique was certainly important if you could practise it yourself – but others could do it for you. The essential thing – which no one else could do for you – was to exercise your judgment and your taste. He taught me how to avoid exposition in dialogue, to make certain that characters never spell out what they're thinking, and that you have to make the public understand what they're really thinking, how to avoid the kind of tedious repetition you find in most movies, even when there are changes in sets or situations.

At the beginning, the camera held the greatest attraction for him and he tended to make it the star of the film. It was only after *Spartacus* that his attitude changed. He had a Technirama camera which couldn't be moved without loss in definition. I think that forced him to concentrate more on actors' movements within the frame. And he realised that he had maybe been too preoccupied with technical brilliance.

Stanley believed that you shouldn't be inhibited by what people are going to think of you, whether they're going to like you or not. For him, every single detail was extremely important and he was ready to give himself up totally to his goal – which was the movie – for you have to live with your work to the end of your life. That's why he preferred to be thought of as a tyrant, as a pain in the neck and to make life difficult for himself, even if it would have been more pleasant to stay on good terms with everyone. For once the movie is finished, everyone else leaves and you are left alone with your footage – forever. I also learned that people would listen to Stanley that much more attentively and work that much harder out of respect for him. Even if he was hard with people, he knew how to get the most out of them.

Do you share his tastes in cinema?

I learned everything from him. I knew only Hollywood movies. Through him I discovered Ophüls, Buñuel, Renoir, Carol Reed's *Odd Man Out*. He's much more of a film buff than I am and sees movie after movie.

Cannes, May 1973

1. *Elisha Cook Jr., Marie Windsor* (The Killing)
2. *James Mason, Shelley Winters* (Lolita)
3. *James Mason* (Lolita)

Ken Adam, designer

*The two films on which you worked with Kubrick are in a sense diametrically opposed: one, a historical film (*Barry Lyndon*), was shot on location; the other, a futuristic film (*Dr Strangelove*), was made in the studio.*

Personally, I prefer *Strangelove* because I was given the possibility of creating an imaginary décor, 'another' reality and, of course, a studio is more suited to that purpose. Especially as the American Army had refused all co-operation and there was no hope of shooting inside the Pentagon. . . . As for *Barry Lyndon*, Stanley wanted it in a way to be a documentary on the eighteenth century. It seemed to him safer, if we were to avoid error as much as possible, to film the architecture of the period. My problem was creating a progression in the sets: for me, the Irish background of Barry Lyndon's youth had to be much more primitive, it had to belong to an earlier period than the scenes in England. And I was very disappointed not to be able to find Irish buildings from that period for it seemed as if they had all been destroyed by revolutions and wars. Finally, we managed to re-create pre-eighteenth-century architecture by combining three different sites: Caher Castle, Ormond House and Huntingdon. It took me a long time to discover them.

Moreover, I wanted Lady Lyndon, who belonged to an old aristocratic family, also to have a house predating the eighteenth century, for if not it would have seemed *nouveau riche*. And I persuaded Stanley to adopt this idea. Though there exist lots of houses from the Elizabethan, Stuart and Jacobean periods, it was difficult to find one of great beauty. Added to which, we were refused permission to shoot in some of the castles. What we did was again to create a kind of composite architecture by using Wilton (Salisbury), Petworth (Sussex), Longleat (Wiltshire) and Castle Howard (York) for the exteriors. But as I say, I am much more interested in the artistic challenge of a film like *Dr Strangelove*.

In the case of Barry Lyndon, *did you begin work the moment the screenplay was finished?*

Basically, we used the novel. Stanley didn't think it was necessary to have a new script based on Thackeray. The original text served as continuity and we worked with it. Of course, Stanley had already prepared a 'montage' in terms of the film itself. The second problem was knowing where and how were we going to shoot the film. When I arrived, Stanley had already worked with another designer. As I recall, their intention was to shoot the whole film at Picketts Manor with the house gradually being transformed. It didn't seem to me at all a practical idea; my feeling about *Barry Lyndon* was that it would have to be made on a larger scale. Then again, Stanley was set against the idea of shooting in the studio and even of mixing studio sets with real ones. He believed it was impossible to recreate the reality of the eighteenth century in a studio, from either a realistic or an economic point of view. As far as I'm concerned, he was wrong, and I spent a lot of time trying to persuade him otherwise. In fact, it was the location shooting that made the film so expensive – what with transport and accommodation costs, overspending on budget, renting the castles, and general expenses.

Were you directly influenced by paintings from the period?

Stanley wanted to make direct reference to the painting. Personally, from my reading of Thackeray's book, I would have preferred to evolve my own conception of the eighteenth century – obviously in agreement with the director – in order to portray what the author was describing in his novel. I don't have to look at the houses or paintings of the period. Whatever book I read, I form an idea of it in my mind. If I'm unfamiliar with the period, I naturally research it, but there comes a moment when I put aside my documentation and begin to work from my own interpretation. Stanley didn't agree at all with this attitude. For him, the safest way – and, knowing how his mind works, I understand him – was to draw our inspiration from painters like Gainsborough, Hogarth, Reynolds, Chardin, Watteau, Zoffany, Stubbs (for the hunting costumes) and, in particular, Chadowiecki, an artist who intrigued both of us, a Pole who worked on the Continent and who was a master of drawing and water-colour, with a marvellously simple style and a remarkable gift for composition. Stanley was also amused by certain weird pictures by Hogarth, I believe, where one could see paintings hung high up on walls and nothing underneath. For me, the research was unending, as were our attempts to reproduce the results of this research – which is not really the way I like to work. During the preparation of a film, I usually make endless drawings, whereas for this one I practically didn't touch a piece of paper. But it was fascinating work all the same. We did research on the toothbrushes of the period, on the contraceptives, on a mass of things which finally didn't appear on the screen. It was an exhausting experience, especially as at the beginning, while we were preparing it, Stanley didn't want to go further than twenty miles from his home, claiming that we never know what we may find at our own front door. But I knew that the most suitable castles were situated further away and that we'd eventually have to go there. As a designer, I think that very often – given his cinematic style and a type of photography that depends on natural light sources – I could have obtained better results in the studio.

How were the scenes in Germany shot?

By the second unit. Stanley never went there. He was sent the maximum of photographic documents and slides from which he made a selection. He has a theory that you don't

Ken Adam's sketch for the War Room set in Dr Strangelove

have to go to a place to judge the lie of the land. Of course, there are no characters in these shots. Likewise, he didn't go to Africa to photograph the landscapes for the first section of *2001*. But, in fact, he is in absolute control of his films, he analyses each photograph and afterwards prefers to shoot in natural light, without any lighting. It was always a joke between us, when we went location hunting, because I would refuse to take a tripod, which is of course indispensable if you are working without a flashlight.

The first part must have given more scope to your imagination.

Yes, it was more fun. Given that we were in Ireland, Stanley, who doesn't like to travel, thought we might as well shoot the Continental sequences there. So I had somehow to find examples of Austrian and German baroque. I was lucky enough to find a spot near Dublin, called Powercourt, in which one could detect a strong German influence. It was there that we shot almost all the battle scenes. Which, up to a certain point, was perfectly acceptable. But there's a kind of contradiction there if you're making a documentary on the period. We compromised in this way until Stanley finally decided that the English scenes would have to be shot in England.

Did you make preparatory sketches for the battle scenes?

Yes, it was practically the only occasion. The reason was that Stanley wanted to see how many soldiers we needed to fill the screen, to create the effect of an attack, and what lenses were going to be used. So we arranged and rearranged lead soldiers from every possible angle.

In the interiors, when you moved from one set to another, it must have posed problems in transition.

We used so many houses to represent that one house that it made a conglomeration that only Stanley could keep in his head. No doubt an art critic might notice the 'jerks' in decoration from one room to another, but for me it isn't very important as there's already a juxtaposition of styles in English castles. At Wilton, for example, there's both the Elizabethan and the eighteenth-century style. The rest is a simple problem of continuity.

In Dr Strangelove, *how did you conceive the War Room set?*

While we were discussing it, I amused myself by scribbling, by doodling on a sheet of paper and Stanley, who was watching me, told me he found it very interesting. And I said to myself that everything people said about him – that he was a difficult person to work with, etc. – was false because he liked my first ideas. He told me to continue along the same lines. For three weeks I developed my ideas and one day, when we were driving to the studio and I was getting ready to have the set built, he told me that it wouldn't work, that he would have to fill the different levels which I had imagined with actors and he didn't know what he'd get them to do, etc. – and he asked me to think of another idea. And all that after encouraging me to develop my conception! For a few hours, I was completely demoralised, because I had already built the set in my head.' That was fourteen years ago and I wasn't as flexible a designer as I am now. It took me some time to calm down; but the strangest thing is that it was that very afternoon that I imagined the War Room as it appears in the film.

The difficulty was justifying to Stanley the shape of the War Room, for with him everything has to have a rational explanation, even if it's the result of instinct or talent. For him, what counts is always how and why. I convinced him that the triangle was a very strong geometrical form, that it would look like an underground atomic shelter, an idea he liked, and that it would be made in reinforced concrete. At which point, I had won the battle. And then he became the perfectionist we all know. He wanted to improve the concept.

And that's very exciting for a designer. You think you've finished, but a creative director can add a whole new dimension to your work, which you wouldn't have thought possible. There's nothing more stimulating than this kind of improvement, whereas often my problem, when I've designed a set, is fighting with the director or the lighting cameraman to insure that my conception of the set gets up there on the screen, without being spoilt. With Kubrick nothing is impossible. For example, he insisted that I build a ceiling for the War Room in concrete to force the director of photography to use natural light instead of the artificial lighting which we use in studios. Before installing my circular lighting, he made tests with the actors to study the height from every possible angle, for all the characters were going to be lit from above. When I thought up that huge circular table, Stanley said to me: 'It's interesting, because it looks like a gigantic poker table. And the president and the generals are playing with the world like a game of cards.' So we developed the idea. He asked me to create a lighting system which would allow him to light the actors *naturally*. We sat someone down on a chair and placed a lamp above him, at a certain angle and at a certain height, until Stanley was satisfied with the lighting. And I conceived that gigantic circle of light which 'duplicates' the table and became the principal source of light for the whole set.

There is a contrast between the realistic scenes at Burpelson Base and the expressionist décor of the War Room.

Stanley was aiming for absolute realism. He was fascinated by the idea of shooting those battle scenes in a newsreel style, with a hand-held camera. We used a large part of Shepperton Studios for the attack on the base. Sterling Hayden's office was designed realistically, as was the interior of the bomber, except for the two atomic bombs – it was the period of the Cuban crisis and we didn't have the co-operation of the authorities for the film! We didn't know what shape they were. I decided to go all out for unreality, for making it larger than life, and Stanley had the brilliant idea of having Slim Pickens sit astride them. For example, this was a sequence for which I made a 'storyboard'.

Dr Strangelove *was originally to end with a custard pie battle.*

It was a very brilliant sequence with a *Hellzapoppin* kind of craziness. Undoubtedly one of the most extraordinary custard pie battles ever filmed. The characters were hanging from chandeliers and throwing pies which ended up by covering the maps of the General Staff. Shooting lasted a week, and the sequence ended with the President of the United States and the Soviet ambassador sitting on what was left of the pies and building 'pie-castles' like children on a beach.

Did Kubrick think of you for 2001?

Yes, but the problem is that I always want to know as much as he does on the subject in hand so that I can discuss it with him on equal terms and present my viewpoint. But he had already worked for a year with experts from NASA and had done a lot of research. I had only three months of preparation at my disposal and was too far behind! Added to which, Kubrick wants everything to be intellectually justified and that would have been difficult, with all those experts around him ready to contradict me!...

When you create a décor for Kubrick, does he offer you the most angles possible for his camera so that he will be freer when he begins to shoot?

For Stanley – and he's right – I have to design each set in terms of the widest possible angle. Of course, he may well ask me later how the set would look with a 40 or 50mm lens. At which point, I sketch it again with the projections he wanted. For large sets, I offer him at least eight possible angles. But normally, for an ordinary set, I know that if I have lines, movements and compositions well-designed from one angle, they will work for all the other angles. Kubrick, though, has a natural distrust of anything he can't see in life-size and I have to give him projections, models, etc. And there's always the possibility of his changing his mind right up to the start of shooting. You have to present him with the widest possible choice.

Peter Sellers in the War Room set in Dr Strangelove

1

2

Ken Adam describes the final sequence of *Dr Strangelove* (lasting about ten minutes) which Stanley Kubrick decided not to include in his final version. Peter Bull (who played the Soviet ambassador) also described it in his memoirs *I Say Look Here* (Peter Davies, London 1965):

Kubrick was no less ruthless with *2001*, from which he cut nineteen minutes after the film's première in Washington (sequences on the space station, on the moon and aboard the *Discovery*). Similarly, only a few days after *The Shining* had been released in the United States, he cut a final sequence of about two minutes in which Ullman, the manager of the hotel, visits Wendy in hospital. The film then came to an end, as in the current version, with the snapshot of the party.

A few weeks later, Kubrick decided to cut two further scenes (a woman doctor's visit to Danny at the beginning of the film; Hallorann's encounter with a gas station attendant on his return from Florida) and tightened up the editing of several other sequences, reducing the length of the film to two hours. It is this version which has been screened all over the world.

The final scene cut from Dr Strangelove
1. and 2. George C. Scott
3. George C. Scott, Peter Sellers
4. Peter Sellers

John Alcott, chief cameraman

How did you begin to work with Stanley Kubrick?

I was Geoffrey Unsworth's assistant and I was naturally brought in to work with him on *2001*. Up to that point, I of course wanted to be a cinematographer, but I was trying to get some pleasure out of it without really succeeding. I would see directors of photography spending hours lighting the sets then just as much time taking their lighting down again, getting rid of mike shadows and things like that. When I arrived on the set of *2001*, it was the first time I had seen a film being shot with natural lighting. What I mean by that is lighting that corresponds to the situation in which one finds oneself. In the case of a spacecraft in orbit, we used the lighting of the centrifugal machine reconstructed in the studio without adding any extra lamps. That's what Stanley wanted, and I immediately got on the same wavelength.

Geoffrey worked from December 1965 to June 1966, in particular on all the scenes with the actors. Then there was an interruption to perfect the special effects. And then my first real job was to film the opening section, 'The Dawn of Man'. We had to shoot it in the studio, as we wanted a very weak light, like that of dawn, and it would have taken months to film each shot in Africa itself. As well as finding some very wide-angle lenses, Stanley constructed a 10″×8″ projector to project the background photographs on a screen measuring thirty metres by ten, the largest of its kind at the time. The transparencies were made up exclusively of photographs taken in Africa on Stanley's precise instructions. But the studio set was so large in the foreground that one really had the impression of being there.

Kubrick used to be a photographer himself. To what extent does he collaborate on the photography of his films?

He knows exactly what he wants. If he were not a director, he would probably be the greatest lighting cameraman in the world. On the set, he works at the camera and you can learn a lot from working with him.

What special problems did the shooting of 2001 *pose?*

I remember the sequence in which William Sylvester goes towards the space station. At the beginning we used an f8 exposure and we ended by fixing it between f2·8 and f4. And the film's brilliant, clear, *white* light is due to that range. I suppose it's less noticeable today because all science-fiction films have adopted the same principle. The brightness extended even to the sets and corresponded to the feeling you're supposed to have in space.

How did you shoot the last sequence, in the eighteenth-century room?

The scene was lit exclusively from beneath, the reflectors were squares with sides of sixty centimetres and they had to be five centimetres thick so that we could walk on them. The heat underneath tended to deform the plastic. We also discovered that the lights generally used in the cinema gave off too much heat. We had to use photographers' lamps, of the 'mushroom' type, which are very simple and much less expensive. There's another example of Stanley's aptitude for always coming up with new ideas.

Did you work on his Napoleon project?

Yes, but not much, because he spends a lot of time preparing a film. You might say that, because of his research, he could tell you virtually where Napoleon was every day of his life, as well as everybody in his entourage. Our discussions on the photography dealt principally with lighting by candles at a period when we didn't yet have the technical equipment which enabled us later to shoot *Barry Lyndon*. I remember we wanted to use reversal stock.

You then worked on A Clockwork Orange.

Yes, after giving up *Napoleon*, he immediately set to work on *A Clockwork Orange*, which was made with a small budget. In the main, we shot it on location with a crew of twenty. It was the opposite of *2001*. Once again, he did a lot of research – to find Malcolm McDowell's apartment, for example. He decided on a block of flats near Borehamwood Studios, but first he preferred to sound out every other possibility to see if there was really nothing better.

The visual style of the film was very eclectic.

The photographic styles were very different – even the opposite of each other. We reverted to 35mm after using 65mm for *2001*. This was obviously for practical reasons, as inside the houses we needed equipment that was more mobile and took up less space. The Arriflex seemed to us best adapted for such shooting conditions, especially for hand-held camerawork. We also used wide-angle lenses a lot and a French lens, the Angénieux, whose minimum aperture is f4. You have to recreate natural lighting on location for if you have only two or three days left to shoot in a particular place, the changes in the weather constantly modify the lighting.

How did you film the speeded-up orgy with the two girls?

There again we experimented. We shot for about twenty minutes, at two images a second. This is the kind of thing Stanley and I discuss before the shooting begins. And it's how every film should be prepared. Most of the time, with other directors, problems arise the moment you start shooting a

John Alcott and Stanley Kubrick (filming The Shining)

scene and it's too late to solve them because time costs money on a set. But Stanley foresees every eventuality a week or two before to eliminate the risk of error. He's prepared even to make tests. But he also likes to keep his options open. Sometimes we'll discuss the placing of the following day's shots the morning before because it could well be too late by the evening, if we have to envisage technical solutions to the problem. But it is, of course, the evening before that we do most of our preparation.

Stanley makes endless notes which he gives to the technicians every morning. He has a good memory, which I haven't, and yet it's he who gets everything down on paper. And that's something else that he taught me: if you want to remember something, note it down. He will always ask you to come back to him in the evening with your answers to his questions, and you can't get out of it. I remember that on other films there were people with wonderful ideas but, when shooting began, they had evaporated, or else no one had thought of the material problems which they would create and which made them impossible to put into effect. With the way Stanley prepares a film, he makes shooting it very easy.

Is he actively involved in setting up a shot?

Yes, particularly for shots filmed with a hand-held camera, because he can see for himself what there is in the frame. He even discovered a simpler, easier way of holding the Arriflex which made it a kind of Steadicam *avant la lettre*. He's the only person I know who has managed to give it such a degree of stability. That comes yet again from the fact that he is, in his heart of hearts, a photographer, and he likes getting the best possible effects out of a camera. As early as in *Paths of Glory*, you can see those extraordinary tracking shots along the trenches, obtained with a dolly which, because of the angle chosen and the general movement of the scene, appears extremely stable.

Does he demand many takes?

Yes, quite often. All the same, he doesn't 'cover' himself, he knows exactly the angle he wants once he has placed the actors in the set. If he requires several takes, it's in order to get the most out of the actors, but the visual composition is also very important to him. On *The Shining* there was a video camera attached to the cameraman which enabled him at every moment to see the frame on the television screen. That enabled him to concentrate wholly on the actors. In *The*

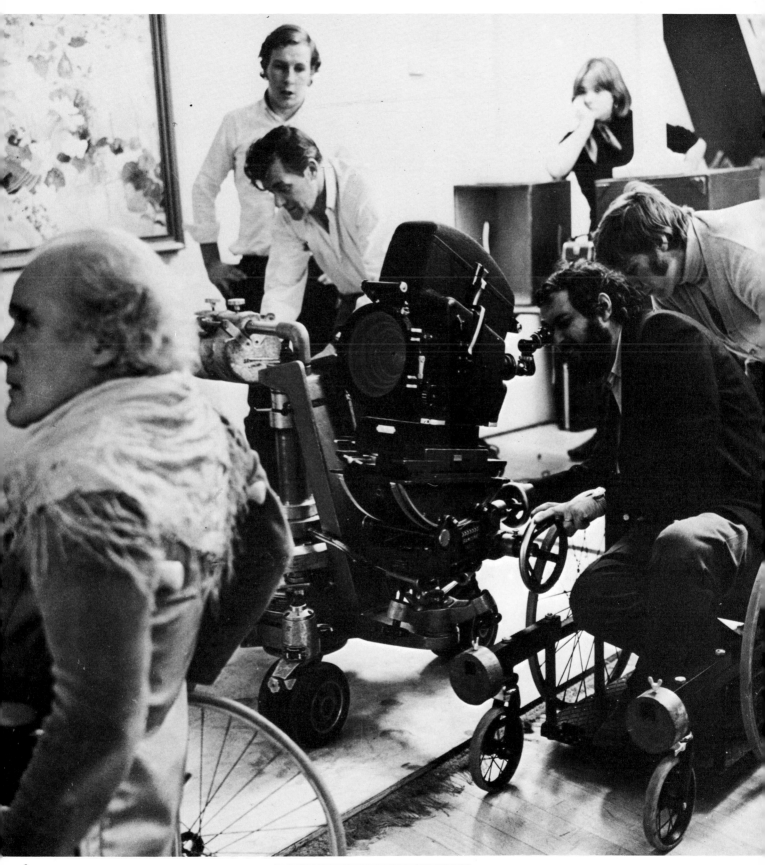

Stanley Kubrick filming A Clockwork Orange:
1. with Miriam Karlin and Malcolm McDowell
2. with Patrick Magee (left)

Shining there were scenes that were very different from a technical point of view and from a performance point of view; the actors had to invest their performances with a great deal of intensity, the shots were sometimes very long and, as always, Stanley was aiming for nothing less than perfection.

For Barry Lyndon, *did you use booster lights?*

Yes, because we shot it mainly in winter and we could only shoot between nine in the morning and three in the afternoon. When there was sun, I used it as natural light. I put tracing paper on the windows and installed lamps so that, the moment the sun went down, we could switch to artificial lighting and continue shooting. But that lighting (six floodlamps or mini-brutes) was still based on natural light.

What kinds of filters did you use?

In the main, low-contrast filters of degree 3, except for the wedding scene when we combined them with a veil to create the kind of pictorial radiance that one associates with happiness. It was when we went to Ireland at the start of shooting that we wanted to lessen the contrasts as the light there is dazzling. So we tried to make it more diffuse. Of course, with the candlelit scenes, we didn't have to do that because the light was naturally soft and the special Zeiss lenses which we used for them had less precise definition.

While shooting *A Clockwork Orange*, Stanley had bought a Mitchell camera for certain scenes as the Arriflex at that time couldn't film more than 100m a take while the Mitchell went up to 300m – which is to say, ten minutes.

And he had the idea of adapting the Zeiss photo lens to his Mitchell while keeping the Arriflex for the daylight scenes. It was Ed di Giulio who adapted the Mitchell so that it would take a lens with such a large aperture. That's the kind of challenge Stanley enjoys and there are few film-makers willing to pose such questions and take the time necessary to solve them. For example, it took three months to perfect the new lens. The problem with the Mitchell is that there's no reflex and you have to depend on the viewfinder at the side of the camera, so that it's more difficult to obtain an exact composition.

What lens did you use for Barry Lyndon?

A 25mm one for most of the interiors. We rarely used the 18mm as we often did for *The Shining*. On the other hand, we used the zoom a great deal. Each time, it became an image in itself and not, as is usually the case, a means of moving from one point in space to another. So each shot was a composition, like the zoom which moved out from the pistol during the duel at the river's edge. The zoom also meant that we did not depend too much on editing and so gave the whole film a kind of softness and fluidity.

Did you use the video system when shooting Barry Lyndon?

We had already done so in the scenes with the wheel in *2001*. No one but the cameraman and his assistant could get inside; and on a television screen Stanley watched the image transmitted by a television camera which would give him more or less the same angle. Video makes for better technical coordination between the camera, the actors' movements and the sets. For *The Shining*, however, video was used as a means of judging the performances and the composition of the image.

Did Kubrick have a large crew on The Shining?

I would say that the official technical crew was undoubtedly smaller than for *A Clockwork Orange*. But there was of course a large special effects team, in particular for the scenes in the snow. For the principal set, there were five enormous windows, each three metres wide, on a thirty-metre-long facade; and when there was a tracking shot in the room, we needed a lot of technicians outside to make the snow fall. But apart from these special cases, there were no more than ten of us in the basic filming area.

What lenses did you choose for The Shining?

Faster lenses even than for *Barry Lyndon*. We used the whole range of the Zeiss lenses, from 18mm to 85mm. On the other hand, we didn't use the zoom much. The set of the hotel and the labyrinth took up almost the whole of Elstree Studios.

How did you envisage colour for The Shining?

In two ways. For the beginning of the film, which takes place in autumn, we wanted, with natural light, to obtain a warm light. Then, with the approach of winter, we switched to one that was colder. I put blue filters on the outside windows and used artificial lighting inside in relation to that blue.

You've worked with Kubrick for more than ten years. How has he evolved during that period?

I think that he has a much wider technical experience now but that his working methods have remained basically the same, which is a very positive thing for those of us who regularly work with him because we know what's expected of us, how we have to adapt and think ahead. I think it would be very difficult for someone starting at the beginning today in an important job for Stanley. With him there can be no excuses and no tricks because he is on to them immediately. It's sometimes happened that I've found myself in a situation with no way out or in which I've made a mistake; and in these cases, it's better simply to tell him, for he'll understand the problem. But don't try to hide it from him!

He's capable of becoming an expert in every field. I remember that during the making of *2001* a technician was amusing himself by throwing a knife at a piece of wood. Within five minutes Stanley, who had probably never played at that in his life, hit the target dead centre.

What is also exciting is the fact that he never ceases to renew himself, he never repeats himself. And he imbues you with so much inner energy that you don't feel time passing. When you're shooting a film with him, it's eight o'clock in the evening before you know it. The fact that he's so intensely involved in his own work explains why he has little time for meeting people from the outside. When he does it, however, he's both very open and very concentrated, very eloquent. He gives himself up totally to the person visiting him. But, as soon as he can, he gets back to his own concerns. Really, working for him is like going to school and being paid for it.

London, February 1980.

The lighting photography of John Alcott and Stanley Kubrick:
The Overlook Hotel (The Shining)

The lighting photography of John Alcott and Stanley Kubrick: The wedding of Redmond Barry and Lady Lyndon (Ryan O'Neal, Marisa Berenson)

The lighting photography of John Alcott and Stanley Kubrick (Barry Lyndon)

4
OSCARS

BARRY LYNDON

en film av
STANLEY KUBRICK

med RYAN O'NEAL MARISA BERENSON
samt PATRICK MAGEE · HARDY KRUGER · DIANA KOERNER · GAY HAMILTON
Exekutiv producent JAN HARLAN
från Warner Bros. A Warner Communications Company

Posters supervised by Stanley Kubrick for the publicity campaigns of his films

Julian Senior, publicity director

What is your exact position?

Officially, I'm in charge of publicity for Warner films in Europe. I met Kubrick for the first time in 1968 when he had finished *2001* and I was working for Metro-Goldwyn-Mayer. He asked me if I would help Roger Caras, who was then managing Hawk Films, Kubrick's company. Caras had already worked on *Dr Strangelove* and had such a remarkable gift for organization that it satisfied even Stanley. After *2001* he launched out into production; Stanley signed a three-film contract with Warner and I joined up with him when he finished shooting *A Clockwork Orange* and was preparing to market the film.

Kubrick knows that his name will appear on the credit titles for ever and that it's in his interest to ensure that the film will be viewed in the best conditions, since it's just as easy to do something well as badly. Stanley's association with Warner Bros. coincided with the takeover of the company by Warner Communications and the arrival of Ted Ashley, John Calley and Frank Wells. They were very aware of the problems of production and wanted the company's policy to be aimed at giving directors the kind of creative freedom they need. This was the spirit of the new triumvirate at the beginning of the 70s: to give film directors the right to the final cut and the possibility, should the occasion arise, of having a say in publicity, sales and distribution. People as varied as Malick, Scorsese, Friedkin and Clint Eastwood also joined Warner Bros. at that period.

In November 1971, when I was working in publicity for the UK, I first made Kubrick's acquaintance. He rang me up to talk about the release of *A Clockwork Orange*. He immediately asked me to call him Stanley when I persisted in calling him Mr Kubrick; and he asked, before coming to see me, if there was a car park near my office and, if so, to reserve him a space. I told him it wasn't necessary as there were always free spaces. And he replied – it's become almost a keynote of our relationship – that it's just when one puts one's trust in past experience that the unexpected happens. 'It's so easy,' he added, 'to reserve a space. Why not do it?'

So he came to see me, sat down opposite me and for six-and-a-half hours he studied in the most minute detail everything that he thought might be important for the release of the film – without once giving me an order. That's the way he works. Likewise, I've never seen him lose his temper – for him it would be a sign of impotence, a cathartic gesture that makes you feel better but solves nothing. He admitted that he didn't know a great deal about advertising techniques, so we had someone brought over from an agency to explain them: posters, newspaper ads, etc. From this first meeting it was already clear how we were going to work together for the next ten years – taking notes, being as precise as possible (he would have made a terrific journalist), never omitting a single detail. He's a very exacting man.

He very quickly learned how publicity operates.

He believes that every essential question can be answered through logic and common sense. I recall very clearly that, at the time of *A Clockwork Orange*, we drew up together what we jokingly referred to as a 'memory jogger' on releasing a film: how many prints should be made, how many trailers, does every cinema possess a projector with a 1·66 mask, do the TV networks prefer video or film, etc. This 'memory jogger' amounted to about thirty pages and for me laid down the definitive guidelines on the matter. As proof of that, I might cite the fact that Stanley asked everybody in the profession to let him know if certain questions seemed useless to them, or if others were impossible to answer – and we didn't receive a single letter in response. According to Stanley, if you pose the question logically and try to answer it logically, there is no problem in publicity that can't be solved. So I became involved with the film's release, not only in England, but in Europe. Then Stanley began working with me again when he finished *Barry Lyndon*.

Does he begin to think of the film's release at an earlier stage of his work, e.g. while shooting or editing?

He'd make a very good general. He's just as capable of checking the details of a trench as of mapping out a whole strategy. For example, when I was waiting for a print of *Barry Lyndon* to be delivered to me for the film's release, I had booked a projection room for the press for thirty or forty evenings – having first, at Stanley's request, tested the projection quality of each available room. And every morning I had to cancel the evening screening as the film wasn't ready. Finally, the great day arrived and I was refused use of the projection room because I had already caused them to lose twenty-five evenings. Then Kubrick personally rang up the projectionist and that was enough for us to have our screening.

Everything is supervised by him. At the moment we are having a problem with photographs for the press. Stanley refuses to have a stills photographer standing beside him, taking photographs of every scene. In his opinion, the photograph which best represents a shot from the film is one enlarged from the print itself. And that's what he's done on all his films since *2001*. All the important magazines, from *Time* and *Newsweek* downwards, have raised objections to this. But Stanley won't be budged, even though it creates a great deal of work for him as he has to view the film frame by frame on a Steenbeck to select the particular one he wants. But for him it's the only way to catch the precise angle and lighting of the shot itself. Naturally, this causes problems, for as long as he hasn't completed editing the film – and he works on it right up to the last minute – it's impossible to give any publicity material to the press.

Another example of his perfectionism: When *A Clockwork*

Orange was about to be released in New York, he discovered that the walls and ceiling of one of the cinemas showing the film were painted in shiny white lacquer which created awkward reflections. Stanley wanted it all repainted, but the cinema manager claimed that with only a few days to the première it would be impossible to find a firm to do the work in the required time. After checking through the Manhattan directory, Stanley sent from London a list of firms capable of installing the scaffolding and changing the colour of the walls. A few days later, he asked what kind of black was being used. No one had realized that a gloss black would create the same problems as before, and they had to repaint it in matte black, as he wanted. That gives you some idea of his precision in technical matters.

For *Barry Lyndon* it was very important – given the experiments in lighting – for the projection equipment to be the best possible. Of course, we had neither the means nor the authority to replace them all, but what we discovered from checking all the principal cinemas in France and Germany was that two thirds of them didn't have a 1·66 mask, something that costs no more than a few pounds. The projectionists told us that the image would overlap a little on the sides. So Kubrick's assistants had all the projectors equipped for a decent screening of the film – and at the same time for every other film!

The other problem is to make a study of each cinema in each city where the film is to be shown. Where is it situated? What sort of clientèle does it have? Once you move away from the central entertainment areas, the choice of a cinema is crucial. Most cinemas have a brand image and Stanley wants to know exactly what it is. On the other hand, audience patterns change from city to city and country to country. For five months he collected figures from the cinemas of every country in the world based on their monthly percentages over several years, because the figures for one year can be misleading owing to some exceptional success.

But there are limits to this kind of logic. It's impossible to check everything. There comes a moment when one has to give up.

The only limits are those fixed by the number of hours' sleep you need. Unlike most producers, Stanley is like a medieval craftsman. He lives and works at home. When he isn't physically at work on his own films, he's viewing other people's so as to know just what's happening in the film world. And he's a great help to young directors, he recommends them to the company if he feels they have talent.

In the same way, he continues to interest himself in his films long after their first release. Two-and-a-half years ago, he called me to his office to talk about Sydney in Australia and the third re-release there of *2001*. He was worried, because although the film had made 58,000 dollars in its first week, the publicity budget for the second week was only 800 dollars. He asked me how much a 30cm ad in a major newspaper would cost; and, after studying the problem, he sent off a telex to MGM in Australia in which he laid out a budget for the distribution of the film. They must have said: 'He's got to be a genius to think of that kind of detail', when it was their job he was doing.

If I should call him while he is in the middle of editing a film, the first question he asks me is always 'Is it urgent? Can it wait?' If I say no, he interrupts the editing and deals with the problem. Most of us react in moments of crisis when we've got to make a quick decision. Few people know how to plan their lives as meticulously and pragmatically as Stanley.

One last anecdote: in Paris *Barry Lyndon* was a greater success in its second week than it had been in the first. I went to see Kubrick for breakfast at about nine o'clock and told him I had very good news concerning takings at such cinemas as

the Hautefeuille, the Gaumont Champs-Elysées, the Impérial, etc. And he said to me: 'Why are you telling me that? I can't do anything if it's good news. It's only when there are problems that I can intervene.'

London, February 1980

A mock-up by Saul Bass

1. and 2. Stanley Kubrick (filming A Clockwork Orange)

Filmography

For several years a man peoples space with images, provinces, kingdoms, mountains, bays, ships, islands, fish, rooms, tools, stars, horses and people. Just before his death, he discovers that the patient labyrinth of lines traces the image of his own face.

Jorge Luis Borges

Shorts

1951 – DAY OF THE FIGHT
A day in the life of Walter Cartier, middleweight boxer. He rises at 6am, attends Morning Mass, looks after his dog, takes a medical for his fight that evening, lunches in a friend's restaurant, enjoys a car trip with his twin brother Vincent, spends a couple of hours on final training. At last, the match. 'For him, it's the end of a working day.'

Photography, editing, sound: *Stanley Kubrick*. Asst.: *.Alexander Singer*. Music: *Gerald Fried*. Commentary: *Douglas Edwards*.
Dist.: RKO Radio.
Length: 16mn. USA.

1951 – FLYING PADRE
Two days in the life of the Reverend Fred Stadtmueller, a Catholic missionary whose New Mexico parish covers four hundred square miles. For six years, he has been piloting his Piper Cub, 'The Spirit of St. Joseph'. The priest attends the funeral of a farmer, reconciles some children, breeds canaries, practises rifle shooting, then takes his aeroplane to fly to a sick baby and its mother 40 miles away and transport them to an airport where an ambulance is waiting.

Photography, editing, sound: *Stanley Kubrick*. Music: *Nathaniel Shilkret*.
Dist.: RKO Radio. Length: 9mn. USA.

Features

1953 – FEAR AND DESIRE
In an abstract war, a military patrol consisting of four men, Lieutenant Corby, Sergeant Mac and two privates, Fletcher and Sidney, find themselves behind enemy lines after their plane has crashed. They advance into the forest, take a couple of enemy soldiers by surprise while they are eating and slaughter them. Then they encounter a young girl and, afraid she will inform on them, tie her to a tree. Sidney stands guard over her while his three comrades proceed to the river to build a raft which, they hope, will take them home. In order to seduce her, Sidney unties the young girl then shoots her when she attempts to escape. Corby, Mac and Fletcher return after discovering an enemy command post held by a general and his aide-de-camp. Mac persuades them to turn back, kill them and steal their plane. While Mac takes the raft downriver to pick up Sidney, Corby and Fletcher approach the post in the dark and kill the general and his aide. The four men are at last reunited.

Prod. Co.: Stanley Kubrick Productions. Prod.: *Stanley Kubrick*. Prod. ass.: *Martin Perveler*. Scr.: *Howard O. Sackler* and *Stanley Kubrick*. Dir. phot. and edit.: *Stanley Kubrick*. Music: *Gerald Fried*. Asst.: *Steve Hahn*. Rehearsal asst.: *Toba Kubrick*. Des.: *Herbert Lebowitz*. Make-up: *Chet Fabian*. Titles: *Barney Ettengoff*. Dir. of prod.: *Bob Dierks*.
Cast: *Frank Silvera* (Mac), *Kenneth Harp* (Lieutenant Corby/enemy general), *Paul Mazursky* (Sidney), *Steve Coit* (Fletcher/aide-de-camp), *Virginia Leith* (young girl), *David Allen* (narrator). Dist.: Joseph Burstyn Inc. Length: 68mn. USA.

1955 – KILLER'S KISS
In the main hall at Grand Central Station, the young boxer Davy Gordon recalls the last few days. Living alone in an apartment, he is attracted to a young girl, Gloria, who leads a no less solitary existence across the courtyard. He leaves for a fight (which he will lose), while she goes to a nightclub where she works as a dancer for its owner, Rapallo. On his return, Davy sees through her window that Rapallo is trying to rape her. He rushes to her aid, Rapallo escapes and Gloria recounts her life-story to Davy. They decide to go off together and stay with Davy's uncle in Seattle. First, however, Davy goes to collect the money owed him by his manager, while she informs Rapallo that she is leaving. Rapallo decides to have Davy killed by his strong-arm men, who mistakenly gun down the manager. Gloria is held prisoner by Rapallo in a warehouse filled with shop-window mannequins. After a chase over New York's rooftops, Davy engages in a life-or-death struggle with Rapallo, kills him and, believing that he has lost Gloria, leaves alone to catch his train. Just as he steps onto the platform, Gloria joins him.
Prod.: *Stanley Kubrick* and *Morris Bousel* (Minotaur). Original story: *Stanley Kubrick*. Scr.: *Stanley Kubrick* and *Howard O. Sackler*. Dir. phot. and edit.: *Stanley Kubrick*. Music: *Gerald Fried*. Chor.: *David Vaughan*.

Cast: *Frank Silvera* (Vincent Rapallo), *Jamie Smith* (Davy Gordon), *Irene Kane* (Gloria Price), *Jerry Jarret* (Albert, the manager), *Mike Dana, Felice Orlandi, Ralph Roberts, Phil Stevenson* (gangsters), *Julius Adelman* (owner of the mannequin factory), *David Vaughan, Alec Rubin* (convention members), *Ruth Sobotka* (Iris, the dancer).
Length: 67mn. USA.
Dist.: United Artists.

1956 – THE KILLING
Johnny Clay, an ex-convict, organizes a two million dollar racecourse hold-up abetted by the cashier George Peatty, the barman O'Reilly, the crooked policeman Randy Kennan and the former alcoholic Marvin Unger, as well as, subsequently, a hired gunman, Nikki Arane, and a wrestler, Maurice. By killing the favourite, Nikki creates a diversion which allows the hold-up to go off smoothly. Back together to divide the spoils, the thieves are surprised by Val Cannon, a gangster and the lovers of Peatty's sex-starved wife Sherry, who had informed him of the robbery. Kennan, O'Reilly and Unger are shot. Peatty, fatally wounded, drags himself home to kill his wife before dying in his turn. Johnny, who did not attend the meeting to which he was supposed to bring the money, prepares to leave town with his fiancée Fay. At the airport, the suitcase containing the banknotes falls open and the money is scattered in all directions. Johnny and Fay are arrested by the authorities.

Prod. Co.: United Artists. Prod.: *James B. Harris*. Scr.: *Stanley Kubrick* and *Jim Thompson*, from the novel by *Lionel White*, 'Clean Break'. Add. Dial.: *Jim Thompson*. Dir. phot.: *Lucien Ballard*. Art Dir.: *Ruth Sobotka*. Cost.: *Rudy Harrington*. Music: *Gerald Fried*. Edit.: *Betty Steinberg*. Sound: *Earl Snyder*. Asst. Dir. and Second Unit Dir.: *Alexander Singer*. Prod. Supervisor: *Clarence Eurist*.
Cast: *Sterling Hayden* (Johnny Clay), *Colleen Gray* (Fay), *Vince Edwards* (Val Cannon), *Jay C. Flippen* (Marvin Unger), *Marie Windsor* (Sherry Peatty), *Ted de Corsia* (Randy Kennan), *Elisha Cook Jr.* (George Peatty), *Joe Sawyer* (Mike O'Reilly), *Timothy Carey* (Nikki Arane), *Jay Adler* (Leo), *Joe Turkel* (Tiny), *Kola Kwarian* (Maurice Oboukhoff), *James Edwards* (parking lot janitor).
Length: 83mn. USA.
Dist.: United Artists.

The two extremes of film-making:
1. Filming Fear and Desire
2. Filming Spartacus

1958 – PATHS OF GLORY

In 1916, on the front, General Broulard persuades General Mireau, who is ambitious for promotion, to launch a suicidal attack on an impregnable German position,' the anthill'. It is Colonel Dax who will lead the attack. Dax's men, exhausted by earlier battles, advance with difficulty, some of them incapable of leaving the trenches. Mireau orders Captain Rousseau to open fire on his own troops. Rousseau refuses. Meanwhile, the attack is a failure. Mireau convinces Broulard that discipline demands a sacrifice: one man will be selected from each of the three companies to be court-martialled, and Colonel Dax will defend them. The prosecutor Saint-Auban has Férol, Arnaud and Paris condemned to death. Dax attempts to save his men by informing Broulard of the order given to Captain Rousseau. Broulard takes no account of it and the three soldiers are executed at dawn. Broulard then reveals his plan: to have an inquiry opened on Mireau and subsequently offer his position to Dax. Dax refuses, and rejoins his men who are listening to a German café-singer.

Prod. Co.: Bryna Prod.: *James B. Harris.* Scr.: *Stanley Kubrick, Calder Willingham, Jim Thompson,* from a novel by *Humphrey Cobb.* Dir. Phot.: *George Krause.* Music: *Gerald Fried.* Des.: *Ludwig Reiber.* Sound: *Martin Muller.* Edit.: *Eva Kroll.*
Cast: *Kirk Douglas* (Colonel Dax), *Ralph Meeker* (Captain Paris), *Adolphe Menjou* (General Broulard), *George Macready* (General Mireau), *Wayne Morris* (Lieutenant Roget), *Richard Anderson* (Major Saint-Auban), *Joseph Turkel* (Arnaud), *Timothy Carey* (Férol), *Peter Capell* (judge), *Susanne Christian* (young German girl), *Bert Freed* (Sergeant Boulanger), *Emile Meyer* (priest), *Ken Dibbs* (Lejeune), *Jerry Hausner* (Meyer), *Frederic Bell* (wounded soldier), *Harold Benedict* (Sergeant Nichols), *John Stein* (Captain Rousseau). Filmed in Munich.
Dist.: United Artists. Length: 86mn. USA.

1960 – SPARTACUS

Spartacus, a Thracian slave, has been brought from Libya by Batiatus, a Roman trader. He is assigned to the Capuan school of gladiators. There he meets Varinia, a beautiful slave from Britain, and they fall in love. When Spartacus's training is almost complete, a Roman general, Marcus Crassus, pays a visit to the school with his protégé Glabrus. He demands that two gladiators fight to the death and Spartacus is chosen to confront the Ethiopian warrior Draba. The latter is victorious but, refusing to finish Spartacus off, turns on Crassus who kills him. Shortly after, Spartacus escapes with his companions and becomes the leader of an army of slaves. He wins a battle against a Roman army led by Glabrus and trains his men in the mountains where Varinia and Antoninus, Crassus's servant, join him. He decides to leave Italy with the other slaves and pays a pirate, Tigranes, to supply him with ships. Meanwhile, in Rome, Crassus is waiting for an occasion to seize power. Gracchus, the leader of the Plebeians, and his ally Julius Caesar oppose him. Arriving with his army on the coast, Spartacus discovers that, bribed by Rome, the pirates will not give him any ships. Unable to withdraw, he is surrounded by three Roman armies led by Crassus. The slaves are routed, slaughtered in their thousands and the survivors, who include Antoninus and Spartacus, led back to Rome to be crucified. Crassus finds Varinia with her newborn baby on the battlefield and befriends her. He fails in an attempt to seduce her and, out of malice, orders Spartacus and Antoninus to engage in a fight to the death, the survivor to be crucified. Antoninus is defeated, Spartacus suffers a slow death on the cross while Varinia, freed through the influence of Gracchus, shows him his son – a Roman citizen.

Co-Dir.: *Anthony Mann* (director of the first sequence). Exec. Prod.: *Kirk Douglas* (Bryna). Prod.: *Edward Lewis.* Scr.: *Dalton Trumbo,* from the novel by *Howard Fast.* Dir. Phot.: *Russell Metty.*

Addit. Phot.: *Clifford Stine* (Super Technirama 70mm. Technicolor). Second Unit Dir.: *Irving Lerner.* Music: *Alex North,* directed by *North* and *Joseph Gershenson.* Prod. Designer: *Alexander Golitzen* assisted by *Roger Furse.* Art Dir.: *Eric Orbom.* Des.: *Russell A. Gausman, Julia Heron.* Edit.: *Robert Lawrence, Robert Schulte, Fred Chulack.* Cost.: *Bill Thomas, Valles.* Titles and Graphics Consultant: *Saul Bass.*
Cast: *Kirk Douglas* (Spartacus), *Laurence Olivier* (Marcus Crassus), *Jean Simmons* (Varinia), *Charles Laughton* (Gracchus), *Peter Ustinov* (Lentulus Batiatus), *Tony Curtis* (Antoninus), *John Gavin* (Julius Caesar), *Nina Foch* (Helena), *Herbert Lom* (Tigranes), *John Ireland* (Crixus), *John Dall* (Glabrus), *Charles McGraw* (Marcellus), *Joanna Barnes* (Claudia), *Harold J. Stone* (David), *Woody Strode* (Draba), *Peter Brocco* (Ramon), *Paul Lambert* (Gannicus), *Robert J. Wilke* (captain of the guard), *Nicholas Dennis* (Dionysius), *John Hoyt* (Roman officer), *Fred Worlock* (Laelius), *Dayton Lummis* (Symmachus), *Jill Jarmyn, Jo Summers.*
Original length: 196mn; current length: 183mn. USA.
Dist.: Universal.

1962 – LOLITA

Humbert Humbert enters the mansion of the television writer Clare Quilty and kills him. He then recalls the four years just passed. A professor of French literature in New Hampshire, he rents a room for the summer in the house of Charlotte Haze, a snobbish widow whose daughter Lolita he finds irresistibly attractive. He marries the mother in order to be closer to the daughter but when Charlotte learns the truth, after reading his private diary, she throws herself in front of a car. Humbert goes to collect Lolita from the summer camp where her mother had sent her and drives her to Ohio where he has a teaching post and where he enrols her in a private school. He discovers that she is taking advantage of her activities in the amateur dramatic society to meet another man. He takes her away on a long car trip across the country without ever managing to rid himself of the feeling that they are being followed. Both of them fall ill and one night Lolita disappears from the hospital. Some years later, Humbert receives a letter from Lolita. She is pregnant and married to a young unskilled labourer. He visits her, and she confesses that she has always been Quilty's girlfriend, even before her first meeting with Humbert: it was he who followed them and persecuted Humbert. When she refuses to leave with him, Humbert gives her his money and goes to kill Quilty. An epilogue informs us that Humbert died in prison of a heart attack.

Prod. Co.: Seven Arts/Anya/Transworld. Prod.: *James B. Harris.* Scr.: *Vladimir Nabokov,* from his novel. Dir. Phot.: *Oswald Morris.* Edit.: *Anthony Harvey.* Art Dir.: *William Andrews, Sid Cain.* Des.: *Andrew Low.* Music: *Nelson Riddle.* Theme song: *Bob Harris.* Sound: *H. L. Bird, Len Shilton.*
Cast: *James Mason* (Humbert Humbert), *Shelley Winters* (Charlotte Haze), *Peter Sellers* (Clare Quilty), *Sue Lyon* (Lolita), *Marianne Stone* (Vivian Darkbloom), *Diana Decker* (Jean Farlow), *Jerry Stovin* (John Farlow), *Gary Cockrell* (Dick), *Suzanne Gibbs* (Mona Farlow), *Roberta Shore* (Lorna), *Cec Linder* (doctor), *Lois Maxwell* (Nurse Mary Lore), *William Greene* (Swine), *Isobel Lucas* (Louise), *Eric Lane* (Roy), *Shirley Douglas* (Mrs. Starch), *Roland Brand* (Bill), *Colin Maitland* (Charlie), *C. Denier Warren* (Potts), *Irvin Allen* (intern), *Marion Mathie* (Miss Lebone), *Craig Sams* (Rex), *John Harrison* (Tom), *Maxine Holden* (receptionist), *James Dyrenforth* (Beale), *Terence Kilburn.*
Dist.: Metro-Goldwyn-Mayer. Length: 153mn. UK.

1964 – DR STRANGELOVE (OR HOW I LEARNED TO STOP WORRYING AND LOVE THE BOMB)

Convinced of a Communist plot to conquer the Free World, General Ripper, the commanding officer of Burpelson military base, launches an attack of B.52's against the Soviet Union. Only he knows the secret code of the attack, and he cuts all communications with his base. When informed of the news, President Muffley summons the Soviet ambassador de Sadesky to the Pentagon War Room and, disregarding the advice of General Turgidson, his head of staff who advocates a limited atomic war, orders Colonel 'Bat' Guano to attack Burpelson. Ripper commits suicide rather than be taken prisoner and Group-Captain Mandrake of the RAF deduces the secret code which will recall the bombers. But one of the pilots, T. J. 'King' Kong, whose radio has been put out of action, determines to proceed with his mission. President Muffley learns from de Sadesky that the Russians have constructed a 'Doomsday Device' which will trigger off all-out nuclear destruction if their country is attacked. Muffley turns to his crippled adviser, the former Nazi Dr Strangelove, who estimates that humanity can survive if a few hand-picked individuals remain for a hundred years in underground shelters. Meanwhile Kong releases the bomb and the world explodes.

Prod. Co.: Hawk Film. Prod.: *Stanley Kubrick.* Ass. Prod.: *Victor Lyndon.* Scr.: *Stanley Kubrick, Terry Southern, Peter George,* from the novel 'Red Alert' by *Peter George.* Dir. Phot.: *Gilbert Taylor* (35mm – Black and white). Camera: *Kelvin Pike.* Art Dir.: *Peter Murton.* Des.: *Ken Adam.* Edit.: *Anthony Harvey.* Music *Laurie Johnson.* Songs: 'We'll Meet Again': *Ross Parker,* music: *Hughie Charles,* sung by *Vera Lynn;* 'Try a Little Tenderness'; 'When Johnny Comes Marching Home'. Sound: *John Cox.* Asst. Dir.: *Eric Rattray.* Dir. of Prod.: *Clifton Brandon.* Continuity: *Pamela Carlton.* Cost.: *Bridget Sellers.* Make-up: *Stuart Freeborn.* Hairdresser: *Barbara Ritchie.* Spec. Effects: *Wally Veevers.* Travelling matte: *Vic Margutti.* Aviation adviser: *John Crewdson.*
Cast: *Peter Sellers* (Group-Capt. Lionel Mandrake/President Muffley/Dr Strangelove), *George C. Scott* (General 'Buck' Turgidson), *Sterling Hayden* (General Jack D. Ripper), *Keenan Wynn* (Colonel 'Bat' Guano), *Slim Pickens* (Major T. J. 'King' Kong), *Peter Bull* (Ambassador de Sadesky), *Tracy Reed* (Miss Scott), *James Earl Jones* (Lieutenant Lothar Zogg), *Jack Creley* (Mr Staines), *Frank Berry* (Lieutenant H. R. Dietrich), *Glenn Beck* (Lieutenant W. D. Kival), *Shane Rimmer* (Captain G. A. 'Ace' Owens), *Paul Tamarin* (Lieutenant B. Goldberg), *Gordon Tanner* (General Faceman), *Robert O'Neil* (Admiral Randolph), *Roy Stephens* (Frank), *Laurence Herder, John McCarthy* and *Hal Galili* (members of Burpelson Defence Team).
Dist.: Columbia. Length: 93mn. UK.

1968 – 2001: A SPACE ODYSSEY

1. The Dawn of Man.
A group of vegetarian apes, threatened by a neighbouring group of carnivores and battling for possession of a waterhole, one morning discover a mysterious black monolith. One of them then learns to use a bone as a weapon and kills to obtain meat.

2. Four million years later, in 2001, an American scientist, Dr Heywood Floyd, goes to the moon to investigate the presence of a black monolith emitting signals towards Jupiter.

3. Mission Jupiter. Eighteen months later. A spacecraft, the *Discovery,* is heading for Jupiter on a nine-month journey. On board are David Bowman and Frank Poole, three other astronauts in hibernation and the computer HAL 9000 which controls the vessel. HAL announces that an external antenna is out of order. When Poole leaves to repair it, he discovers that the information is false; but HAL cuts off his link with the spacecraft, maroons him in space and causes the three hibernating astronauts to die. After endeavouring to save his friend, Bowman returns to the *Discovery* to lobotomise HAL.

4. Jupiter and Beyond Infinity.
Bowman continues his flight and encounters the monolith in Jupiter's orbit. Entering a new spatio-temporal dimension, he passes through a succession of landscapes and colours. He arrives in an eighteenth-century room, sees himself progres-

sively grow older, is once more confronted with the black monolith and is reborn as an astral foetus floating above the earth.

Prod. Co.: Metro-Goldwyn-Mayer. A *Stanley Kubrick* Production. Ass. Prod.: *Victor Lyndon.* Scr.: *Stanley Kubrick, Arthur C. Clarke*, from the latter's short story '*The Sentinel*'. Dir. Phot.: *Geoffrey Unsworth.* Add. Phot.: *John Alcott.* Camera: *Kelvin Pike.* Art. Dir.: *John Hoesli.* Prod. Designer: *Tony Masters, Harry Lange, Ernest Archer.* Edit.: *Ray Lovejoy.* Music: *Gayaneh Ballet Suite: Aram Khatchaturian*, played by the Leningrad Philharmonic Orchestra; *Atmospheres, Lux Aeterna, Requiem: György Ligeti; The Blue Danube: Johann Strauss; Also Sprach Zarathustra: Richard Strauss.* Sound: *A. W. Watkins.* Asst. Dir.: *Derek Cracknell.* Cost.: *Hardy Amies.* Make-up: *Stuart Freeborn.* Spec. Phot. Effects: *Stanley Kubrick, Wally Veevers, Douglas Trumbull, Con Pederson, Tom Howard, Colin J. Cantwell, Bryan Loftus, Frederick Martin, Bruce Logan, David Osborne, John Jack Malick.* (35mm and 70mm, Super Panavision – Technicolor and Metrocolor). Scient. Adviser: *Frederick I. Ordway III.*
Cast: *Keir Dullea* (David Bowman), *Gary Lockwood* (Frank Poole), *William Sylvester* (Dr Heywood Floyd), *Daniel Richter* (Moonwatcher), *Douglas Rain* (voice of HAL 9000), *Leonard Rossiter* (Smyslov), *Margaret Tyzack* (Elena), *Robert Beatty* (Halvorsen), *Sean Sullivan* (Michaels), *Frank Miller* (Mission Controller), *Penny Brahms* (stewardess), *Alan Gifford* (Poole's father), *Vivian Kubrick* (Dr Floyd's daughter), *Glenn Beck, Edwina Caroll, Bill Weston, Mike Lovell, Edward Bishop, Ann Gillis, Heather Downham, John Ashley, Jimmy Bell, David Charkham, Simon Davis, Jonathan Daw, Peter Delmar, Terry Duggan, David Fleetwood, Danny Grover, Brian Hawley, David Hines, Tony Jackson, John Jordan, Scott Mackee, Laurence Marchant, Darryl Paes, Joe Refalo, Andy Wallace, Bob Wilyman, Richard Wood.*
Dist. MGM. Length: originally 160mn., reduced to 141mn. UK.

1971 – A CLOCKWORK ORANGE
England in the near future. Alex Delarge and his three droogs, Dim, Pete and Georgie, successively attack a tramp, a rival gang led by Billyboy and the isolated house of a writer and politician, Mr Alexander, whose wife they rape. The following day, while his parents are at work, Alex receives a visit from the social worker Deltoid, then meets two girls in a record store and enjoys a quick orgy with them. After he has reasserted his leadership of the gang, they break into the house of the Cat Lady who manages to alert the police seconds before Alex kills her. He is arrested and receives a fourteen-year sentence; two years later, however, he agrees to undergo shock treatment initiated by the government in their war against crime. After agreeing to be brainwashed, he is released and can no longer countenance any form of violence. He discovers that a lodger has appropriated the room which he occupied in his parents' house, is set upon by tramps and beaten up by his former droogs who have since become policemen. He seeks refuge with Mr Alexander who, combining personal revenge with a desire to discredit the government, drives Alex to an attempted suicide. Alex escapes and recovers in hospital. There the Minister offers him a lucrative job which will allow him once more to indulge his violent instincts.

Prod. Co.: Warner Bros., Polaris Productions. Prod.: *Stanley Kubrick.* Ass. Prod.: *Bernard Williams.* Asst. Dirs.: *Derek Cracknell, Dusty Symonds.* Scr.: *Stanley Kubrick*, from the novel by *Anthony Burgess.* Dir. Phot.: *John Alcott* (colour). Edit.: *Bill Butler.* Des.: *John Barry.* Asst. Dirs.: *Russell Hagg, Peter Shields.* Paintings and sculptures: *Herman Makkink, Liz Moore, Christiane Kubrick.* Electronic music: *Walter Carlos.* Music: *Music for the Funeral of Queen Mary: Purcell; William Tell Overture: Rossini; Time Steps: Walter Carlos; Beethoviana: Walter Carlos*, after *Purcell* and *Beethoven: Molly Malone: James Yorkston; The Thieving Magpie Overture: Rossini; Singin' in the Rain: Arthur Freed, Nacio Herb Brown*, sung by *Gene Kelly; Pomp and Circumstance Marches No. 1 and 4: Elgar; Sheherazade: Rimsky-Korsakov; Overture to the Sun: Terry Tucker; I Want to Marry a Lighthouse Keeper: Erika Eigen; Beethoven's Symphony No. 9*, arranged by *Walter Carlos.* Cost.: *Milena Canonero.* Sound Edit.: *Brian Blamey.* Tech. Adviser: *Jon Marshall.* Stunts: *Roy Scammel.*
Cast: *Malcolm McDowell* (Alex DeLarge), *Patrick Magee* (Mr Alexander), *Michael Bates* (Chief Guard), *Warren Clarke* (Dim), *John Clive* (actor), *Adrienne Corri* (Mrs Alexander), *Carl Duering* (Dr Brodsky), *Paul Farrell* (tramp), *Clive Francis* (lodger), *Michael Gover* (Prison Governor), *Miriam Karlin* (Cat Lady), *James Marcus* (Georgie), *Aubrey Morris* (P. R. Deltoid), *Godfrey Quigley* (Prison Chaplain), *Sheila Raynor* (mother), *Madge Ryan* (Dr Branom), *John Savident* (conspirator), *Anthony Sharp* (Minister), *Philip Stone* (father), *Pauline Taylor* (psychiatrist), *Margaret Tyzack* (conspirator), *Steven Berkoff* (Constable), *Lindsay Campbell* (Inspector), *Michael Tarn* (Pete), *David Prowse* (Julian), *Jan Adair, Vivienne Chandler, Prudence Drage* (handmaidens), *John J. Carney* (C.I.D. man), *Richard Connaught* (Billyboy), *Carol Drinkwater* (Nurse Feeley), *Charyl Grunwald* (rape girl), *Gillian Hills* (Sonietta), *Barbara Scott* (Marty), *Virginia Wetherell* (actress), *Katya Wyeth* (girl), *Barrie Cookson, Gaye Brown, Peter Burton, Lee Fox, Craig Hunter, Shirley Jaffe, Neil Wilson.*
Dist.: Warner. Length: 136mn. UK.

1975 – BARRY LYNDON
Ireland in the eighteenth century. After the death of his father in a duel, Redmond Barry is raised by his mother. He falls in love with his cousin, Nora Brady; challenging her suitor, the English officer Captain Quin, to a duel and convinced that he has killed him, he flees. He is robbed by highwaymen and forced to enlist in the army. While taking part in the Seven Years War, he learns from a former friend, Captain Grogan, that Quin is not dead but married to Nora. Barry deserts, but meets a Prussian ally, Captain Potzdorf, who sees through his disguise and forces him to enlist in the Prussian army. Ordered to spy on the Chevalier de Balibari, an Irishman like himself, he confesses his mission to him and becomes his protégé. At a gaming table, he meets the rich countess, Lady Lyndon, who marries him after her husband's death and gives him her name. He is unfaithful to her, incurs the enmity of his stepson, Lord Bullingdon, and, following a public brawl between the two, loses all hope of being raised to the peerage. After the death of his own son Bryan, he becomes estranged from his wife who attempts to commit suicide. Bullingdon challenges him to a duel in which he is seriously wounded. Barry is obliged to leave England.

Prod. Co.: Hawk/Peregrine, for Warner Bros. Prod.: *Stanley Kubrick.* Scr.: *Stanley Kubrick*, from the novel by *William Makepeace Thackeray.* Dir. Phot.: *John Alcott* (colour; *Carl Zeiss* lens for the candlelit scenes, adapted by *Ed di Giulio*). Music: *Leonard Rosenman*, after extracts from works by *J. S. Bach (Concerto for Double Harpsichord and Orchestra), Frederick II ('Hohenfriedberger' March), G. F. Handel (Saraband), W. A. Mozart (Idomeneo), G. Paisiello (The Barber of Seville), F. Schubert (German Dance No. 1, Piano Trio), A. Vivaldi (Cello Concerto in E Minor).* Irish traditional music and music by *Sean O'Riada*, played by *The Chieftains.* Prod. Designer: *Ken Adam.* Art Dir.: *Roy Walker.* Edit.: *Tony Lawson.* Cost.: *Ulla-Britt Soderlund, Milena Canorero.* Wigs: *Leonard.* Exec. Prod.: *Jan Harlan.* Assoc. Prod.: *Bernard Williams.* Asst. Prod.: *Andros Epaminondas.* Asst. Dir.: *Brian Cook.* Make-up: *Ann Brodie, Alan Boyle, Barbara Daly, Jill Carpenter, Yvonne Coppard.* Choreog.: *Geraldine Stephenson.* Historical adviser: *John Mollo.* Gambling adviser: *David Berglas.* Stunts: *Roy Scammel.* Fencing coach: *Bob Anderson.* Horsemaster: *George Mossman.* Armourer: *Bill Aylmore.*
Cast: *Ryan O'Neal* (Barry Lyndon – Redmond Barry), *Marisa Berenson* (Lady Lyndon), *Patrick Magee* (Chevalier de Balibari), *Hardy Kruger* (Captain Potzdorf), *Steven Berkoff* (Lord Ludd), *Gay Hamilton* (Nora Brady), *Marie Kean* (Mrs Barry), *Diana Koerner* (young German woman), *Murray Melvin* (Reverend Samuel Runt), *Frank Middlemass* (Sir Charles Lyndon), *André Morell* (Lord Wendover), *Arthur O'Sullivan* (highwayman), *Godfrey Quigley* (Captain Grogan), *Leonard Rossiter* (Captain Quin), *Philip Stone* (Graham), *Leon Vitali* (Lord Bullingdon), *Dominic Savage* (young Bullingdon), *David Morley* (little Bryan), *John Bindon, Roger Booth* (George III), *Norman Mitchell* (Brock), *Billy Boyle, Jonathan Cecil, Peter Cellier, Geoffrey Chater, Anthony Dawes, Patrick Dawson, Bernard Hepton, Anthony Herrick, Barry Jackson, Wolf Kahler, Patrick Laffan, Hans Meyer, Ferdy Mayne, Liam Redmond, Pat Roach* (Toole), *Frederick Schiller, George Sewell, Anthony Sharp* (Lord Harlan), *John Sharp, Roy Spencer, John Sullivan, Harry Towb, Michael Hordern* (narrator).
Exteriors filmed in England, Ireland and Germany. Post-synchronization at the EMI Studio, Elstree (UK). Dist. Warner Bros. Length: 187mn. UK.

1980 – THE SHINING
Hoping to write a novel there, a former teacher, Jack Torrance, accepts the post of janitor for the winter at the Overlook Hotel, which is closed for the season and totally isolated from the outside world. The manager, Ullman, warns him that in 1970 a janitor named Grady killed his wife and two daughters before committing suicide. Jack Torrance settles in with his wife Wendy and son Danny, who possesses both extrasensory powers and a 'double', Tony, who speaks to him. Before leaving the hotel, Hallorann, the head cook, 'communicates' with Danny and warns him that, for those like them who possess 'the shining', certain events leave traces which can be dangerous. He particularly warns him not to enter Room 237. Becoming increasingly nervous and irritable, Torrance cuts himself off to work. He begins to frequent the hotel's gilded lounge where he has conversations with a barman Lloyd. His son's visions become more and more frequent, and he receives a strange wound on the neck; then Torrance in his turn encounters a woman in Room 237. In the hotel's toilets, during an evening which is really taking place in the twenties, an attendant named Grady advises him to be stricter with his wife and son. Torrance becomes more and more brutish in his relations with his family and Danny enters into contact with Hallorann who is vacationing in Florida. Hallorann rushes back to save them but is killed on his arrival by Torrance, who proceeds to chase his son through the snow-covered labyrinth in the grounds of the hotel. He dies of cold, however, before he can kill him.

Prod. Co.: Hawk/Peregrine for Warner Bros. Prod.: *Stanley Kubrick.* Scr.: *Stanley Kubrick* and *Diane Johnson*, from the novel by *Stephen King.* Exec. Prod.: *Jan Harlan.* Dir. Phot.: *John Alcott.* Prod. designer: *Roy Walker.* Edit.: *Ray Lovejoy.* Music: *The Shining* and *Rocky Mountains: Wendy Carlos* and *Rachel Elkind; Lontano: György Ligeti; Music for Strings, Percussion and Celesta: Béla Bartok;* Extract from *Utrenja: The Awakening of Jacob* and *De Natura Sonoris No. 2: Krzysztof Penderecki;* Song: *Home: Henry Hall.* Dir. of Prod.: *Douglas Twiddy.* Asst. Dir.: *Brian Cook.* Cost.: *Milena Canonero.* Steadicam operator: *Garrett Brown.* Helicopter Phot.: *MacGillivray Freeman Films.* Art Dir.: *Les Tomkins.* Make-up: *Tom Smith.* Personal Asst. to S.K.: *Leon Vitali.* Hairdresser: *Leonard.* Cameramen: *Kelvin Pike* and *James Devis.* Second Unit Phot.: *Douglas Milsome.* Sound: *Ivan Sharrock.*
Cast: *Jack Nicholson* (Jack Torrance), *Shelley Duvall* (Wendy Torrance), *Danny Lloyd* (Danny), *Scatman Crothers* (Hallorann), *Barry Nelson* (Ullman), *Philip Stone* (Grady), *Joe Turkel* (Lloyd), *Ann Jackson* (doctor) (I), *Tony Burton* (Durkin) (I), *Lia Beldam* (young woman in bathtub), *Billie Gibson* (old woman in bathtub), *Barry Dennen* (Watson), *David Baxt* and *Manning Redwood* (Rangers), *Lisa Burns* and *Louise Burns* (Grady's daughters), *Robin Pappas* (nurse) (I), *Allison Coleridge* (secretary), *Burnell Tucker* (policeman), *Jana Sheldon* (hostess), *Kate Phelps* (receptionist), *Norman Gay* (injured guest).
Dist.: Warner. Length: 120mn. (Original length: 146mn, then 144mn.) UK. (I) Role cut from the final version.

Bibliography

The secret of being boring is to say everything.

Voltaire

This bibliography – already sizable – is limited to texts published in France, the United Kingdom and the United States and, for the most part, in magazines. A complementary and extremely detailed bibliography will be found in Wallace Coyle: *Stanley Kubrick, a guide to references and resources*, G. K. Hall, Boston 1980. For an Italian bibliography, see the works of Ghezzi[2] and Toffetti[5] and the Italian edition of this work. For a German bibliography, see the volume on Kubrick in the Reihe Film series published by Carl Hanser Verlag (to appear in late 1982). With few exceptions, I have not included the countless articles, sometimes of great interest, which have appeared in daily or weekly newspapers, as their numbers made listing them impossible in a book of this kind. Similarly, I have not listed the numerous histories, dictionaries and encyclopaedias of the cinema, all of which contain entries on Kubrick.

Books about Stanley Kubrick

1. – De Vries (Daniel), *The films of Stanley Kubrick*. William B. Eerdmans Publishing Company, Grand Rapids, Michigan, 1973, 76 p.
2. – Ghezzi (Enrico), *Stanley Kubrick*. Il Castoro Cinema n. 38. La Nuova Italia, Florence, June 1977, 168 p.
3. – Kagan (Norman), *The Cinema of Stanley Kubrick*. Holt, Rinehart and Winston, New York, 1972, 206 p.
4. – Phillips (Gene D.), *Stanley Kubrick, A Film Odyssey*. Popular Library, New York, 1975, 190 p.
5. – Toffetti (Sergio), *Stanley Kubrick*, Contemporanea Cinema, n. 12. Moizzi editore, Milan, 1978, 92 p.
6. – Walker (Alexander), *Stanley Kubrick Directs*, Harcourt Brace Jovanovich, New York, 1971, 272 p., revised edition, 1973, Davis-Poynter Ltd, London, 1972..

Books partially about Stanley Kubrick

7. – Kolker (Robert Philip), *A Cinema of Loneliness*, Oxford University Press, Oxford – New York, 1980, p. 69–138.
8. – Kuhns (William), *Movies in America*, Dryton-Pflaum, 1971, p. 226–229.
9. – Taylor (John Russell), *Directors and Directions*, Eyre Methuen Ltd, London, 1975, pp. 100–135.

Interviews with Stanley Kubrick

10. – Bean (Robin), *How I learned to stop worrying and love the cinema, Films and Filming*, June 1963.
11. – Ciment (Michel), *L'Express*, 17–23 April 1972, on *A Clockwork Orange*, reprinted in this book.
12. – Ciment (Michel), *Positif* n. 139, Ju e1972, on *A Clockwork Orange*, reprinted in this book.
13. – Ciment (Michel), *L'Express*, 30 August–5 September 1976, on *Barry Lyndon*, reprinted and expanded in this book.

14. – Gelmis (Joseph), in *The Film Director as Superstar*, Doubleday, New York, 1970, p. 293–316.
15. – Haine (Raymond), *Cahiers du cinéma*, n. 73, July 1957.
16. – Houston (Penelope), *Saturday Review*, 25 December 1971, on *A Clockwork Orange*.
17. – Houston (Penelope) and Strick (Philip), *Sight and Sound*, Spring 1972, on *A Clockwork Orange*.
18. – Kohler (Charles), *Eye*, August 1968, on *2001*.
19. – Kubrick (Stanley), Words and movies, *Sight and Sound*, Winter 1960–61, on *Lolita*.
20. – Kubrick (Stanley), Ten questions to nine directors, *Sight and Sound*, Spring 1964.
21. – Norden (Eric), *Playboy*, September 1968.
22. – Phillips (Gene), *Film Comment*, Winter 1971–72.
23. – Rapf (Maurice), *Action*, January–February 1969, reprinted in *Directors in Action*, The Bobbs Merrill Co., New York, 1973, edited by Bob Thomas.
24. – Romi (Yvette), *Le Nouvel Observateur*, 23 September 1968, on *2001*, reprinted in *70 interviews du Nouvel Observateur*, Le Terrain Vague, Paris, 1969.
25. – Siskel (Gene), *Chicago Tribune*, on *A Clockwork Orange*.
26. – Walter (Renaud), *Positif*, 100–101, December 1968–January 1969.

General articles on Stanley Kubrick

27. Appel Jr. (Alfred), The eyehold of knowledge: voyeuristic games in film and literature, *Film comment*, May–June 1973.
28. – Bernstein (Jeremy), Profile: how about a little game, *New Yorker*, 12 November 1966.
29. – Burgess (Jackson), The anti-militarism of Stanley Kubrick, *Film Quarterly*, Autumn 1964.
30. – Ciment (Michel), L'Odyssée de Stanley Kubrick, *Positif* n. 98, October 1968, reprinted and expanded in this book.
31. – Ciment (Michel), Entre raison et passion (Between Reason and Passion), *Positif*, n. 186, October 1976, reprinted and expanded in this book.
32. – Deer (Harriet and Irving), Kubrick and the structures of popular culture, *Journal of Popular Film*, Summer 1974.
33. – Feldmann (Hans), Kubrick and his discontents, *Film Quarterly*, Autumn 1976.
34. – Hofsess (John), Mind's Eye, *Take One*, May–June 1971.
35. – Milne (Tom), How I learned to stop worrying and love Stanley Kubrick, *Sight and Sound*, Spring 1964.
36. – Moskowitz (Ken), Clockwork violence, *Sight and Sound*, Winter 1976–77.
37. – Noble (Peter), Killers, kisses and Lolita, *Films and Filming*, December 1960.
38. – Russel (Lee), Stanley Kubrick, *New Left Review*, Summer 1964.

39. Sineux (Michel), Maestro, musique! (Image et son dans le cinema de Stanley Kubrick), *Positif*, n. 186, October 1976.
40. – Spinrad (Norman), Stanley Kubrick in the 21st century, *Cinema* (U.S.A.), December 1966.
41. – Stewart (Garrett), Close encounters of the 4th kind, *Sight and Sound*, Summer 1978.

The Films

FEAR AND DESIRE
42. – Owens (Iris), It's movies for me, *Modern Photography*, September 1953.
43. – Tyler (Parker), A dance, a dream and a flying trapeze, *Theatre Arts*, 1953.
44. – (anonymous), *Motion Picture Herald*, April 4, 1953.

KILLER'S KISS
45. – Lambert (Gavin), *Sight and Sound*, Spring 1956.
46. – *Monthly Film Bulletin*, March 1956.

THE KILLING
47. – Baker (Peter), *Films and Filming*, September 1956.
48. – Croce (Arlene), *Film Culture*, Vol. 2, 3, 1956.
49. – Godard (Jean-Luc), *Cahiers du cinéma*, n. 80, February 1958.
50. – Lambert (Gavin), *Sight and Sound*, Autumn 1956.
51. – Sternberg (Jacques), *Positif*, n. 21, February 1957.
52. – Tailleur (Roger), *Positif*, n. 29, Autumn 1958.

PATHS OF GLORY
● *Books*
53. – Cobb (Humphrey), *Paths of Glory*, a novel, Viking Press, New York 1935, new edition, Dell 1957, William Heinemann Ltd, London.
54. – Hughes (Robert), in *Film: Book 2. Films of Peace and War*, Grove Press, New York, 1962, p. 256.
● *Articles*
55. – Baker (Peter), *Films and Filming*, February 1958.
56. – Baumbach (Jonathan), *Film Culture*, February 1958.
57. – Cluny (Claude-Michel), *Cinéma 75*, n. 194, January 1975.
58. – De Ville (Bernard Luc), *Cinéma 58*, n. 27, May 1958.
59. – Ferrari (Alain), *Téléciné*, n. 198, April 1975.

Adolphe Menjou, Kirk Douglas (Paths of Glory)

60. – Ferro (Marc), *Jeune Cinéma*, n. 86, April 1975.
61. – Garel (Alain), *La Revue du cinéma*, n. 308, September 1976.
62. – Kubrick (Stanley), Letter to *L'Express*, 5 March 1959.
63. – Lambert (Gavin), *Sight and Sound*, Winter 1957–58.
64. – Lefèvre (Raymond), *Image et son*, ns. 140–141, April–May 1961.
65. – Lefèvre (Raymond), *La Revue du cinéma*, n. 295, April 1975.
66. – Martin (Marcel), *Ecran*, n. 36, May 1975.
67. – Rabourdin (Dominique), *Cinéma*, n. 198, May 1975.
68. – Seguin (Louis), in *Une critique dispersée*, '10/18', Paris 1976, pp. 89–94.
69. – Vitoux (Frédéric), *Positif*, n. 143, October 1972.

SPARTACUS
● *Book*
70. – Fast (Howard), *Spartacus*, a novel, Crown, New York, 1951, Panther Books, London, 1959.
● *Articles*
71. – Cooper (Duncan), *Cinéaste*, Vol. 6, n. 3, 1974.
72. – Cutts (John), *Films and Filming*, January 1961.
73. – Dyer (Peter John), *Sight and Sound*, Winter 1960–61.
74. – Gilson (René), *Cinéma 61*, n. 61, November–December 1961.
75. – Legrand (Gérard), *Positif*, n. 45, May 1962.
76. – Lightman (Herb A.), Filming Spartacus in super-Technirama, *American Cinematographer*, January 1961.
77. – Miller (Claude), *Téléciné*, n. 393.
78. – Török (Jean-Paul), *Positif*, n. 43, January 1962.

LOLITA
● *Books*
79. – Appel (Alfred), *Nabokov's Dark Cinema*, Oxford University Press, 1974.
80. – Nabokov (Vladimir), *Lolita*, a novel, McGraw-Hill Book Company, New York, 1955, Weidenfeld and Nicolson, London, 1959.
81. – Nabokov (Vladimir), *Lolita, a screenplay*, McGraw-Hill Book Company, New York, 1974.
● *Articles*
82. – Croce (Arlene), *Sight and Sound*, Autumn 1962.
83. – Durgnat (Raymond), *Films and Filming*, November 1962.
84. – French (Brandon), in *The Modern American Novel and the Movies*, edited by Gerald Peary and Roger Shatzkin, Frederick Ungar Publishing Company, New York, 1978, pp. 224–235.
85. – Kael (Pauline), in *I Lost it at the Movies*, Little Brown and Company, New York, 1965.
86. – Marcorelles (Louis), *Cahiers du cinéma*, n. 141, March 1963.
87. – *Monthly Film Bulletin*, October 1962.

DR STRANGELOVE
● *Books*
88. – George (Peter), *Dr Strangelove, or How I Learned to Stop Worrying and Love the Bomb*, a novel, Bantam Books, New York, 1964, Transworld Publications, London, 1963.
89. – *Film*, screenplay in German, n. 8, June–July 1964.
● *Articles*
90. – Burgess (Jackson), *Film Quarterly*, Spring 1964.
91. – Cohn (Bernard), *Positif*, Autumn 1964, n. 64–65.
92. – Forbes (Bryan), *Films and Filming*, February 1964.
93. – Linden (George W.), in *Nuclear War Films*, edited by Kack G. Shaheen, Southern Illinois University Press, 1978, pp. 58–67.
94. – Macklin (F. A.), *Film Comment*, Summer 1965.
95. – Milne (Tom), *Sight and Sound*, Winter 1963–64.
96. – *Monthly Film Bulletin*, February 1964.
97. – Narboni (Jean), *Cahiers du cinéma*, n. 155, May 1964.
98. – Philippe (Pierre), *Cinéma 64*, n. 86, May 1964.
99. – Suid (Lawrence), in *American History/*
American Film, edited by John E. O'Connor and Martin A. Jackson, Ungar Film Library, New York, 1979, pp. 219–236.
100. – Suid (Lawrence), in *Guts and Glory, the Great American War Movies*, Addison Wesley Publishing Company, Reading, Massachusetts, 1978, pp. 190–194.
101. – Taylor (Stephen), *Film Comment*, Winter 1964.
102. – Wolfe (Garry K.), *Journal of Popular Film*, Vol. 5, n. 1, 1976.

2001: A SPACE ODYSSEY
● *Books*
103. – Agel (Jérome), *The Making of Kubrick's 2001*, Signet Classics, The New American Library, New York, 1970, 368 p.
104. – Clarke (Arthur C.), *2001: A Space Odyssey*, a novel, Hutchinson, London, 1968, 224 p.
105. – Clarke (Arthur C.), *The Lost Worlds of 2001*, Signet, New American Library, New York, 1972, 240 p.
106. – Clarke (Arthur C.) and Kubrick (Stanley), *2001: A Space Odyssey*, Scenario, L'Avant-scène du cinéma, n. 231–232, 1–15 July 1979.
107. – Dumont (Jean-Paul) and Monod (Jean), *Le Foetus astral*, Christian Bourgois, Paris, 1970, 318 p.
108. – Geduld (Carolyn), *Filmguide to 2001: A Space Odyssey*, Indiana University Press, 1973, 88 p.
● *Articles*
109. – Abet (André), Oms (Marcel) and Talvat (Henri), *Cahiers de la Cinémathèque*, n. 7, Summer 1972.
110. – Austen (David), *Films and Filming*, July 1968.
III. – Boyd (David), Mode and Meaning in *2001*, *Journal of Popular Film*, Vol. 6, n. 3, 1978.
112. – Capdenac (Michel), *Les Lettres françaises*, 2 October 1968.
113. – Cluny (Claude Michel), in *Dossiers du cinéma*, Film I, Casterman, 1971.
114. – *Cinéma 68*, Round table, n. 131, December 1968.
115. – Daniels (Don), A skeleton key to *2001*, *Sight and Sound*, Winter 1970–71.
116. – Daniels (Don), A new myth, *Film Heritage*, Summer 1968.
117. – Eisenschitz (Bernard), *Cahiers du cinéma*, n. 209, February 1969.
118. – Fischer (J.), *Film Journal*, September 1972.
119. – Flatto (Elie), The eternal renewal, *Film Comment*, Winter 1969.
120. – Goimard (Jacques), *Fiction*, n. 179, November 1968.
121. – Greenberg (Harvey R.) in *The Movies on Your Mind*, Saturday Review Press/E. P. Dutton, New York, 1975, pp. 257–262.
122. – Hofsess (John), *Take One*, May–June 1968.
123. – James (Clive), Kubrick vs Clarke, *Cinema* (G.B.), n. 2, March 1968.
124. – Kozloff (Max), *Film Culture*, Winter–Spring 1970.
125. – Lightman (Herb A.), Filming *2001: A Space Odyssey*, *American Cinematographer*, June 1968.
126. – Macklin (F. A.), The comic sense of *2001*: *Film Comment*, Winter 1969.
127. – McKee (Mel), *2001*, out of the silent planet, *Sight and Sound*, Autumn 1969.
128. – Madsen (Axel) and Spinrad (Norman), *Cinema* (U.S.A.), Summer 1968.
129. – *Monthly Film Bulletin*, June 1968.
130. – Robinson (David), Two for the Sci-fi, *Sight and Sound*, Spring 1966.
131. – Sand (Luce), *Jeune Cinéma*, November 1968.
132. – Shatnoff (Judith), *Film Quarterly*, Autumn 1968.
133. – Sineux (Michel), *Positif*, n. 104, April 1969.
134. – Strick (Philip), *Sight and Sound*, Summer 1968.
135. – *Take One*, Interview with Wally Gentleman, Special Effects Supervisor, *Take One*, May–June 1968.
136. – Trumbull (Douglas), The Slit-scan process, *American Cinematographer*, October 1969.
137. – Youngblood (Gene), in *Expanded Cinema*, Studio Vista, London, 1970, pp. 139–150.

A CLOCKWORK ORANGE
● *Books*
138. – Burgess (Anthony), *A Clockwork Orange*, W. W. Norton and Co., New York, 1963, William Heinemann Ltd, London, 1962.
139. – Kubrick (Stanley), *A Clockwork Orange*, Lorrimer, London, 1972.
● *Articles*
140. – Barr (Charles), *Straw Dogs, A Clockwork Orange* and the critics, *Screen*, Summer 1972.
141. – Benayoun (Robert), Stanley Kubrick, le libertaire, *Positif*, n. 139, June 1972.
142. – Bourget (Jean-Loup), Les avatars du cercle, *Positif*, n. 136, March 1972.
143. – Boyers (Robert), *Film Heritage*, Summer 1972.
144. – Burgess (Anthony), Letter to *The Los Angeles Times*, republished in French in *Positif*, n. 139, June 1972.
145. – Burgess (Jackson), *Film Quarterly*, Spring 1972.
146. – Burks (John), Feldman (Seth) and Krassner (Paul), *Take One*, January–February 1971.
147. – Cluny (Claude Michel), *Cinéma 72*, n. 166, May 1972.
148. – Cocks (Jay), Kubrick: degrees of madness, *Time*, 20 December 1971.
149. – Daniels (Don), *Sight and Sound*, Winter 1972–73.
150. – Evans (Walter), Violence and film: the thesis of *A Clockwork Orange, Velvet Light Trap*, n. 13, Autumn 1974.
151. – Gow (Gordon), *Films and Filming*, February 1972.
152. – Gumenik (Arthur), *Film Heritage*, Summer 1972.
153. – Hughes (Robert), The Decor of Tomorrow's Hell, *Time*, 27 December 1971.
154. – Isaacs (Neil D.), Unstuck in time: *A Clockwork Orange* and *Slaughterhouse Five*, *Literature and Film Quarterly*, April 1973.
155. – Kolker (Robert Philipp), Orange, Dogs and the Ultra-violence, *Journal of Popular Film*, Summer 1972.
156. – Lefèbvre (Jean-Pierre) and Leroux (A.), *Cinéma Québec*, March–April 1972.
157. – Mamber (Stephen), *Cinema* (U.S.A.), Winter 1972–73.
158. – Martin (Marcel), *Ecran 72*, n. 6, June 1972.
159. – *Monthly Film Bulletin*, February 1972.
160. – Moskowitz (Kenneth), The vicarious experience of *A Clockwork Orange, Velvet Light Trap*, n. 16, Autumn 1976.
161. – Oudart (Jean-Pierre), A propos d'*Orange Mécanique*, Kubrick, Kramer et quelques autres, *Cahiers du cinéma*, n. 293, October 1978.
162. – Seguin (Louis), in *Une critique dispersée*, '10/18', Paris, 1976, pp. 104–109.
163. – Strick (Philip), *Sight and Sound*, Winter 1971–72.
164. – Tournès (Andrée), *Jeune Cinéma*, n. 63, May–June 1972.
165. – Zimmerman (Paul), Kubrick's Brilliant Vision, *Newsweek*, 3 January 1972.

BARRY LYNDON
● *Book*
166. – Thackeray (William Makepeace), *Barry Lyndon*, Penguin Books, London, New York University Press, New York.
● *Articles*
167. – Cluny (Claude Michel), *Cinema 76*, n. 214, October 1976.
168. – Craven (Jennie), *Films and Filming*, February 1976.
169. – Dempsey (Michael), *Film Quarterly*, Autumn 1976.
170. – Garel (Alain), *La Revue du Cinéma*, n. 308, September 1976.
171. – Gastelier (Fabian), *Jeune Cinéma*, n. 97, September–October 1976.
172. – Houston (Penelope), *Sight and Sound*, Spring 1976.
173. – Lightman (Herb), Interview with John Alcott, *American Cinematographer*, March 1976.
174. – Oudart (Jean-Pierre), *Cahiers du cinéma*, n. 271, November 1976.

175. – Rosenbaum (Jonathan), The pluck of *Barry Lyndon*, *Film Comment*, March–April 1976.
176. – Segond (Jacques), Le hasard et la nécessité (Chance and necessity), *Positif*, n. 179, March 1976.
177. – *Time*, Kubrick's grandest gamble, 15 December 1975.
178. – Wiswell (Frank), *Films and Filming*, October 1977.

THE SHINING
● *Book*
179. – King (Stephen), *The Shining*, Doubleday and Company Inc., New York, 1977, New English Library, London, 1977, 448 p.
● *Articles*
180. – Anderson (Pat) and Wells (Jeffrey), *The Shining*, two views, *Films in Review*, August–September 1980.
181. – Barbier (Denis), Interview with Diane Johnson (scenarist), *Positif*, n. 238, January 1981.
182. – Benayoun (Robert), Tous les fous n'ont pas l'air d'être fous (Not all madmen look like madmen), *Le Point*, 20 October 1980.*
183. – Bourget (Jean-Loup), Le territoire du Colorado (Colorado Territory), *Positif*, n. 234, September 1980.
184. – Brown (Garrett), The Steadicam and *The Shining*, *American Cinematographer*.
185. – Chute (David), King of the Night: an interview with Stephen King, *Take One*, January 1979.
186. – Ciment (Michel), Oui, il y a des revenants (Yes, there are ghosts), *L'Empress*, 18 October 1980 (reprinted and expanded in this book).*
187. – Garsault (Alain), Les deux visages du fantastique (The two faces of the fantastic), *Positif*, n. 238, January 1981.
188. – Hofsess (John), Stanley Kubrick strikes back with *The Shining*, *International Herald Tribune*, 25–26 October 1980.*
189. – Jameson (Richard T.), Kubrick's *Shining*, *Film Comment*, July–August 1980.
190. – Jeffress (Lynn) and Leibowitz (Flo), *Film Quarterly*, Spring 1981.
191. – Kael (Pauline), Devolution, *The New Yorker*, 9 June 1980.
192. – Kennedy (Harlan), Kubrick goes Gothic, *American Film*, June 1980.
193. – Kroll (Jack), Stanley Kubrick's horror show, *Newsweek*, 2 June 1980.
194. – Lenne (Gérard), *La Revue du Cinéma*, n. 355, November 1980.
195. – Le Pavec (Jean-Pierre), *Cinéma 80*, n. 263, November 1980.
196. – Lofficier (Jean-Marie), Une odyssée de l'épouvante (An Odyssey of Terror), *L'Ecran fantastique*, n. 15, November–December 1980.
197. – Maslin (Janet), *The New York Times*, May 24 1980.
198. – Masson (Alain), L'indifférence et le goût (Indifference and Taste), *Positif*, n. 238, January 1981.
199. – Mayersberg (Paul), The Overlook Hotel, *Sight and Sound*, Winter 1980–81.
200 – Molinax Foix (Vicente), Interview with Stanley Kubrick, *Cahiers du cinéma*, n. 319, January 1981.*
201. – Moraz (Patricia), Une rencontre avec Stanley Kubrick (An encounter with Stanley Kubrick), *Le Monde*, October 23 1980.*
202. – Nave (Bernard), *Jeune Cinéma*, n. 131, December–January 1981.
203. – Oudart (Jean-Pierre), Les inconnus dans la maison (Strangers in the house), *Cahiers du cinéma*, n. 317, November 1980.
204. – Schickel (Richard), Red herrings and refusals, *Time*, 2 June 1980.
205. – Sineux (Michel), La symphonie Kubrickienne (image et son dans le cinéma de Stanley Kubrick: notes complémentaires), *Positif*, n. 239, February 1981.
206. – Titterington (P.L.), Kubrick and *The Shining*, *Sight and Sound*, Spring 1981.

Stanley Kubrick and Jack Nicholson (filming
The Shining)

207. – Veillon (Olivier-René), *Cinématographe*, November 1980.
208. – Walker (Alexander), Here's Jack!, *Evening Standard*, 23 May 1980.

*Interviews

RECOLLECTIONS

209. – Chateau (René), Interview with Dalton Trumbo (scenarist), *Positif*, n. 64–65, Autumn 1964.
210. – Ciment (Michel), Interview with Ken Adam (decorator), *Positif*, n. 191, March 1977, reprinted in this book.
211. – Ciment (Michel) and Tavernier (Bertrand), Interview with Kirk Douglas, *Positif*, n. 112, January 1970.
212. – Ciment (Michel), Interview with James B. Harris (producer), *Positif*, n. 158, April 1974, reprinted in this book.
213. – Gow (Gordon), An interview with Malcolm McDowell, *Films and Filming*, October 1975.
214. – Gow (Gordon), An interview with Keir Dullea, *Films and Filming*, November 1976.
215. – Hanson (Curtis Lee), Interview with James B. Harris (producer), *Cinema* (U.S.A.), December 1965.
216. – Hudson (Roger), Three designers (one of whom is Ken Adam), *Sight and Sound*, Winter 1964–65.
217. Hudson (Roger), Putting the magic in it, Interview with Anthony Harvey (editor), *Sight and Sound*, Spring 1966.

VARIOUS

218. – Arc (L'), *Nabokov*, n. 24, Spring 1964, 104 p.
219. – Boie (Bernhild), *L'Homme et ses simulacres*, José Corti, Paris, 1979, 360 p.
220. – Brown (Norman O.), *Life Against Death*, Wesleyan University Press, 1959, Routledge and Kegan Paul, 1959, 366 p.
221. – Buraud (Georges), *Les Masques*, Club des éditeurs, Paris, 1961, 234 p.
222. – Caillois (Roger), *Cohérences aventureuses*, 'Collection Idées', Gallimard, 1976, 282 p.
223. – Caillois (Roger), *Man, Play and Games*, Free Press of Glencoe, 1961, 208 p.
224. – Chevalier (Jean) and Gheerbrandt (Alain), *Dictionnaire des symboles*, 4 volumes, Seghers, Paris, 1973.
225. – David (Aurel), *La Cybernétique et l'humain*, 'Collection Idées', Gallimard, Paris, 1965, 192 p.
226. – Freud (Sigmund), *Introductory Lectures on Psycho-Analysis*, Hogarth Press, London, 1963, 496 p.
227. – Heisenberg (Werner) *The Physicist's Conception of Nature*, Harcourt Brace Jovanovich, New York, 1970, 192 p.
228. – Lenne (Gérard), *Le Cinéma 'fantastique' et ses mythologies*, Editions du Cerf, Paris, 1970, 232 p.
229. – Rorvik (David M.), *As Man Becomes Machine*, Abacus, London, 1975, 206 p.
230. – Santarcangeli (Paolo) *Il libro dei labirinti*, Vallecchi, Florence, 1967.
231. – Starobinski (Jean), *The Invention of Liberty, 1700–89*, Skira, Geneva, 1964, 222 p.
232. – Todorov (Tzvetan), *The Fantastic*, Cornell University Press, 1975, 180 p.

Discography

Spartacus	Decca 9092
Lolita	MGM SE 4050
Dr Strangelove	Colpix 464 S
2001: A Space Odyssey	MGM 2315 034
A Clockwork Orange	RCA LSB 4057
Barry Lyndon	Warner K 56189
The Shining	Warner HS 3449

'The promise of immortality': the last shot of The Shining

Overlook Hotel
July 4th Ball
1921

Acknowledgements

My thanks go to

Stanley Kubrick for the hours he was willing to spend with me and for the hitherto unpublished frame enlargements which he had specially printed for this book;

Julian Senior (Warner Bros, London) for the extensive and varied assistance which he has afforded me over a period of several years;

Jean-Loup Bourget, Mary Corliss (of the Museum of Modern Art, New York), Caroline Decriem and Claude Venin (Cinema International Corporation, Paris), Olivier Eyquem, Anabel Herbout, Jean-Claude Missiaen, Dominique Rabourdin, Michelle Snapes (and the British Film Institute, London) for having enabled me to complete my iconography;

David Meeker (British Film Institute) and Didier Moncel (Warner Bros, Paris) for screening some of Stanley Kubrick's films;

L'Express and the magazine Positif for having authorised the reprinting of certain texts (corrected and supplemented) and interviews which originally appeared in their pages (see the bibliography in this book);

my wife Jeannine for her precious and permanent collaboration.